Inequality and Teacher Education:
An International Perspective

Inequality and Teacher Education:
An International Perspective

Edited by

Gajendra K. Verma

The Falmer Press

(A Member of the Taylor & Francis Group)
London • Washington, D.C.

UK   The Falmer Press, 4 John St, London WC1N 2ET
USA   The Falmer Press, Taylor & Francis Inc., 1900 Frost Road, Suite 101, Bristol, PA 19007

First published 1993

A catalogue record for this book is available from the British Library

Library of Congress Cataloging-in-Publication Data are available on request

ISBN 075070 224 9 cased
ISBN 075070 225 7 paperback

Jacket design by Caroline Archer
Typeset in 9^{1}/$_{2}$/11pt Times
by Graphicraft Typesetters Ltd, Hong Kong

Printed in Great Britain by Burgess Science Press, Basingstoke on paper which has a specified pH value on final paper manufacture of not less than 7.5 and is therefore 'acid free'.

To
John Turner
in recognition of his
international contribution
to
Teacher Education

Gajendra Verma

Contents

Contents

Tables and Figures

Foreword

Given the increasing cultural and social diversity of society today, it becomes all the more urgent that education is able to make a response that is in keeping with that diversity and enables tomorrow's citizens to find the four freedoms of which Roosevelt spoke in 1941. He sought a world in which there was freedom of speech and expression, of worship, from want and from fear — everywhere in the world.

If education is to be better placed to make that response (and those ideals are to be attained), much rests on the way in which teachers are prepared for their manifold roles in the classroom. This book is about teacher education and inequality and seeks to offer an international perspective on the ways in which the issues of inequality are perceived and addressed.

Apart from the timely need for such issues to be re-assessed, it seems fitting to dedicate this book to a man who has done a great deal, both here in Britain and abroad, notably in Africa and Asia, to awaken consciousness of those issues and to strive to foster the development of programmes of teacher education that are responsive to the needs of that social and cultural diversity. John Turner, to whom this book is dedicated, has a distinguished record as a teacher educator, not just here at the University of Manchester, where he has been the Sarah Fielden Professor of Education, Dean of Education and, currently, Pro Vice-Chancellor, but also in many parts of the world, notably in Africa. From 1981 to 1984 he was Vice-Chancellor of the University of Botswana and was recently Chair of the Presidential Commission on Higher Education in Namibia. He has twice been elected to the Chair of UCET (Universities Council for the Education of Teachers), and served on a number of international committees on education.

In dedicating this book to John Turner, I am hopeful that his contribution to the world of teacher education will continue to be a source of inspiration to us all.

Gajendra Verma

Chapter 1

Teacher Education and Inequality

Gajendra K. Verma

This book presents a series of invited chapters relating to Teacher Education and Inequality. In this first chapter a framework for the themes those chapters cover is set out.

The subject of inequality/inequalities in education is not a new one. There is a considerable body of literature both in Britain and other parts of the world that bears testimony to this. Much of that writing reflects concern that sections of the population either get no access to any schooling at all or only access to one in which the dice are loaded against their chances of success. Viewed from the macro-level many of the factors involved transcend the boundaries of the education system itself and relate to the socio-economic structure of particular societies.

In this book narrower frames of reference are used, not to deny the work that has gone before but because it was considered that a narrower focus could highlight aspects of the problems associated with educational inequality from within the immediate context of the education system. This focus was not selected to discount the needs for broader action on education. It was chosen to address issues related to inequality from within the educational process itself. Such a choice was based on the premise that education is an invaluable commodity important not only to individuals but also to the society in which they live. Given its being invaluable to both, much rests on the quality of the education offered. While that quality is no doubt affected by the level of financial input into the system, much also rests on the quality of the teaching force available to provide that education. It is considered irrefutable that the quality and effectiveness of that teaching force is conditioned in no mean part by the quality of the training that the teaching force receives.

Well-honed teaching skills can make a significant contribution to making the education process, operating under whatever present restraints (political and/or politico-financial), more efficient and more effective. While those teaching skills are heavily reliant on the personal and other qualities of the teacher, there remains the important consideration that teacher education has a vital role to play in ensuring that those skills are optimally focused.

It is an inescapable fact that in the present day and age, the demands placed on teachers are greater than ever before. In a rapidly changing world, the educational process also has to reflect that change and teachers need to be able to respond to that change/those changes.

In earlier times, it was possibly appropriate merely for teachers to be launched into their careers equipped as transmitters of accepted knowledge. Thus the emphasis was on the launch process i.e., on what is now referred to as initial training. Although its contribution is important, no longer does initial training suffice to equip the teacher for a lifetime of service. As the curriculum and skill requirements change in step with (or ahead of?) the needs of society, so there is both the need for initial training that is more flexible than before and for a career-long programme of supportive 'in-service training'.

Inequality is both a relativist and a generic term when considered in the context of education (or any other sphere of activity where assessment rests heavily on value judgments rather than absolutes). Nevertheless, the term has a useful part to play in any debate on the effectiveness of the education process. It serves as an umbrella term to embrace a variety of dimensions, in which there are imbalances in any education system. Typically, the term inequality is employed to refer to matters of ethnicity/race, socio-economic status/social class, sex/gender and inter-regional (e.g., urban/rural) differences. Such issues are very much at the heart of the 'equal opportunities' debate in western countries. Typically, they arise out of claims/arguments about the relative chances of success as measured by educational outcomes of different sections of the population. Fuelling such debate may well be evidence put forward to support views that youngsters from within an 'identifiable' element of a given society are not being given a 'fair chance'. The statistics of inequality in such debates are often subjects of some controversy in themselves. So too, if not more so, are factors/practices considered as being linked (causally or by correlation) to that inequality or as being essential for the alleviation of it.

There is also a relativist element inherent in the term inequality, particularly within the context of this book. The authors contributing to this book comment on the experience of education in different parts of the world. No doubt the type of inequalities considered above as falling under the inequality umbrella could be demonstrated as being present in all the countries to which reference is made. Where the relativist element enters is not so because on comparison, a particular group is evidenced as being less favourably treated than another but because much depends on the reference points. The latter may well be conditioned by levels of expectation and of priority.

For example, it is a matter of concern that the post-education life chances of girls may not be as good as those of boys. A variety of factors, in-school and out-of-school in a given society could be shown to be accountable for, or con-tributory to, that inequality. Yet, if there were other sources of inequality also present in that society, which should be given the greater priority in terms of alleviating measures? Consider the situation reported by Roger Iredale in some developing countries (see Chapter 3) or by David Freer in the black 'independent states' within South Africa (see Chapter 4). In a number of societies female enrolments were considerably smaller than male ones and the inequality became more pronounced beyond the basic level of education. Socio-cultural factors were held to be largely instrumental in this against a background of poverty, the education of sons was held to be more important to the family's well-being than that of daughters. Such inequalities would be considered scandalous in many societies, especially those with a fully developed education system and with a high level of public consciousness about equal opportunities. Even in those apparently sophisticated societies in which parental choice on matters of education was given a high political profile, tolerance would hardly extend to condoning resultant inequality between the sexes in educational access and opportunity.

Yet, while one would not wish to let male–female inequalities go unchallenged, wherever these occurred, how much importance should be attached to that challenge if their source was not the result of structural features in the education system of a society, where other inequalities were structural, i.e., they arose out of failings directly related to the education system or its processes? Given a country in which the education system did not extend to the whole country, for example, to rural areas, or to a particular section of society such as elements of South Africa's black population, which inequality should be given the greater priority?

However, it is not proposed to make a judgment on the relative importance of particular issues of inequality, merely to illustrate the point about the relativist element of the term. Moreover, it is also worth mentioning that there are likely to be socio-cultural factors that will influence the weighting of relative priorities in any given society.

This book looks at inequalities presented from a teacher-education perspective. Not every chapter treats the issues of teacher education as the primary focus, but all chapters have important implications for the orientation of teacher education. While schools cannot be expected to be able to 'compensate for society', there remains a lot that schools can do to ensure that their teaching and organization does as much as they can to ensure that they do not exacerbate inter-group inequalities. If schools are going to move toward the achievement of such a goal, then much depends on the vision, quality and purpose of the teacher-training institutions. They have a critical role to play in the equipping of teachers, both in initial and in-service training to act as a positive force in the classroom.

Teacher education needs not only to focus on the classroom, in terms of the 'mechanics' of teaching and learning, but also on the impact of these on classroom interaction. That impact has important implications for the wider societal processes, especially as far as the reduction of inequalities is concerned. Teachers need to be aware that the teaching–learning processes are not neutral and are heavily cultural in character. This has an important bearing not only on what is learned (and on how effectively it is learned) but also on how pupils perceive themselves, their fellow pupils and other people. It is important that we understand more about how the cultural messages implicit in the teaching–learning processes affect those perceptions, for then it may be possible to improve the focus of our teaching.

In this respect, it is interesting to look at the two contrasting models — one considered by Frankrijker (see Chapter 11) and Campbell (see Chapter 12) and the other by Rizvi and Crowley (see Chapter 13). Both models represent attempts to prepare the trainee teacher for life in the culturally pluralist classroom but differ in their approach to its challenges.

The Dutch model, discussed by Friedrijker and Campbell, seems largely a prescriptive but none the less pragmatic one. It focuses on the cultural and ethnic background of particular groups whom the teacher is likely to meet in his or her work. It would seem legitimately argued, that, armed with that understanding, the teacher would be better equipped to respond sensitively to the needs of his or her pupils and to enable them to make the most of their educational opportunities.

The other model, considered by Rizvi and Crowley, is the product of a different setting, namely Australia. Its focus is not on the pupils but on the teacher as an individual and it targets the 'culturalization' process. In essence, the model seeks to build on the development of awareness in the trainee teacher of the part played by personal, social and cultural factors in his or her identity and perceptions of other people. In support of that model, it is argued that such an awareness will sensitize the trainee teacher to the effect of such factors on those with whom he or she comes into contact.

Neither model is without imperfections in terms of the universality of its application. For example, the Dutch model rests on the exposure of the trainee teacher to five particular ethnic/cultural backgrounds, those five being predominant in the location where the teacher is to work. Even allowing for the possibility that he or she might at some stage move to another part of the country where the ethnic composition is different, the potentially greater weakness in that type of model is the conservatism of all educational institutions. It is, as I have argued elsewhere, (Verma, 1990) all too easy for culture and ethnicity to be treated as static entities rather than as dynamic ones. There is a danger in casting a course describing the characteristics of a particular culture or ethnic group in such a way that it becomes 'immutable' and does not allow for the subtle and on-going changes that occur when that culture/ethnic group comes into constant contact with other groups. Then the knowledge generated from such a course becomes stultified, with all the attendant dangers of stereotyping; this is harmful both to teacher and pupils.

On the surface, the culturalization model seems more attractive since its starting point is the trainee teacher and builds from his or her subjectivity; enabling individuals to understand what contributes to their cultural make-up would apparently focus on the dynamic elements of culture and this would be welcome. However, the development of that cultural sensitivity in the individual may not be easy to achieve, placing great demands on the skill of the trainer. Moreover, it would still appear problematic as to whether that training would necessarily enable the recipient to read cultural 'manifestations' in others not of his or her background.

Despite the reservations expressed, both models would appear worthy of further and careful consideration. They highlight the need for further exploration into the impact of the ways in which we teach if we are to maximize teacher effectiveness in the classroom and to optimize the benefits to be gained by pupils.

This leads on to another important point. While the central focus of teacher education must be on the preparation of trainees to equip them for the classroom, the importance of feedback on the effectiveness of their training programmes to the training institutions cannot be overlooked. To ignore mounting their own research to evaluate what they teach, (not just doing research for the sake of research), is detrimental to the quality of the training they offer. This is all the more important in an age of rapid change and the increasing cultural complexity of modern society.

Such is the thrust of modern technological progress that a good education is at a premium if one is to benefit from its fruits, in terms of career opportunities and self-fulfilment. Consequently, the penalty for not having had a good education becomes all the greater, with reduced chances of finding and retaining employment with the implications for self-fulfilment. Where the distribution of educational opportunity across the population is uneven, whether measured in terms of ethnicity, sex or social class, three of the currently widely used yard-sticks, it is hard to develop social cohesiveness and, more importantly, to avoid the creation of subgroups which are grossly disadvantaged, condemned to a cycle of poverty and effectively reduced to the status of second-class citizens.

Viewed at the world level, inequality, however real it may be for individuals or particular sections of a given society, also has important implications. There already exists a gulf in terms of national opportunity between the so-called de-veloped countries and the under-developed/developing ones. It seems almost certain that this gulf will widen further, with the latter countries ever more de-pendent financially and economically, through aid packages and trade agree-ments, on countries in the former group. This also represents a considerable challenge to all involved in teacher education. While arguably their immediate loyalties may lie within the national system they serve, teacher educators surely ought to have a moral obligation to promote the exchange of information on good practice and its universal development.

It should not be forgotten that, given its nature, inequality will never disap-pear, for it is both generic and relativist. As the range of provision expands, which, we may hope, will reduce the present inequalities, so new ones will emerge to be confronted. Already in developed countries, ageism is emerging as an issue of concern. Perhaps, if in ten years' time one were to review inequality, disparities in educational opportunity on the basis of age, might well have become an im-portant issue, with other new issues appearing on the horizon. One suspects, how-ever, that the issues of inequality referred to earlier will continue to dominate discussion.

Technology and improved communications mean that there is now a global awareness of inequality. Regrettably, there is no equality among nations in their ability to reduce the inequalities they perceive. Rich nations with ample resources and well-established governmental machinery can address the issues – if the political will is there. Countries with fewer resources and weaker internal struc-tures have other imperatives. Inequality will be ever-present, though how it will manifest itself will constantly change. Perhaps the only conclusion is that those involved in education must constantly struggle with it, whatever form it takes in time and space.

It is easy to argue that the education system should not be held responsible for all the ills of the broader society, since these were beyond its direct control. Nonetheless, it remains unalterably true that the education system should not close its eyes to those inequalities and seek to isolate itself from them. Teacher education must give the lead in the battle against inequality. It needs to focus not only on the classroom processes but also on its own and, through a resultant synthesis, to build on one it has already achieved and so to play its full part in pushing back the frontiers of inequality.

Chapter 2

Educating Teachers to Combat Inequality

John Eggleston

Children come to school with different physical, mental and emotional capabilities. They also come with a bewildering variety of expectations and attitudes that may enhance or diminish the full realization of their capability. These expectations and attitudes are to a large extent a product of their social, gender and ethnic background and spring from the value systems of their parents, their extended families and the adults and other children in the communities. They are important not only because they have a formative effect on the children but also because they interact with the expectations and attitudes of teachers. Often teachers, despite much effort to the contrary, end up by reinforcing the differentiating consequences of these underlying values, not infrequently to the disadvantage of children. A key task of teacher education is to break this cycle of reinforcement by helping students to identify them, to recognize their source and to devise ways of combating the negative effects. And, of equal importance, students must be helped to recognize their own assumptions and prejudices.

There are three main categories into which these underlying value systems, with their representative attitudes and expectations, may be placed: social class, gender and race. Here their effect on work in the classroom and hence their crucial importance in the work of teacher education is examined.

Social Class

A clear example is provided at the outset of schooling. Let us imagine two children entering school from different ends of the social class structure. They are coming into the reception class of a first school serving a catchment area that spans the social spectrum.

On the first morning Kate, from an affluent suburban home, arrives with Kylie, from a much less affluent inner-city family. They enter a well-equipped modern classroom supervised by a newly trained teacher who is enthusiastic to help all the children in her class to maximize their capability. Yet Kate will start with many advantages. She will be familiar with the equipment, having almost certainly met it in her home and pre-school playgroup. She will be relaxed with teachers, as she and her parents are likely to know teachers socially and to 'speak the same language'. So she is likely to use her new environment effectively and immediately and to be posting the bricks in the correct slots in the postbox without waiting to be asked. Meanwhile, Kylie has probably been sent to school with the injunction 'Make sure you do what the teacher tells you', and is waiting patiently for the teacher to tell her when to use the unfamiliar equipment for the first time. It is very difficult for the teacher, armed with her developmental check-list, generated in her training course, to resist evaluating Kate as 'bright and quick' and Kylie as 'dull and slow' in the first few hours, when the crucial early (and often persistent) diagnoses are made. The diagnosis is very likely to be reinforced by Kate's greater familiarity with books in the home and the strong probability that her parents have already taught her to read.

Gender

Similar prejudgments are all too easy to make on gender issues. Boys, encour-aged in home and community to be more dominant, assertive and adventurous and to enjoy approval for such behaviour, will behave differently in the classroom from girls, who have often received a very different early encouragement. In particular, as most teachers acknowledge, boys tend to be much more effective in claiming teachers' attention, with predictable consequences for teachers' evaluation. Indeed much the same may be happening in the teacher-training course itself!

Race

The same kind of experience can happen when children from different ethnic backgrounds enter the classroom; their different languages and cultural back-grounds may make it less easy for them to relate to the 'mainstream' knowledge and understanding they are offered. In consequence their achievements may be seen to be lower and their capabilities in their own home language and culture may go unrecognized. The situation may well be presented as inevitable and unalterable to the beginning student as Francis O'Reilly makes clear, writing in *The Independent* on 13 September 1990:

> The Maths teacher introduces the student teacher to the class and briefs her. Before leaving, she points out a girl sitting on the back row and says, 'Oh, by the way, Jhamari won't understand anything. Give her some additions to do.'

> In French, where they have to label parts of the body, Jhamari steals a glance at her neighbour's book and earns the snarling response 'Buzz off, stop copying!' In Humanities they are discussing the Reformation and Jhamari is asked to draw a picture of Henry VIII. In science 'sir' need not keep a wary eye on her as she sits, devoid of mischief and curiosity. She goes from class to class in a dream — eyes not fearful or expectant, but dead.

> Jhamari is not handicapped or mentally disturbed. She is simply Bengali. She and many like her go through the school day and the school year as

through a great sterile desert, uncomprehending, shut off, neither gaining nor giving. What potential they have is never realized, because it
goes unrecognized . . .

The presence of silent passengers in the classroom means a failure of
education, wasted childhoods and demoralized or desensitized teachers.
It should at very least become an immediate focus of research, debate
and policy.

The crucial point in these three simplified examples of class, gender and race is
that whilst the capability and potential of the children may be similar, the teacher's evaluation is likely to be different and to have crucial consequences in
subsequent actual achievement. This is because of the formative nature both of
children's self-image and of teachers' expectations. In addition, other children in
the classroom are quick to reinforce the teacher's expectations.

It is essential for teacher educators to challenge these assumptions, yet, at
the same time to emphasize that this is not an argument for 'putting down'
middle-class children, boys or white pupils. There is no place in the classroom for
negative experiences. Advantaged children must be helped to build on their
advantage; the disadvantaged must be given full opportunity to match them by
whatever means the teachers can make available.

Socialization

If trainee teachers are to become effective in delivering equality of opportunity
they need a conceptual and theoretical understanding of the issues to underpin
the practical suggestions for work in the classroom. Perhaps the best and certainly the most accessible is to be found in the concepts and theories of
socialization.

A major underlying reason for the differences between children before and
during schooling is the process of socialization that occurs in family community
and school (and continues through adult life), in which new members of society
learn the culture — the values, attitudes, language and general life skills — that
enables them to survive. It is an essential process of growth, but unlike physical
social growth it does not occur 'automatically'; it has to be learned from other
human beings. And whilst there are aspects of common culture that virtually all
members of society know and share, such as language, diet, religion and law, very
many aspects are specific to groups within it. These subcultures, with recurring
variations from the mainstream culture, can lead to widely varying life chances
and prospects. And the main subcultures in virtually all societies are those of
social class, gender and race.

There are of course many others, usually less permanent, such as the subcultures of a workplace, a club, a school, or even a school class. Human beings
commonly put a great deal of effort into learning the appropriate culture patterns
of social groups in which they find themselves or which they aspire to join. Unless
they succeed they will never have the recognition of full membership and as a
result will be confined to low, marginal roles and status or will even be 'outsiders'.
All teachers know children who never quite 'make it' in classroom acceptability
and have seen the distress and anxiety such children experience.

The process of learning the culture or subculture is known as socialization, and it is a process which can bring individuals together in behaviour and opportunity — or differentiate them. For many years teachers have reinforced not only the learning of common culture but also the process of differential socialization, helping middle-class children to become middle-class adults, boys to be men and girls to be women and, often, ethnic-minority community children to occupy marginal adult roles. More recently, however, teachers have come to see more clearly that this process can lead not only to a kind of social stability but also to great injustice. It is a fundamental assumption of this chapter that teachers wish to maximize the full capacity of all their pupils. There are many reasons but three will suffice:

- justice to young people;
- the needs of all modern societies for developed human capability; and
- the professional satisfaction of the teachers themselves.

Language

Let us now look at some aspects of socialization particularly relevant to the understandings of the beginning teacher. One is language. We are in debt to Basil Bernstein (1961) for reminding us that there are two strikingly different kinds of language usage. His famous story of the two children on the bus is well known. There are many versions, but all involve two mothers and their equal concern for the safety of their respective children when the bus moves off. Mother A says, 'Sit down now, darling'. Her child says, 'Why?' and mother explains the risk of falling over in careful detailed ways. After several more 'whys' mother is close to discussing centrifugal force. But when the bus actually moves she has to turn her request into a command. Mother B also asks her child to sit down; faced with 'Why?' she responds with 'I told you to sit down' and soon reaches 'If you don't sit down I'll knock your head off'.

In Bernstein's terminology, child A is being helped to acquire an elaborated code, with complex syntax and extended vocabulary so that eventually every subtlety of meaning can be expressed by words alone. It is a language that middle-class parents use in work and leisure, but also, more crucially, it is the language of the classroom, the textbook and the examination room. Without it success in mainstream education is difficult, even impossible. Child B is experiencing a restricted code of language, one with simple syntax and limited vocabulary. Full meaning requires the words to be augmented by gesture, expression or context. A good example is the building site, where workers may often use the 'f' word for almost every adjectival or adverbial use, and yet achieve full communication. There are countless restricted codes; almost every permanent social group has its own. Most families have their own version and their use plays an important role in family bonding. Yet teachers' preferences for elaborated codes, though understandable and largely necessary, should not lead them into the easy belief that these are always superior to restricted codes, which can convey, with non-verbal augmentation, a full range of subtle meanings.

Labov (1969) made the point clearly in his study of New York children. He showed that many had been identified by their teachers as being virtually without language capability and that test results confirmed this view. Such children were seen as virtually ineducable by teachers, and their schooling had little prospect. The children responded with low motivation, low attendance and low cooperation with their teachers. Yet when Labov mixed with the children out of school he found that in their language they were able to conduct extended discussions and arguments involving complex issues of sport, popular music, community relationships, often much more demanding than the verbal reasoning required of them in the classroom. Yet sadly this capability remained unrecognized in their schooling and its assessment. It does not take many comments such as 'You cannot use that language in the classroom' to turn children into non-verbal members of the class. This point was recognized by the Working Group on English (1989), which urged teachers not to be over-insistent on the use of standard English at all times. The extent to which that injunction can and should be implemented and in what situations must be a major item of the agenda of all teacher-education programmes.

Social Control

But the work of Bernstein and Labov alerts us not only to how language is used but to the significant consequences of its different uses. This is an issue of control. Child A on the bus was not only learning how to use elaborated language but also learning that by understanding and reason it is possible to control one's relationship with the environment and to use it to personal advantage. Child B was learning that personal behaviour is controlled by others; personal understanding is unnecessary, even irrelevant. The experiences point to different future lifestyles, lifestyles probably very similar to those of the children's parents: the first based on ability to control situations and having power over others, the second controlled by others. To use conceptual terms, the difference is between learning inner-directedness and other-directedness. Using our concept of socialization, it could also be seen as the difference between two distinct patterns of anticipatory socialization.

Most teachers recognize the importance of inner-directedness. It is after all, a crucial element of the teacher's own role as every new teacher learns to recognize. Similarly, all children need to feel they can control some parts of their own lives and enjoy their own 'space'. If children are precluded from, or feel unable to respond to, the opportunities the teacher is offering them for personal space and control, then they are likely to set up alternative subcultures in which they can achieve it, as Labov's work clearly shows. For this reason teachers are often faced with the 'anti-group' in schools who find ways of 'counting for something' by adopting deviant, teacher-provoking ways of dress, hairstyle, language or behaviour which may be matched by delinquent and deviant behaviour out of school (e.g., Patrick, 1973).

Reinforcing Expectations

This discussion of language has focused on social-class differences, though in the case of Labov's study the ethnic factor is also relevant since many of the children were black. Brandis and Henderson's study of primary schools (1974) offered information that is crucial to teacher education. They found that, contrary to widespread expectations parents from all social backgrounds were actively interested in teachers' views of their children and paid keen attention to them. However, there was a marked difference in the response of parents from different social groups. Middle-class parents faced with a less than enthusiastic commentary on their children sought to change the appraisal by giving extra assistance and support to the children and seeking to encourage the teachers to change their views. Working-class parents were equally concerned but tended to defer to the view of the teacher as the expert and to accept the situation. The inevitable consequence was a widening class gap as the differentiation was reaffirmed and built upon. Following the 1988 Education Reform Act, and the Citizen's Charter of 1992, all parents in England and Wales will now receive regular information on their children's achievements in National Curriculum subjects. It will be vital for teachers to ensure that all parents are helped to respond effectively to the information they receive.

Many other writers have reaffirmed the class, gender and racial differentiation that is arbitrarily built upon very rapidly assumes permanent dimensions. Douglas (1964) documented how teachers' class-linked perceptions of children of similar ability led to wide variations in actual achievement through the period of primary education. Jackson and Marsden (1960) noted how schools handicapped parents who had little knowledge of the school curriculum and examinations by failing to recognize and remedy their need for better information, thereby diminishing their capability to support and guide their children's education or even to ask appropriate questions.

Delamont (1986), like many other writers, has shown how the expectations teachers hold about the education of girls are different from those they hold about boys and lead to familiar differences in subject choice. In every university the results are clearly to be seen on degree day: very few women receive degrees in engineering and technology, and not infrequently the lone woman engineering graduate receives a special round of applause, much as would be received by a severely handicapped student! Conversely, numbers of male students obtaining a professional qualification in early-years teaching are still very small. Sex stereotypes abound throughout education: 'Boys don't cry', 'Girls don't get dirty'. All readers will know these and many similar exhortations; they are indeed part of the culture of our society and as such are highly formative.

Eggleston *et al.* (1986) in a study of black young people and their parents showed how teachers underestimated and undervalued the capability and motivation of black children, even though in many cases the schools themselves had reliable evidence of it. In several of the schools which the researchers investigated, able black children were assigned to lower-achieving groups; when challenged, teachers argued that this was done 'for social reasons'. At the heart of the 'reasons' were expectations that black children lacked the persistence, ambition and endurance to 'make it' academically, assumptions that the research team demonstrated to be unfounded.

Eggleston and Sadler (1988) in a study of technical and vocational education found that schools were disappointed that black children and their parents were not more enthusiastic about the new opportunities on offer. But the research found that relatively little information was effectively reaching the parents:

letters sent home with pupils were often not reaching the home, and even when they did, the letters' standard, formal English was often interpreted inaccurately or incompletely to the parents by the pupil. Conversely, the schools were receiving little or no information about the aspirations of parents and their support for education through such means as supplementary schooling or books and computers in the home. Thus erroneous assumptions about the lack of black parents' enthusiasm and support went unchallenged and once again formed the basis for decisions on examination entry, school reports and thereby, life prospects. Smith and Tomlinson (1989) present clear evidence that, when schools break through these assumptions, the achievement of *all* pupils, white and black, can be enhanced and that the key variable is good teaching not race. Much the same conclusion about social class is recorded by Mortimore *et al.* (1987):

> Those schools which were effective for one group tended to be effective for the other. Conversely, those which were ineffective for one group were also usually ineffective for the other. Our results show, therefore, that effective schools tend to 'jack up' the progress of all pupils, irrespective of their social class background, while ineffective schools will usually depress the progress of all pupils.

One of the main reasons for the perpetuation of the negative assumptions we have reviewed can be the needs of teachers! In a study by Sharp and Green (1975), 'Mrs Lyons' sees her pupils as:

> the products of largely unstable and uncultured backgrounds, with parents who are, in various combinations, irresponsible, incompetent, illiterate, 'clueless', uninterested and unappreciative of education, and who, as a result, fail to prepare their children adequately for the experiences they will be offered in school.

> The parents, especially the mothers, tend to be spoken of very disparagingly. The mothers are perceived as generally immature and unable to cope, having too many young children either by accident or design whilst they are still too young. The teacher declares that many mothers go to work to help pay off rent arrears and electricity bills incurred through bad management. She castigates them for creating latchkey children and for frittering away their conscience money on toys and unsuitable clothes in an attempt to relieve 'their guilt' at neglecting them.

'Mrs Lyons' is illustrating a rationalization often used by teachers: holding children's backgrounds to blame for low achievement in school. There are some situations where this may be true, but to see it as the end of the matter is to condemn children to the constraints of their backgrounds. And of course it may well be that some of the factors listed by 'Mrs Lyons' do not exist at all or, if they do, are not constraints!

At the heart of the issues raised in this chapter there is one issue: Should education really make a significant difference to the experience of child, parent and teacher? Or should it simply transmit to each new generation the social distinctions of class, gender and race? Should it in fact be simply a process of social and cultural reproduction as Bourdieu (1973) has described? If teacher education is to enhance equality of opportunity, then its students must be convinced that it should not and need not be; but that unless teachers are constantly vigilant it will be. It is facile, misleading and generally untrue to say that middle-class parents value education more than working-class parents, to say that the education of boys is seen to matter more than that of girls, or to say that black parents have lower understanding and expectation of education than white parents. On close examination, these assumptions turn out to be false; most of the evidence suggests that the differences are non-existent.

If education is to provide real equality of opportunity then all the understandings and misunderstandings we have listed in this chapter have to be re-examined. Such re-examination can best be begun in the teacher-training course and the school-practice classroom. To do it teacher trainers need awareness of social and cultural backgrounds and a willingness not just to recognize but to understand and value alternative forms of knowledge, language and culture so that they can base the work of the classroom upon a positive analysis of all the children in it.

Conclusion

This chapter has examined the role of the teacher in class, race and gender socialization and indicated the crucial need to help trainee teachers to break through stereotypes of class, gender and race. If teachers cannot lead in this then many children have little hope of real achievement. If teachers succeed then they will have made education matter — identifying feasible and rewarding achievements for each child, and delivering them. The teacher education course can provide them with the practical understanding and the theoretical and conceptual underpinning to do so.

References

BERNSTEIN, B. (1961) 'Social class and linguistic developments', in FLOUD, J., HALSEY, A.A. and ANDERSON, C.A. (Eds) *Education and Society*, Glencoe, Illinois, Free Press.
BOURDIEU, P. (1973) 'Cultural reproduction and social reproduction', in BROWN, R. (Ed) *Knowledge, Education and Cultural Change*, London, Tavistock.
BRANDIS, W. and HENDERSON, D. (1974) *Social Class, Language and Communication*, London, Routledge and Kegan Paul.
DELAMONT, S. (1986) *Sex Roles and the School*, London, Methuen.
DOUGLAS, J.W.B. (1964) *The Home and the School*, London, MacGibbon and Kee.
EGGLESTON, J., DUNN, D. and ANJALI, M. (1986) *Education for Some*, Stoke-on-Trent, Trentham Books.
EGGLESTON, J. and SADLER, S. (1988) *The Participation of Ethnic Minority Pupils in TVEI*, Sheffield, The Training Agency.
JACKSON, B. and MARSDEN, D. (1960) *Education and the Working Class*, London, Routledge and Kegan Paul.
LABOV, W. (1969) 'The logic of non-standard English', in ATLATIS, J. (Ed) *School of Languages and Linguistics Monograph*, 22, Washington D.C., Georgetown University Press.

MORTIMORE, P. *et al.* (1987) *School Matters: The Junior Years*, London, Open Books.

PATRICK, J. (1973) *A Glasgow Gang Observed*, London, Eyre Methuen.

RUTTER, M. (1987) 'School effects on pupil progress', *Child Development* 34, 1, pp. 1–9.

SHARP, R. and GREEN, A.G. (1975) *Education and Social Control*, London, Routledge and Kegan Paul.

SMITH, D.J. and TOMLINSON, S. (1989) *The School Effect*, London, Policy Studies Institute.

'WORKING GROUP ON ENGLISH' (1989) *English for Ages 5–16*, London: Department of Education and Science.

Chapter 3

Global Apartheid: Disadvantage and Inequality

Roger Iredale

Global Disparities in Access to Education

The 1990 annual report of the United Nations Children's Fund took as one of its propositions that 'a new world order should oppose the apartheid of gender as vigorously as the apartheid of race.' (Grant, 1992, p. 57). The word 'apartheid', effectively if dramatically, describes the very real barriers that exist between male and female opportunity; but it could with equal appropriateness describe barriers that separate other groups of people across the global community. The purpose of this chapter is to review some of the significant gaps in opportunity and access to education that exist today, to examine what needs to be done or is being done to redress them, and to consider their implications for the training and support of teachers.

The obvious and major disparities are those between low-income and high-income countries where the most elementary educational indicators show the disparities of opportunity for all but the sons and the daughters of the wealthy. The statistics of under development are far too well-known to need reiterating, but a few drawn selectively from the UNESCO *World Education Report 1991* (UNESCO, 1991, pp. 31–3) illustrate the bleakness of the opportunities that lie before the child of parents in most countries in Africa, the Caribbean, Latin America, or southern Asia. In Latin America and the Caribbean only 55 per cent of children enrolled in the first class of the primary school will reach year 4; for sub-Saharan Africa the figure is a little better at 67 per cent, while in South Asia the figure is 63 per cent. At secondary level the gross enrolment rate in 1990 averaged 44.10 per cent for all developing countries, 17.50 per cent for sub-Saharan Africa, and 93.60 per cent as an average for all developed countries (Northern America 98.90 per cent; Europe/USSR 93.10 per cent).

Behind these figures lie enormous physical, economic and social constraints on children's prospects of obtaining even the least acceptable level of educational opportunity. They conceal schools with virtually no books or writing materials; classrooms with holes in the roof, no chairs, no desks, no storage space for the teacher to use; teachers with little initial training and virtually no in-service opportunities or advisory support, often irregularly and/or inadequately paid; pupils

15

who have to walk long distances to reach even a primary school, let alone a secondary school (the attendance of which might require them to lodge with a distant relative); parents who desperately need the services of any able-bodied child, not only at harvest time, but (especially in the case of girls) often throughout the year for the carrying of water, care of younger children, and the grinding of meal; mothers who, never having stayed at school long enough to acquire even the most basic literacy, place relatively little value on its merits and advantages.

Disparities within Countries

While it is not easy to overlook the obvious disparities between developing and developed countries, the disparities within countries, and especially between rural and urban, between rich and poor and between males and females are less immediately evident. Although two-thirds of the people in developing countries live in rural areas the percentage differences as between rural and urban in their access to the three key facilities of health care, water, and sanitation are 45.88 per cent, 41.79 per cent and 14.61 per cent respectively (UNDP, 1992, pp. 29–33).

A comparable educational indicator is not as readily available, but there is little reason to believe that it would significantly differ in terms of access and quality of provision. Illiteracy, the best documented educational indicator, is twice as high in rural as in urban areas in selected countries in Africa and Asia; in Latin America three women in rural areas will be illiterate for every female illiterate city dweller, and four illiterate men for every one urban male illiterate. In Brazil in 1979, 74 per cent of the urban children but only 26 of the rural children were enrolled in school, and similar demonstrable disparities are documented for Sudan and Indonesia (Baum and Tolbert, 1985, p. 121).

The average income disparities between richest and poorest groups of people were estimated by UNDP in the 1990 *World Development Report* as around 140 to one (pp. 34–8), but these hide much wider differentials between the wealthiest and poorest in individual societies. In Namibia, for example, it has been estimated that 5 per cent of the population earn more than 70 per cent of Gross Domestic Product, while the poorest 55 per cent earn only 3 per cent. Moreover, globally the disparities are generally in the process of widening rather than narrowing. Educational and other opportunities for the poor, rural and female are worsening rather than improving. In practical terms, this means that, without positive interventions to improve their lot economically and alter social and other attitudes which stand in their way, the children — especially female children — of the poor in developing countries will increasingly lose any foothold they temporarily gain on the educational ladder.

The poor, whether rural or urban, are markedly disadvantaged in all societies, but in developing countries, where facilities are many times more unequal than in the developed world, the extent of their inequality can be quite markedly demonstrated. UNDP's *World Development Report* of 1992 provides a number of examples which include a difference in life expectancy in Brazil of twelve years between the bottom-income groups, who can expect to live only to fifty, and those with more than $400 per annum, whose life expectancy is sixty-two; in rural

Punjab child mortality among the landless is 36 per cent higher than for land owners, while in rural South India Brahmins can enjoy a literacy rate of 90 per cent compared with the Harijans' 10 per cent (UNDP, 1992, pp. 32–3).

Implications for Teacher Training

Two different but related conclusions offer themselves. *The World Declaration on Education for All*, of the *1990* World Conference called for an education that achieves tolerance towards social, political and religious systems that differ from one's own and empowers individuals to 'work for international peace and solidarity in an interdependent world'; in terms of teachers in metropolitan (developed) countries this suggests a need to appreciate in depth the issues of underdevelopment, not simply in terms of economic facts, but in terms of the social and cultural values of the people most in need of support so that they can pass on to their pupils a sense of the urgency, depth and complexity of the problems involved. The importance of training teachers in such skills is discussed at the end of this chapter.

The second, on which the first is predicated, is to consider the nature of the problem and what national governments, aid donors, charities and other non-governmental organizations should be doing about redressing the disparities referred to above. Though the problems and their solutions are infinitely varied from culture to culture and even location to location, there are common strands. To begin with, while it will be evident that the teacher is a key operator in the educational equation, and that his/her training is a crucial element, it is equally important to remember that the teacher is often as much a victim of the system as the pupils themselves, and can usually only make improvements where a range of other issues is tackled simultaneously. To give but one example, as Hugh Hawes (1979, p. 103) comments in his celebrated *Curriculum and Reality in African Primary Schools*, 'because the examination is set on knowledge and abilities required for secondary school entry, and because all children do aspire to such entry, it forces teachers to cover material with their pupils whether they are able to understand it or not; the very antithesis of sound pedagogy.' He cites the then Botswana science examination in which forty-nine out of fifty questions required only recall of factual information.

Improved teacher education therefore has to go hand in hand with sensible curriculum improvements that are both relevant and teachable, with adequate remuneration and teaching conditions for teachers, with proper professional supervision, with the supply of at least basic learning materials including textbooks, with community involvement in the school; all this has to take place within the much wider context of overall community development that includes adult literacy classes for parents, especially women, with the creation of employment opportunities for school-leavers, and with the kind of overall economic development that enables families the 'luxury' of sending their children to school instead of requiring them to undertake domestic work or provide an income from local labour. The realization that significant improvements can be effected only through an overall concentration on a whole range of changes in the education sector of a country has begun to be appreciated by aid donors, who are increasingly concerned to engage ministries of education (and related line ministries) in constructive dialogue about improvements to the whole system (Avalos, 1991, p. 18).

Rural/Urban Disparities

Before we examine the issues facing teachers and their employers in developing countries, we need to look in more detail at the two major areas of disparity: rural–urban; female–male. Of the two, the rural–urban distinction is not as well documented as the female–male, though in many ways the two are inseparable parts of the same spectrum of inequality. The lack of rural opportunity documented by UNDP and cited above underlies the difficulties which many of the poor face in developing countries. In educational terms, some of the difficulties are represented by:

- lack of housing and other general facilities for teachers; the village is probably not on a tarmac road, it lacks shops, it may lack electricity and main drainage, possibly piped water; medical care may be at a distance and so not readily available; it will be dark at night, and particularly difficult therefore for a woman living on her own, and hence female teachers are likely to be available only when they are married and their husband is posted (for reasons of *his* work) to the area.
- poor school buildings; where the education system is centralized, rural school buildings will tend to be neglected and rarely visited by administrators or inspectors (who will often lack transport or the fuel to enable them to make a journey);
- minimal teacher support (for the reasons given above) often accompanied by school closures resulting from teacher absences (which are frequently unauthorized);
- general shortage of learning materials because of transport or distribution difficulties;
- a centralized curriculum and related examinations written in a curriculum development centre situated in the capital city; consequently, many examples in science lessons are likely to appear theoretical and removed from realities of everyday life;
- the need for pupils to walk long distances to school, often returning home in the dark; like many of the other disadvantages referred to above, this particular difficulty is often detrimental to girls, whose parents are concerned for their safety; in addition, pupils are physically tired and often hungry by the time they get to school, as well as wet through in the rainy season;
- interference with the school year at harvest times; the children of the poor are usually needed in the fields when harvesting takes place, and few education systems yet provide the flexibility that allows school holidays to coincide with this key period; with the inflexibility of school examinations arrangements a pupil who has been withdrawn for seasonal work may fail the end-of-year examination and be forced to repeat the year, or drop out.

This rural–urban divide is fundamental to the problems of poor people in developing countries and especially teachers (Avalos, 1991, p. 9). The urban poor are frequently as badly off as those in rural areas, and urban deprivation can be as acute as rural; nevertheless, the urban environment, while lacking amenities, does not suffer from the same range of problems because access is generally easier. The daunting difficulties faced by female teachers in rural areas are to an extent (but only an extent) mitigated in the urban context. Yet in both rural and urban situations education must be the main means by which the poorest are enabled to make some progress. The 1990 Report of the Bangladesh Rural Advancement Committee makes the point that a functional education course is obligatory for all group members under the rural development programme since 'it plays a crucial role in conscientizing the target people and unlocking their hidden potential to tackle the problems they encounter every day.' (BRAC, 1990, p. 13). The particular problems of rural schools and the training of teachers to cope with, and take advantage of, the rural environment merit further research.

Gender Disparities

Gender differences are the best documented of inequalities in most developing countries. Literacy rates among females over the age of fifteen, compared with those of men, provide one of the clearest indicators of the considerable gap between men's and women's educational opportunities. In 1990 male literacy in sub-Saharan Africa stood at 59 per cent against 36 per cent for women; the difference between countries in southern Asia was even more dramatic at 59 per cent against 32 per cent (UNESCO, 1991, p. 26). The same inequalities exist at school level: Estimates by UNICEF suggest that in the second half of the 1980s the gender gap in primary-school enrolment was approximately 29 per cent in South Asia, 20 per cent in sub-Saharan Africa, and 18 per cent in the Middle East (Grant, 1992, p. 4). Apart from the loss of opportunity and human potential, the economic cost is acknowledged to be high (World Bank, 1989, p. 79).

Considerable attention is being given by aid donors to the huge loss of talent represented by the serious neglect of women's educational opportunity. UNICEF have already produced two popular digests of past experience in an effort to persuade all concerned — national governments, donors, non-governmental organizations, local authorities and individuals — to focus on the problem; UNICEF pick out twenty-nine countries, where fewer than 30 per cent of women can read or write, and note that over 70 per cent of female illiteracy is concentrated in the six populous countries of Bangladesh, China, India, Indonesia, Nigeria and Pakistan (UNICEF, 1992, p. 16).

An analysis of the difficulties faced by girls in gaining access to education appears in an unpublished research study by Colin Brock and Nadine Cammish (1991) commissioned by the Overseas Development Administration. The study analyzes the barriers to female participation in six selected countries and reviews them under the headings of geographical, socio-cultural, health, economic, religious, legal, political/administrative, and educational; it also outlines the initiatives being taken in each country to redress identified disparities.

Generalizing from their country studies Brock and Cammish (1991, pp. 3–6) analyze the barriers to female education as follows:

- geographical: patchy physical location of schools, lack of provision of single sex institutions, poor transport, combined with physical difficulties in travel, are major factors; lack of provision is particularly acute in the rural context;
- socio-cultural: the near-universal cultural bias in favour of males, combined with patriarchal systems of social organization, early marriage, early pregnancy and heavier subsistence duties for females represent a major influence;
- health: boys often get preferential feeding and girls have to work harder domestically; pregnancy and other sexual activity disadvantage girls;
- religious: this tends to be a positive rather than a negative force, especially in relation to Christian mission schools, but also in Islamic areas;
- legal: though most systems have introduced suitable legislation, traditional sanctions continue to operate unchallenged, especially in the employment of young children;
- political/administrative: the political will to carry through equal opportunities commitments is often weak; and
- educational: poor teacher quality and morale, and the frequent lack of female teachers in rural areas are cited, along with the incompatibility between the timetable and the requirements of local economies. Scholarship schemes for girls and secure boarding facilities are among the needs identified.

It will be apparent that the major inequalities of poverty–wealth, rural–urban and female–male identified above are intertwined with each other. On balance, the most disadvantaged position that any group of human beings can occupy is to be born female to poor and illiterate parents in the rural part of a developing country. No single intervention is likely to be able to redress such an imbalance, as Brock and Cammish point out in their discussion of school accessibility: the problem 'can only be overcome by more sophisticated and multivariate spatial analysis of educational needs and the planning and implementation of integrated development projects . . . Educational planning on its own would be futile.' (ibid., p. 3).

How Should Teachers Be Trained?

The need for a multifaceted approach has to be kept constantly in mind in any discussion of teacher preparation. While it can be argued that effectively prepared and supported teachers are the single most important contribution to assisting in the development of people's abilities, teacher quality is only one part of a complex mosaic of factors and influences. However effective a teacher may be he or she is of no value to children who are not at school. That said, the ability of the teacher is a crucial factor in retaining those who do enrol.

Teacher education in relation to the inequalities described above has become an increasing preoccupation with ministries of education and their donor partners. Of these, gender is the most pressing and important issue. In a paper written recently for a conference sponsored by the Rockefeller Foundation in May 1992, Katherine Namuddu refers to research indicating that in the African classroom textbooks and the curriculum more than frequently tend to trivialize women's roles, or at least subordinate them to those of men. She suggests that during lessons teachers perpetuate and reinforce patriarchal values through speech and behaviour (Namuddu, 1992, p. 5). As a first step in teacher training it is necessary to ensure that teachers are made aware of the inevitable tendency for materials to portray women as less important, as stereotyped in trivial roles, and as less involved in the key areas of science, mathematics and the use of international languages such as English, French or Portuguese. Female retention rates clearly begin here.

The more traditional and rural a society the more complex the issue is. Teachers and curricula cannot simply operate as though women will not be as-signed traditional tasks within the family context. It is more a question of ensuring that those tasks are not perceived as trivial, less important and that the education of girls as well as boys is seen as having a real economic value in terms of family health, size and behaviour (Brock and Cammish, 1991, p. 8). The task of convey-ing such messages within the already overcrowded and often unreal college cur-riculum is a challenging task (Hawes, 1979, p. 133).

The Need for Female Teachers

Teacher preparation is not, however, the only issue. The very absence of female teachers from classrooms in many countries or parts of countries reduces the opportunities for girls to find suitable role models. One of the UNICEF docu-ments cites figures of only 20–45 per cent for the numbers of teachers even at primary level in Asia, Africa and the Middle East (UNICEF, 1991, p. 33). This very absence of female teachers, like that of science and mathematics teachers, feeds the problem by starving the system of suitably qualified candidates for training at the upper levels of the system. The absence of female pupils higher up the educational systems of developing countries and in the professions manifests itself in the low numbers of women nominated for training overseas under donor assistance programmes. A figure of only 20 per cent female participation in over-seas training is common across developing countries, and reflects the problems which women have in reaching the upper levels of the educational and profes-sional pyramid.

In many developing countries it is essential, therefore, to increase the number of female teachers as any part of the effort to provide greater access to education for girls. Brock and Cammish assert the importance of more female teachers, single-sex schools and secure boarding accommodation, especially in Muslim and Hindu areas in the Sub-Continent (Brock and Cammish, 1991, p. 30). But even where female teachers do exist, they and their pupils may well be exposed to disadvantages that become evident only on close enquiry. For example, a recent unpublished study of conditions for teachers in slum areas in Faisalabad reports how many male teachers have lucrative after-schools private-tuition classes for boys enrolled in government and municipal primary schools, while their female counterparts are not able to participate in this activity because girls are not allowed out at night to attend extra classes. Undesirable in one sense as the practice may appear in principle, it nevertheless has the effect of disadvantaging both girls and their female teachers relative to males.

Increasing female access to education has to be a multipronged effort. It should include:

- non-formal education opportunities for girls outside the formal school curriculum; in India, non-formal education classes in poor urban and rural areas operate outside school hours, often in the room of a house, with a (usually female) instructor from the local community who takes the pupils through a syllabus that is different from that of the formal day schools but which eventually provides certification that is formally recognized as equivalent to school-based examinations. Because the classes take place within the community, parents are willing to release their daughters (and sons) to participate; the system leaves the pupils free to take paid employment or work in the home, if necessary, during the day;
- entry to teacher training that discriminates in favour of female recruits by allowing them to enter college with lower qualifications, supplemented by additional tuition (though there is always the paradox that such a system, if not sensitively handled, will be detrimental to the eventual standing of female teachers by branding them as less well qualified than their male counterparts);
- teacher training that also helps male and female trainees to perceive gender bias in both books and their own teaching styles; training that emphasizes the practical aspects of teacher training and draws on experienced teacher trainers who are more than theoreticians;
- female literacy classes led by imaginatively trained *animatrices*; a short publication of the National Institute of Adult Continuing Education describes a number of highly innovative projects involving women in various developing countries, such as a group in a 'Women's Laundry' in Santiago, Chile, who wrote a 200-page book about their lives as part of a cooperative endeavour that included organizing themselves, learning book keeping, running credit clubs, and finally developing their own literacy workshops (McGivney and Murray, 1991, pp. 51–3) The training of literacy workers to assist in this kind of development requires an innovative approach that transcends traditional teacher training.
- other interventions such as bursaries and scholarships for girls to encourage increased school attendance, grants for books, materials and uniforms, and in certain societies health education to provide them with the knowledge and means to reduce the risk of early pregnancy and, increasingly importantly, of sexually acquired diseases and viruses.

Training Teachers in Rural Areas

The rural–urban divide is of a different nature and in many ways more difficult to redress. The nature of the rural environment in developing countries is such that *ipso facto* it militates against equality of opportunity and provision. Many projects supported by major aid donors are aimed precisely at seeking to redress this imbalance. The Indian government has, for instance, encouraged donors to develop educational projects in a number of states aimed specifically at rural disadvantaged groups, both school-age pupils and adults. The Andhra Pradesh

Primary Education Project, supported by the British bilateral aid programme, aims to provide in-service training to every primary-school teacher in the State, to continue the support through local teachers' centres, to stimulate the provision of simple classroom materials and upgrade school buildings, and to help local research into the development of primary education — an important initiative itself, given the hitherto low status of primary education locally and the lack of indigenous research experience in the field.

A similar development, also supported by the British bilateral programme, is the active-learning primary-school project in Indonesia (King and Singh, 1991, p. 64). The project involves the in-service training of primary-school teachers so that they adopt an activity-based and problem-oriented approach, with support from head teachers and supervisors as an integral element in the design of the activities. As with the Andhra Pradesh project, the idea is to cascade the teaching style from the centre to the rural periphery through intensive workshops, simultaneously raising teacher morale by making the task of teaching more interesting for the teacher as well as more insightful for the pupil.

The resistances to such innovations at all levels should not be underestimated. In both the projects referred to above, it has not been easy to change pre-service teacher training to take account of the new approach because initial teacher training comes under a different part of the Ministry from in-service; additionally, in one of them, it was discovered that a quite separate unit of the Ministry of Education was continuing to encourage the development of textbooks that took no account at all of the parallel developments already taking place in virtually all the classrooms throughout the education system.

Moreover, the training of the trainers is itself a challenge if they are to understand at depth the nature and purpose of the changes of teaching style that are being developed (Lockheed and Verspoor, 1990, p. 69). Traditional teacher training in many colleges tends to be theoretical and based on urban assumptions. It may be necessary to include some work in the rural community alongside a planned period of rural teaching practice, and even to make success during a probationary period dependent on acceptance of the teacher by community members (Avalos, 1991, p. 18). Certainly an understanding of, and sympathy with, the nature of rural life and community are an essential part of teacher training in virtually all developing countries.

One particular area of disadvantage for rural pupils lies in the key area of language. The acquisition of literacy should necessarily take place in the mother tongue, but children and adults who are not able to operate in whatever language the normal medium of communication in government and business is, even if that language is a second or foreign one such as English or French, will inevitably be disadvantaged, both materially and psychologically. Teacher training must therefore include adequate tuition in the skills of teaching the nationally adopted language so that these can be passed on to pupils, whether urban or rural. In the rural situation, where a local language or dialect is normally used in all social contexts, particular attention will need to be given to ensuring confidence in the use of a language that gives access to the wider community.

Other interventions to try to redress rural–urban disparity were discussed by ministers of education and donors at the *International Consultative Forum on Education for All* held in Paris in December 1991. Ideas included children's literacy groups, improved sensitivity of schooling to the child's culture (hence presenting teacher trainers with a major challenge), and expansion of special education services, combined with decentralization of education management to the local level in order to enhance community participation in the educational process (UNESCO, 1991, p. 12).

Potential Teacher Shortages and the Use of Distance Learning

None of this takes account of a hitherto largely unconsidered threat to rural schools: AIDS. The extent to which the disease will affect future population growth is highly controversial; but one possible outcome of the disease's impact on populations could be the loss of key mid-career professionals in the public sector in urban areas, both teachers and administrators in other fields. The teaching profession forms a natural pool of educated manpower for the replacement of such losses, and the resultant vacuum at the centre may well draw rural teachers in towards it, further depriving rural schools (already in many places short of qualified or experienced staff) of their teachers. In such a situation not only may innovative and urgent methods of training teachers be required, including distance learning, but the development of distance learning may well be needed to provide the very lessons themselves, especially at secondary level (Lockheed and Verspoor, 1990, p. 46). As the record of the Consultative Forum puts it:

> timetabling 40 minute slots for each subject and seating children in militant rows are common practices that may not always be pedagogically sound. Furthermore, although technological advances contribute to improved production in many sectors, there is relatively little application of modern technology to enhance learning and to reach underserved groups. (Lockheed and Verspoor, 1990, p. 13)

The challenges of using a highly diversified approach to the provision of education for the underprivileged in rural societies, both male and female, will require a major rethink of how teachers are trained, supported and deployed.

The Role of Aid Donors

It would not be surprising if this area of activity becomes a major focus for ministries of education and aid donors in a large number of countries in the near future. The challenges will be great, and the need for an imaginative approach to unconventional and varied forms of teacher preparation will be considerable. The *Framework for Action* accompanying the World Declaration on Education for All in 1990 recognized the importance of the teacher's role:

> The pre-eminent role of teachers as well as of other educational personnel in providing quality basic education needs to be recognized and developed to optimize their contribution. This must entail measures to ... improve their working conditions and status, notably in respect to their recruitment, initial and in-service training, remuneration and career development possibilities. (World Declaration, 1990, par. 33)

The *Framework* goes on to relate the efforts of the teacher to the resources of the community and non-governmental organizations. It emphasizes the importance of libraries — another resource often lacking in the rural environment and in rural schools — and of pre-school educational provision. In addition to all this teachers in developing countries need to be provided with the skills to diagnose different kinds of learning difficulty and know what to do to help the sufferers who represent yet another group of largely ignored underprivileged members of society.

The disparities analyzed above represent a major challenge to the world community and, as has been indicated, they are the subject of comprehensive programmes of assistance from a wide range of agencies from collossi like the World Bank to non-governmental organizations like the Bangladesh Rural Advancement Committee (BRAC) which operates its own systems of educational and other social provision, which parallel those of the government. In between are other multilaterals, including the Regional Development Banks, UNICEF, UNESCO, and a score of bilateral aid agencies including Britain's Overseas Development Administration which currently spends about £2 billion per annum on programmes in developing countries, of which educational projects form a significant element. Additionally a considerable amount of educational assistance, particularly at the community level, is provided through national and international non-governmental organizations like Action Aid, Oxfam, Save the Children and Voluntary Service Overseas. Teacher education, both pre-service and in-service, is a major component of many projects funded by multilateral and bilateral donors.

Disparity and Teacher Education in Developed Countries

The disparity we have not analyzed is that between developed and developing countries. Given the increasing inter-relatedness of the global community and the role of the media in portraying life in other parts of the world, pupils in developed countries cannot but be aware of the problems facing those who live in different cultures and environments from themselves. What they are often not so clear about are the reasons underlying those problems, nor are they so often conscious of the pluses as well as the minuses of cultural diversity. Unfortunately, the British National Curriculum as it currently stands does little to assist in the process of helping pupils to understand the social and cultural dimensions of development. The nearest it gets is the geography curriculum which, however, is heavily biased towards the economic and physical dimensions of developing countries. Attainment Target 2, level 4e, requires the description of how the daily life of a locality in an economically developing country is affected by its landscape, weather and wealth (DES, 1991, p. 8). Only a particularly gifted, experienced or imaginative teacher is likely to be able to develop the associated lessons into a study of how daily life is also likely to be affected by traditional values, assumptions, perceptions and customs and how behind that daily life, there is an enormous richness and diversity.

Yet these are important if we are to understand and learn from other people's experiences. Teacher trainers therefore also face the important challenge of assisting future British teachers both to look for opportunities to introduce cross-cultural studies into their teaching and to do so with sympathy and understanding.

The kinds of facts and information provided in essays such as the present one represent one method; but the question remains how teachers can also represent to their pupils the kind of insights provided by this passage from Francis Selormey's story of education as perceived through the eyes of a new pupil in Ghana:

> As I stood and gazed at them, I heard my own name called. I was to go into Class 3. I found that Classes 2 and 3 shared one classroom and one teacher. I walked shyly into the room. It seemed to me very overcrowded and all the boys looked large and rough . . .
>
> I noticed that none of the children with whom I had played and eaten mangoes during the week before were in school, and asked where they were. I was told, rather scornfully, that they were not schoolboys, but farm-children. I realized then why those children had stared at my neat clothing. But they had been friendly. They were free as the birds. How I envied them!
>
> I asked what the farm-children did all day.
>
> 'They go to the farms with their parents and work all day,' I was told.
>
> 'What do they eat? Only mangoes?' I asked.
>
> 'Oh, no!' my informant said. 'They have huts in their farms, and they keep yams and cassava and corn there. And they pick fresh pepper and tomatoes and mushrooms from their fields, whenever they want them.'
>
> . . . Oh, how I envied those children: their carefree, outdoor life. No examinations, no inspections, no cane. (Selormey, 1966, pp. 63–5)

References

AVALOS (1991) *Approaches to Teacher Education: Initial Teacher Training*, Commonwealth Secretariat, London.

BAUM, W.C. and TOLBERT, S.M. (1985) *Investing in Development: Lessons of World Bank Experience*, Washington, D.C. Oxford University Press for the World Bank.

BRAC (1990) *BRAC Report 1990*, Bangladesh Rural Advancement Committee, Dhaka.

BROCK, C. and CAMMISH, N. (1991) 'Factors Affecting Female Participation in Education in Six Developing Countries', Unpublished research report for the Overseas Development Administration, London.

DEPARTMENT OF EDUCATION AND SCIENCE (1991) *Geography in the National Curriculum (England)*, London, HMSO.

EDUCATION FOR ALL (1990) *World Declaration on Education for All and Framework for Action to Meet Basic Learning Needs*, Inter-Agency Commission for the World Conference on Education for All, New York, Article I, 3.

GRANT, J. (1992) *The State of the World's Children 1992*, Oxford University Press for UNICEF.

HAWES, H. (1979) *Curriculum and Reality in African Primary Schools*, London, Longman.

KING, K. and SINGH, J.S. (1991) *Quality and Aid*, Commonwealth Secretariat, London.

LOCKHEED, M.E. and VERSPOOR, A.M. (1990) *Improving Primary Education in Developing Countries: A Review of Policy Options*, The World Bank, Washington, D.C.

McGIVNEY, V. and MURRAY, F. (1991) *Adult Education in Development: Methods and Approaches from Changing Societies*, National Institute of Adult Continuing Education, Leicester.

NAMUDDU, K. (1992) 'Constraints to the Achievement of African Women', Unpublished paper prepared for the Conference on Women's Human Capital and Development, Bellagio, sponsored by the Rockefeller Foundation, May.

SELORMEY, F. (1966) *The Narrow Path*, London, Heinemann.

UNDP (1990) *World Development Report*, New York.

UNDP (1992) *World Development Report 1992*, New York.

UNESCO (1991) *World Education Report 1991*, Paris.

UNESCO (1991) *Final Report, International Consultative Forum on Education for All*, Secretariat for the EFA Forum, Paris.

UNICEF (1991) *Strategies to Promote Girls' Education*, Education Section, Programme Division, New York.

UNICEF (1992) *Educating Girls and Women: A Moral Imperative and Strategies to Promote Girls' Education*, Education Section, Programme Division, New York.

WORLD BANK (1989) *Sub-Saharan Africa: From Crisis to Sustainable Growth*, Washington, D.C.

WORLD DECLARATION ON EDUCATION FOR ALL (1990) *Framework for Action*.

Chapter 4

The Residuals of Apartheid: Impediments to Teacher Development in South Africa

David Freer

Despite the reforms of the late 1980s which accelerated after State President de Klerk's initiative in 1990, many of the racially divisive structures erected in the apartheid era continue to exert a profound influence on all forms of social and economic life in South Africa. 'Petty apartheid' has virtually collapsed and the majority of public transport facilities, cinemas, hotels and restaurants now admit people of all races. Residential areas no longer embody racial restrictions and many employers in commerce and industry are seeking to recruit qualified people for management roles irrespective of their racial background. In spite of these significant moves towards an open and non-racial society, many of the bureaucratic structures designed to implement separate development or 'grand apartheid' are still visible and continue to exert a malign influence, particularly in the sphere of education.

The architects of apartheid were determined to divide the inhabitants of South Africa so that political and economic power remained the prerogative of people classified as 'white', that is people of European descent. A vital element in such a policy was to construct an educational system in which white children would be educated to fill the most prestigious roles in social and economic affairs. Children of African or Bantu descent, initially classified as 'Bantus' but latterly as 'Blacks', were deliberately and cynically allocated resources so small that they would be unable to challenge the ascendant position of Whites. Basic human rights were ignored and legislation was progressively enacted which created a class structure based upon what might be described as a continuance of colour. Black children had no compulsory schooling and the voluntary institutions open to them offered an education designed to fit them largely for labouring tasks on farms and mines. Coloured children, which in South Africa means children of mixed racial characteristics, received a slightly more generous provision and could therefore generate slightly higher employment aspirations. Children of Indian descent were closely aligned to the provision accorded to Whites which enabled them to enter segregated but nevertheless reasonably high-status occupations. In this starkly hierarchical structure, the norm or standard was traditionally delineated by perceived white needs and from a white apex, systematically scaled down for the other racially defined classes.

To give credence to this policy, a system of forced removals and oppressive influx-control measures sought to diminish the size of the black population so that in vast regions of South Africa the Whites would become the majority population and so have a legitimized right to political control. As part of the drive to achieve legitimacy, the Nationalist Government undertook a redefinition of South Africa's historical boundary which then became so complex as to be reduced to geographical absurdity. These geographic absurdities have become serious obstacles to rational and national educational reforms. In outlining the context of schooling in South Africa, it is vital to consider the unnecessary wastage of resources because of the erection of a multiplicity of bureaucracies designed to sustain apartheid and which still retain important executive functions.

The Context of Schooling in South Africa

In mid-1992 currently fourteen separate departments of education coexist, each with a different minister of education and each reporting to one of fourteen legislative bodies. Eleven departments administer schools and tertiary institutions for Blacks. The remaining three administer departments for the groups designated coloured, Indian and white. To further complicate this administrative structure, four black communities have been designated 'independent states' with all the paraphernalia of national borders, customs barriers, civil-service officials, national armies and national police forces. A further six ethnic groups have been declared 'self-governing national states' each with its own civil service including a department of education. Technically 'self-governing states' remain within the borders of South Africa. Despite pressures from central government, the 'self-governing central states' have consistently voiced an intention to remain South African.

The eleventh department involved in black education has the responsibility for providing schooling and tertiary education for all black people living in South Africa who are not resident in the two former groups of 'states'. As referred to earlier, the intention of the planners of apartheid was to create enclaves in which South African Blacks would have citizenship and therefore be enfranchized within an 'independent' or 'self-governing' state and so could be regarded as foreigners in 'white' South Africa. By definition Whites would then form a majority group in those areas of south Africa declared to be neither 'independent' or 'self-governing'.

The map of southern Africa's educational regions in Figure 4.1 illustrates the unequal distribution of land by area and the geographical fragmentation of the 'independent' and 'self-governing' states.

The basis for these 'independent' and self-governing' states rests upon the criteria of ethnicity and language. The ten 'states' have predominantly black populations and the basis for their formation relates to historic tribal affiliations and languages. As examples, the people of Kwa-Zulu are predominantly Zulu speakers whereas the people of Ciskei are predominantly Xhosa speakers. Invariably the areas in between the splintered boundaries that comprise 'states' such as Bophuthatswana or Kwa-Zulu are rich farmlands or important mining areas that have characteristically remained under white control in order that they can continue to contribute to the economic well-being of the white population.

Figure 4.1: Educational Regions of Southern Africa

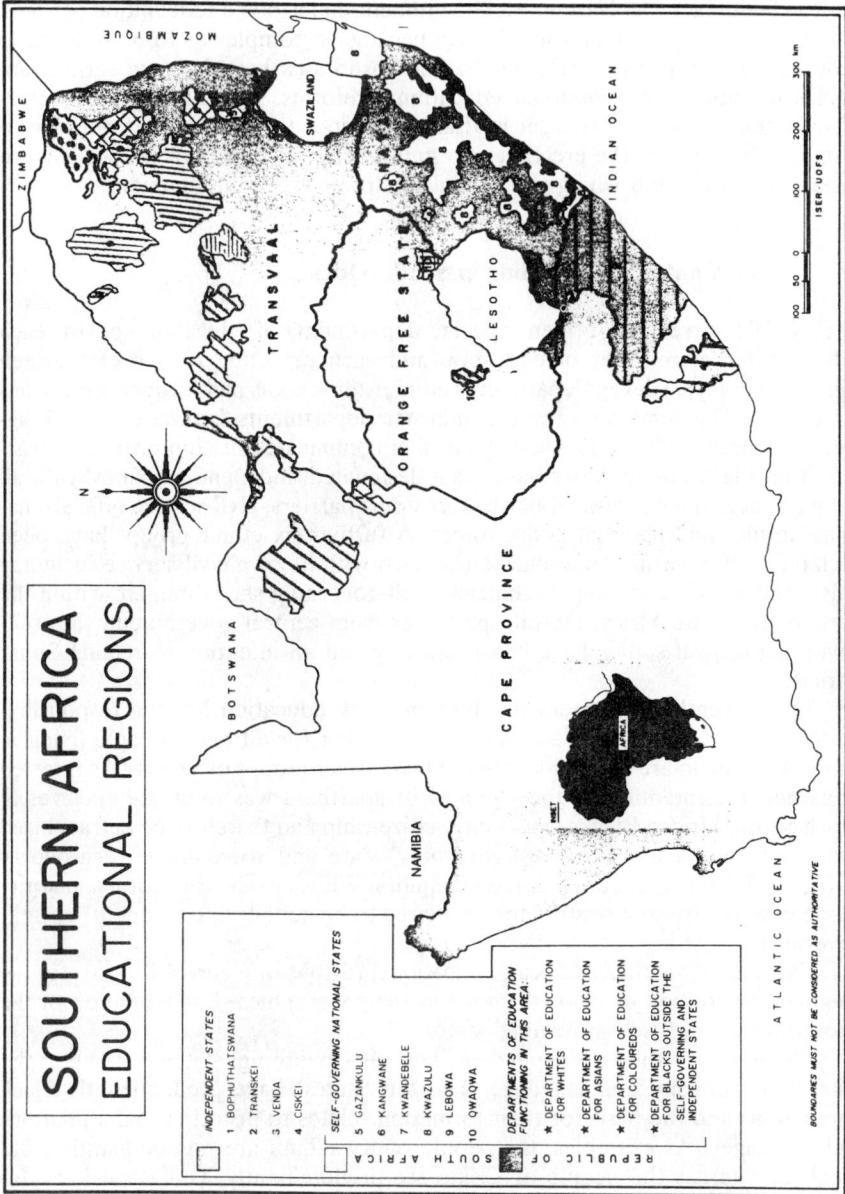

SOUTHERN AFRICA
EDUCATIONAL REGIONS

Source: Research Institute for Educational Planning, University of the Orange Free State, Bloemfontein

Table 4.1: Enrolment of Children in Schools in South Africa

Education Departments	Public Ordinary Schools	Special Schools	Private Schools	Totals
Whites	939,558	14,830	60,008	1,014,396
Indians	245,619	5,747	2,866	254,232
Coloureds	847,619	6,599	3,140	857,358
Blacks (not in 'self-governing' or 'independent' states)	2,060,733	4,430	19,859	2,085,022
Blacks in 'Self-governing' States	3,178,110	1,840	6,835	3,186,785
Blacks in 'Independent' States	2,100,984	1,595	6,454	2,109,033
Totals	9,372,623	35,041	99,162	9,506,826

Source: Statistics published by Department of Education in the Republic of South Africa, Pretoria, 1992

Evidence of the failure of this unrealistic attempt to promote a white majority is revealed in the 1989 figures for the Enrolment of Children in Schools in South Africa shown in Table 4.1. When further separated into particular state enrolments not one of the ten 'states' has a black school population that approaches the two million black children who attend school in 'white' South Africa and despite attempts to reduce the black population of white South Africa through influx control and forced removals to the ten 'states', twice as many black children as white reside in 'white' South Africa.

Using the historic, pre-1948 internationally recognized borders as the criterion to determine South African nationality, white children comprise 11 per cent of the school population (in the country as a whole). However in the allocation of resources they have enjoyed such a highly privileged educational advantage that the cutting edge of many of the popular mass movements for reform has been generated and sustained within black schools and among black student organizations. The impoverished rural areas allocated for the establishment of the ten 'states' have been unsuitable for the development of viable economies able to sustain adequate schooling systems and every 'state' has become reliant upon central government subsidies. These subsidies in turn have been totally inadequate to meet the social and economic needs of residents in those states.

Table 4.2 indicates per-capita expenditure on pupils classified by race for the period 1970–1990. Although Blacks living outside the ten states received slightly better financial allocations, the generally depressed provision for Blacks is indicative of the inability of the states to support adequate schooling systems. Above all, Table 4.2 demonstrates a remarkable adherence to racially biased funding which, although showing some percentage change during the past twenty years, still markedly favours white schooling.

Table 4.2: Per-Capita Expenditure on School Pupils by Race 1970–1990

	1970	1980	1990
Blacks	25 rands	91 rands	930 rands
Coloureds	94 rands	234 rands	1,983 rands
Indians	124 rands	389 rands	2,659 rands
Whites	461 rands	1,169 rands	3,739 rands

Note: 1992 rates: 5 rands = £1 sterling (approximately)
Source: South African Institute of Race Relations, *Race Relations Survey 1992*, Johannesburg

Table 4.3: Estimates of Pupil–Classroom Ratios in 1990

Racial Classification of Pupils	Primary Classrooms	Secondary Classrooms
Blacks	51:1	41:1
Coloureds	26:1	23:1
Indians	29:1	27:1
Whites	24:1	19:1

Source: South African Institute of Race Relations (1992), *Race Relations Survey 1991/92*

Teachers and Teacher Education

The per-capita inequity exemplified in Table 4.2 can be explained to some extent by salary differentials commonly applied in South Africa. Teachers' salaries are closely related to qualifications with lowly-qualified teachers receiving very low salaries. In addition, black children are invariably taught in very large groups. Table 4.3 indicates the extent to which a racially-determined funding strategy has led to vast differentials in classroom populations.

On average black children are taught in classes twice as big as their white counterparts and this obvious educational handicap for Blacks is accentuated by the low formal qualifications held by majority of black teachers. The racially hierarchical nature of the per-capita allocation is repeated in teachers' qualifications which in turn are reflected in teachers' salary structures. White teachers normally complete four-year pre-service programmes following twelve years of primary and secondary schooling. Generally white primary teachers enrol for non-graduate college courses and white secondary teachers for university-based courses. In contrast black primary teachers and many secondary teachers enrol for three-year courses with a very small group following four-year university programmes. Coloured and Indian primary teachers follow the three-year primary pattern but in general secondary teachers enrol for four-year courses. However only in very recent years have black teachers had the opportunity for twelve years of schooling followed by three years of college education. Table 4.4 demonstrates the considerable backlog of black teachers who are regarded as underqualified. It can be assumed that the majority of this group of over 70 per cent of black teachers have had a maximum of ten years of schooling followed by two years at a low-level teachers' training institution.

Table 4.4: Teacher Qualifications According to Race 1989

Teachers' Race Classification	Below 3 Yrs of Tertiary Education	Standard 3 Yrs	Qualification 4, 4+ Yrs	Total
Blacks	134,066	39,745	9,451	183,262
Coloureds	16,013	15,217	4,676	35,906
Indians	257	6,450	5,098	11,805
Whites	785	8,997	43,256	53,038
Totals	151,121	70,409	62,481	284,011

Source: South African Institute of Race Relations Survey for 1991/2 (1992) and *Education and Manpower 1990*, Research Institute for Education Planning (1991)

Nationwide, salary structures and promotion criteria are very closely linked to qualifications. Qualifications determine salary structures which are common to the 'independent' and 'self-governing' states, and to all the central-government education departments. Teachers holding substandard qualifications, that is any certificate below that of a three-years standard qualification, receive salaries at a level barely sufficient to breach the poverty datum line. For example new entrants to the teaching profession with four-year qualifications and no prior experience receive salaries approximately double that of teachers with substandard qualifications.

As black teachers hold the lowest qualifications, they receive the lowest salaries. Because teacher–pupil ratios are highest in black schools because of persistent long-term inequities in per-capita provision, they teach the largest classes. Crudely expressed, many black teachers receive half the salaries of their white counterparts yet teach classes twice as large. Because of low qualifications such teachers have the least prospects for any form of promotion.

To aggravate this distressing situation, many black secondary-school pupils have become highly politicized and aggressively militant because of the struggle that has continued since 1976 between the Nationalist Government and popular mass movements. Many of the leaders of popular mass-opposition groups gain their grass-roots support from older school pupils. A spin-off from the power structures created among such pupils has had a severely detrimental effect upon normal teacher–pupil relationships. Traditional teacher role models have been challenged and the use of schools as sites of popular protest has led to a massive decline in teacher morale, particularly in large urban areas such as Soweto. Increasingly pupil dissent has been matched by teacher dissent, sometimes in sympathy with the children, or alternatively in support of mass protests. At times teachers have taken strike action, euphemistically termed 'chalk downs' to support their own particular demands. Not surprisingly in such a climate, black teacher organizations have developed a greater affinity to workers' unions than to the professionally orientated associations espoused by most white teachers.

Government departments responsible for black teachers have made efforts to improve the qualifications of teachers up to at least a three-year tertiary level but the programmes they have introduced have been unrealistically long and unimaginative in that there has been little attention given to exploiting teachers' previous teaching experience, or in improving their professionally orientated knowledge and skills. It could be argued that the courses accepted by government

David Freer

Table 4.5: College of Education Enrolment: 1987–1990

Racial Classification	1987	1988	1989	1990
Blacks	29,297	38,700	46,096	46,247
Coloureds	7,901	8,527	8,331	7,636
Indians	625	1,111	1,235	734
Whites	13,606	12,281	10,714	9,467
Total	51,429	60,619	66,376	64,084

* Includes estimates for the 'independent states'
Source: South African Institute of Race Relations (1992)

as valid for salary and promotion purposes have in reality served as detractors to classroom efficiency. Many black primary teachers hold the qualification known as the Primary Teacher's Certificate which was awarded after two-year certificate courses following eight years of primary and secondary schooling. The first step these teachers have to take to improve their status is to gain a school-leaver's certificate based upon the current norm of twelve years of formal schooling. Dependent upon the marks and subjects chosen this examination also confers matriculation or university-entrance status. It is a broadly based six-subject examination. Only after successful completion of this school-leaving examination can teachers enrol for a number of university credit courses, which are essential for salary enhancement purposes. Such a process may require a reasonably competent primary teacher to engage in four to five years of part-time study beyond their original certificate course to achieve a qualification recognized as three years of tertiary teacher education. In some cases, teachers have been observed completing their tutorial assignments whilst supervising classes of children. Teachers themselves have commented that they have very little time for normal teaching preparation whilst they are engaged upon such upgrading courses. The problem that has arisen and has been widely recognized outside formal government agencies was that the upgrading courses were personally orientated rather than professionally orientated and no credit has been allocated for teachers for the length and extent of their previous teaching experience or their teaching ability. Far less bureaucratically designed and professionally focused upgrading programmes are an urgent priority to correct this misdirection of teachers' efforts. Some universities and non-governmental agencies have introduced professionally focused programmes but as teachers receive no financial reward for such courses there has been little incentive for teachers to complete such courses.

As the political pressures have increased, the South African government has made substantial efforts to improve teacher supply and so lower teacher–pupil ratios in black schools. To meet the high teacher–pupil ratios, there has been a substantial increase in enrolments in black colleges of education compared with those of other race groups. Table 4.5 indicates that the extent of this increase is in the region of 56 per cent over the four-year period 1987 to 1990, whereas white enrolment has declined by 30 per cent.

However, because rationalization of teacher supply has been conducted along racially segregated lines a number of well-resourced white colleges have been closed and many well-qualified teacher educators either retrenched or induced

Table 4.6: Degrees and Diplomas Awarded at South African Universities 1987

Racial Qualification of Students	Law	Medicine	Com- merce	Engineering and Architect- ure	Natural Sciences and Maths	Arts	Educa- tion	Total
Blacks	280	507	227	34	231	2,298	4,188	7,765
Coloureds	19	81	66	26	89	402	291	974
Indians	93	236	221	51	206	1,241	747	2,795
Whites	1,784	2,725	4,592	1,954	3,436	11,460	4,443	30,394
Total	2,176	3,549	5,106	2,065	3,962	15,401	9,669	41,928

Source: South African Institute of Race Relations (1992)

into early retirement. This failure to utilize good human and material resources is a direct consequence of the failure to abandon racially divided educational structures. An obvious alternative course of action would have been to utilize these colleges on a national and non-racial basis to further augment the supply of much needed teachers in black schools.

In contrast to the divided teachers' colleges, the liberal English-language universities have sought to provide teachers on a non-racial basis and a substantial number of teachers are educated through various university routes. The majority of university courses are of four years' duration. There are three-year degrees followed by a one-year teaching diploma, four-year concurrent degrees in which a teaching course is included and a number of specialist four-year non-graduate diplomas. However a further concern that has obvious implications for economic development is the paucity of black graduates in specific fields such as science and mathematics. Estimates of school-leavers suggest that approximately 70,000 white and 250,000 black pupils annually complete the full complement of twelve years of primary and secondary schooling. However the inequality of the education offered within a racially divided system becomes apparent in the final school-examination results. A survey by the South African Institute of Race Relations (1992, p. 208) indicates that only 8 per cent of 1990 black school-leavers, compared with 20 per cent of coloureds, 45 per cent of Indians and 41 per cent of Whites achieved passes at a level that qualified them for university entrance. More striking disparities emerge when the award of university degrees and diplomas are classified by race. Whereas 40 per cent of the white school-leaving cohort received university qualifications in 1987, only a tiny minority of Blacks, a mere 3 per cent achieved a similar level of success. Even more disturbing was the minute number who were successful in faculties that offered mathematical and scientifically related qualifications. Approximately a thousand black students graduated in the faculties of medicine, commerce, engineering and science at all the universities of South Africa. This is less than a half per cent of the black school-leavers' cohort. In contrast, approximately 18 per cent of the white school-leavers' cohort graduated in those faculties.

In addition to the scientifically orientated faculties, students who qualified in the field of education included some graduates or diplomates with a mathematical or scientific strength but the numbers should be assumed to be insignificant. The majority of education graduates or diplomates choose subject combinations from disciplines in the humanities, social sciences and fine arts. In the 1990 school examinations the South African Institute of Race Relations' survey (1992) indicated that of the 253,623 black candidates only 26 per cent were entered for the mathematics papers and 16 per cent for the physical-science papers. In the examination as a whole, 21,000 black candidates achieved university entrance. If the mathematics and physical-science candidates conformed to the 8 per cent overall pass rate then the probability has to be assumed that even optimistically barely 2 per cent of the black school-leavers achieved a pass in mathematics and less than one and a half per cent in physical science.

The disastrous impact of these figures for education cannot be overemphasized. The very small numbers eligible to enter universities in scientifically related fields have tended to apply for the high-status faculties of medicine, engineering and commerce. Very few black candidates in scientifically related fields have viewed teaching as a desirable career. Because of the virtual dearth of black graduate teachers of mathematics and science, there is depressingly little hope of rapidly improving the quality of teaching in black schools. Only in a desegregated school system can there be any likelihood of improving this situation and although there is a shortage of white teachers in mathematics and physical science, it is nothing like as catastrophic as the shortage prevailing among black graduates.

Black colleges of education have been unable to address the 'mathematics and science' problem in any meaningful way. The racial demarcation has extended to produce an intellectually inferior curriculum and, characteristically in most of South Africa, the courses implemented in black and white colleges have very little in common. The syllabuses and mode of teaching in majority of the black colleges have been of a low level, unstimulating and have to be regarded as a major factor contributing to the inadequate education received by most black children. Whereas the four-year courses in white colleges have been related to university validation processes and have included a number of courses comparable to university courses, a very different pattern prevails in black colleges. Black colleges have offered their students courses which essentially were repetitions of the three final years of an already impoverished secondary programme. Commonly, students have used school textbooks and enjoyed little that could be identified as challenging or insightful. Salmon and Woods (1991) in a review of seven black colleges in Kwa-Zulu, Natal sought the views of college principals, academic staff and students through questionnaires and interviews. The consensus they recorded from all the strata of college respondents was that the academic content of college diplomas were 'shallow, unchallenging and not likely to stretch the student beyond standard ten level' (p. 64). Normal school organization in South Africa consists of grades 1 and 2 followed by standards 1 to 10. Responses also indicated the extent to which the colleges failed to offer learning situations designed to develop mature and professionally responsible attitudes towards learning.

> Both the primary teachers' diplomas and the secondary teachers' diplomas share a common busyness; students are expected to do many subjects with primary diploma candidates taking as many as eighteen subjects per annum. The atomized timetable resembles the pigeonhole model common at secondary schools. There are no free periods, lectures are 35 to 40 minute sessions, and clear distinctions which separate rather than integrate subjects are emphasized. (Salmon and Woods, 1991, p. 64)

It was evident that when students emerged from such institutions they were unlikely to have received anything like the professional preparation for teaching enjoyed by students fortunate enough to have been enrolled at the predominantly white colleges.

In addition to these overt disparities between black and white colleges there has been an underlying ideological factor that has distanced many black colleges from the English-language tertiary institutions. The first language of three-fifths of the white population and of many coloured people is Afrikaans. Of the ten predominantly white enrolled universities, only four, Cape Town, Natal, Rhodes and the Witwatersrand teach through the medium of English. The remaining six have not only been aligned to an Afrikaans culture, literature and lifestyle but have also fairly consistently supported the Nationalist Government. Moreover, there is very little evidence of them challenging or criticizing government policy in the sphere of education.

Not surprisingly, they have been regarded as enthusiastic implementers of a racially divided education system. Within the faculties of education of the Afrikaans-speaking universities a theoretical position has evolved, known as 'fundamental pedagogics' and this has been translated into a schooling policy known as 'Christian National Education'. This particular narrow perspective has underpinned the majority of the black schools and colleges which have been maintained under the direct control of government education departments. A narrow, almost fundamentalist view of Christianity has been linked to a form of school discipline and authority designed to encourage unquestioning compliance and acquiescence to the State and the Dutch Reformed Church. Not surprisingly both 'fundamental pedagogics' and 'Christian National Education' have achieved little credibility in the liberal English speaking universities whose academics have consistently attacked them as part and parcel of the ideological apparatus of the State. In contrast the English institutions have developed eclectic approaches to philosophy, sociology and psychology similar in character to education faculties in the United Kingdom or the United States. Such is the distance between Afrikaans and English university departments of education that very little academic interaction has taken place between them. The dichotomy has been transmitted to all forms of pre-service teacher education. The black colleges under the direct control of government departments have been staffed very largely by academics owing adherence to 'fundamental pedagogics' whereas colleges linked to the English-medium universities have taken liberal and radical theoretical positions. As the vast majority of black colleges have been administered directly by government departments a consequence has been that the majority of black teachers have been subjected to a prescriptive and narrow form of educational theory.

However, overarching all these racial and ideological problems, has to be the major economic question of how to correct years of deprivation. In the period 1988–91, annual budgets have included a share of approximately 20 per cent for primary, secondary and tertiary education. Estimates of the amount necessary to raise black schooling to a level comparable with white schooling suggest that the allocation might have to rise to something in the region of 40 per cent. As housing, health, state pensions and other social welfare services have also been targeted as urgent priorities, it appears unlikely that state funding for education can be increased to any significant extent. Yet the shortages are daunting. The South

African Institute of Race Relations' (1992) survey estimated that to provide universal compulsory schooling in the immediate future required 120,000 new teachers and 110,000 new classrooms. The classroom shortfall has been accentuated by school violence and unrest. An estimated 6,000 classrooms have been destroyed or severely damaged during the past few years and new building programmes have rarely exceeded 2,000 units per year.

In summary, the residuals of apartheid which continue to exert a detrimental influence on teacher development can be identified as:

- historic underfunding for black schools resulting in inacceptably high teacher–pupil ratios and inadequately trained teachers;
- the multiplicity of geographically irrational administrative structures which have dissipated educational resources;
- bureaucratic barriers to innovative programmes of in-service education;
- the dearth of candidates for pre-service mathematics and science teachers' courses;
- limitations related to a narrow ideological focus commonly projected in many black colleges of education; and
- competing priorities for a number of social services which have been perceived as traditionally underfunded for black people.

Perspectives and Prospects

The attitudes of distrust, suspicion and fear which many black people hold in regard to state structures have been generated by decades of discriminatory practices. Changes in the statute book heralding the prospect of drastic reforms are unlikely to invoke a rapid reversal of people's perceptions. Nevertheless before major reforms in South African education are introduced, essential political and constitutional steps have to be taken. Such has been the dissent leading to turmoil and violence in black secondary and tertiary institutions that only the leaders of a popularly elected government have any chance of persuading black militant youth to return to schools prepared to submit to the authority that characterizes normal teacher–learner relationships. Only when a learning ethic re-emerges in institutions which are currently centres of black resistance can there be any reasonable hope of implementing a process of educational reform.

However if student militancy declines and some form of educational sanity begins to surface, the prospects for a fundamental reform of teacher education are not unencouraging and even within the divided colleges there are potentials for fairly rapid change. Human resources in the form of college-based teacher educators are in good supply. National Education (1992) records that staff-student ratios in white colleges approximate to one to ten, in coloured colleges one to thirteen, in Indian colleges one to eleven and in black colleges one to ten. In comparison universities and institutions of technology have far less favourable ratios averaging one to nineteen. The college ratios if reorganized to meet national priorities rather than remaining limited by racial and ethnic considerations should be a platform from which to launch a greatly enhanced supply of teachers and to reduce unacceptably high classroom ratios. There seems little reason why college enrolments could not be increased by 50 per cent, which would lead to a substantial improvement in teacher supply within a few years. The favourable college staffing ratios might also enable lecturer in-service training schemes to be introduced. Liberal grants of sabbatical leave should enable staff to improve their knowledge and skills with the objective of improving the qualifications awarded at the former black colleges.

Reorganization of the curricula in colleges of education could be spearheaded by establishing close links between universities and colleges. Alternatively, groups of colleges might establish inter-college curriculum networks and create 'in house' validation procedures. In either shape of development it appears essential that colleges become largely autonomous institutions able to provide stimulating, tertiary-level pre-service courses. Examples of expansions of college–university links are beginning to flourish but as yet no national policy designed to introduce full tertiary status for all colleges of education is evident.

Several predominantly white-enrolled colleges of education have attracted increasing numbers of black students. With their well-equipped laboratories and well-endowed library facilities these colleges could play key roles as models for improving the quality of pre-service education.

With an imaginative redistribution of teacher educators and a relatively small increase in college lecturer–student ratios it should be feasible to improve the supply of teachers without any significant increase on the budgetary allocation for education. However it will have to be accepted that the generous funding previously available for white schooling may be impossible to replicate in the non-racial schools of a future South Africa. A compromise level of provision should be possible which might reduce national teacher–pupil ratios to approximately one to thirty-five in primary schools and one to thirty in secondary schools. Once these suggested teacher–pupil ratios have been approached, the second priority of improving the professional skills of underqualified serving teachers could be addressed. Optimistically, as a well coordinated in-service programme is developed consequential status and salary improvements for teachers would lead to an improvement in morale.

The deliberate and cynical impoverishment of black education during the past forty years has created generations of young black people who have been confined to the lowest economic level in the industrial and commercial workplace in stark contrast to the myriad of opportunities open to white people. Class differences have been concealed by race laws which have been designed to promote white supremacy. Pessimistically, it could take a further forty years before a society is developed in which the suspicions associated with notions of racial inferiority and superiority totally disappear. To achieve a non-racial society it is essential that racial discrimination is not only removed from the statutes but that direct action is taken against people who continue to pursue racist practices.

The impact of segregated schools has led to a situation in which very few teachers will have had any experience of working in other than segregated classrooms. Generally white teachers have taught white children, Indian teachers Indian children, coloured teachers coloured children and black teachers black children. Colleges of education have also been largely segregated so that newly qualified teachers not only lack teaching experience but also will have received little guidance or introduction to strategies appropriate to multicultural education. It becomes evident that a major task has to be the development and implementation of college curricula which will facilitate multicultural teaching. In the reconstruction of society, teachers will have vital roles in creating learning climates which are tolerant, purposeful and which promote harmonious interactions between children whatever their colour. Lecturers in universities and colleges face the awesome responsibility of imbuing teachers with the attitudes and enthusiasm essential to facilitate progress to a non-racial society in South Africa.

References

DEPARTMENT OF EDUCATION AND TRAINING (1992) *Annual Report for 1991,* Pretoria, Government Pointer.

DEPARTMENT OF NATIONAL EDUCATION (1991) *Preliminary Education Statistics for 1991,* Pretoria, Department of National Education.

DEPARTMENT OF NATIONAL EDUCATION (1992) *Education in the Republic of South Africa 1989,* Pretoria, Department of National Education.

RESEARCH INSTITUTE FOR EDUCATION PLANNING (1991) *Education and Manpower Development 1991,* 11, Bloemfontein, Faculty of Education, University of the Orange Free State.

SALMON, C.M.R. and WOODS, C.A. (1991) *Colleges of Education: Challenging the Cliché,* Durban, Education Research Unit, University of Natal.

SOUTH AFRICAN INSTITUTE OF RACE RELATIONS (1992) *Race Relations Survey 1991/92,* Johannesburg, Institute of Race Relations.

Chapter 5

The Multicultural Preparation of US Teachers: Some Hard Truths

Carl A. Grant

Teacher education in the United States should be addressing the issue of multi-cultural education. In fact, it rarely does. In the majority of our teacher education programmes there is little or no attention to the issues of racial and ethnic diversity, socio-economic and social-class disparities, and gender discrimination. Even those programmes that purport to address multicultural education, or specific issues imbedded in multicultural education usually do so in a minimal or perfunctory manner.

Accurately describing multicultural teacher education or how teacher educa-tion programmes deal with issues of equity in the United States is a very difficult task. There are three major reasons for this: the United States does not have a national educational system; the geographic location of a college or university and the interests of its faculty influence the nature of the teacher preparation toward the multicultural education it offers; and there is very little written de-scription or analysis of multicultural teacher-education programmes.

The United States Constitution does not refer directly to education or delegate power to the federal government for participation in education areas. According to the Tenth Amendment, 'The powers not delegated to the United States by the Constitution, nor prohibited by it to the States, are reserved to the States respec-tively, or to the people.' Each of the fifty states, therefore, has its own legislative mandate from its state government for teacher preparation. Although there is commonality, these mandates differ somewhat. Many Americans, like myself, believe this is good, because, in theory, it allows the people of each state, indi-viduals who are closer to the children and the schools, to make the policy decisions, and to recommend the curriculum and instruction that best meet the needs of the children of each state. In addition, the lack of a national educational system celebrates a basic and fundamental ideal of American life, which is to 'praise diversity'.

There are approximately 1,200 colleges and universities that prepare teachers. Some teacher-preparation institutions are located in urban areas, and give par-ticular attention to preparing teachers to work with students who live in the inner city or the barrio. Some teacher-preparation institutions are located in small towns or rural areas and prepare teachers to work with the specific type of popu-lation indigenous to the nearby region. Still other teacher-preparation institutions are located in major research universities and reflect the research efforts and interests of the teacher-education faculty.

Although legislative mandates under the auspices of the state-education agencies exist, for example, Human Relations Code Points (Wisconsin) and Multicultural Standards (California) there is very little substantive description and analysis of teacher-education programmes from an equity or multicultural perspective. Similarly, the National Council for Accreditation of Teacher Education (NCATE) which is responsible for accrediting teacher-education programmes, reports mixed messages about what institutions report they are doing in self-report surveys and what is actually found by an accrediting team during a site visit (Gollnick, 1992).

Although, these reasons rightly suggest that my observations should be read with a cautionary note, I nevertheless strongly believe that multicultural advocates, who are in what Gordon (1988) refers to as a 'war for the heart and mind of people of color', need to continually inform one another about the progress (or lack of progress) that is being made to prepare society's teachers to teach from a multicultural perspective.

This chapter will include three sections. The first section describes the context of teacher education. Included is a discussion of multicultural policy and teacher preparation; the significance for multicultural education of the location of a teacher-education programme; teacher-education reform efforts, with a focus of The Holmes Group and educational equity; multicultural research on teacher-preparation programmes; and teacher-education students and multicultural education. The second section presents some of the challenges facing teacher-education programmes. Included is a discussion of the teacher-education faculties; the importance of defining multicultural education in teacher-education programmes; the impact of academic ethnocentrism and elitism on advocates of multicultural education; and the development and production of multicultural education knowledge. The third and final section presents my response to the challenges confronting the establishment of teacher-education programmes.

Context

Policy

In the late 1960s and 1970s the American Association of Colleges for Teacher Education (AACTE) provided the informal policy on multicultural teacher-education programmes. Smith's (1969) book, *Teacher for the Real World,* written on behalf of the organization, was seen by many teacher educators, especially proponents of multicultural education as providing guidelines to which teacher-education programmes should adhere. Smith argued:

> Education is beyond repair! What is needed is radical reform. This reform is to include the nature of the schooling process, the system which control educational policy, and the institutions which prepare persons to be teachers. In teacher training, reform must be undertaken in the selection of teachers. There must be more adequate representation of the poor, the black, the Mexican, and the Indian in teaching ranks. (Smith, 1969, p. 9)

Following this publication, and the establishment of a commission on multicultural education in 1970, AACTE 1972 published its widely heralded 'No One Model American' statement, which includes the following:

Multicultural education recognizes cultural diversity as a fact of life in American society and it affirms that cultural diversity is a valuable resource that should be reserved and expended. It affirms that major education institutions should strive to preserve and enhance cultural pluralism. *To endorse cultural pluralism is to endorse the principle that there is no one model American.* (my emphasis) (AACTE, 1972)

Although since the mid 1970s AACTE has sponsored at least seven publications on multicultural teacher education and has had them distributed to its nearly 800 institutional members, the organization (like most other educational organizations and associations) has not been as active and as forceful in its overall multicultural efforts. Instead, the organization has focused its attention on the decreasing number of people of colour joining the teaching force, on encouraging the recruitment of teachers of colour, and on promoting the need to identify 'best practices' for teaching students of colour. These efforts are important, but remove AACTE from the firestorm of the multicultural 'war'.

The National Council for Accreditation of Teacher Education (NCATE) is the only agency recognized by the Council on Post-secondary Accreditation (COPA) and the United States Department of Education to accredit professional education units (post-secondary institutions) that are responsible for preparing teachers to work in at any level from pre-school to high school (Gollnick, 1992). NACTE conducts on-site reviews of most teacher-preparation programmes every five years to determine the extent to which they are meeting eighteen professional standards. Important to this discussion is *Standard 2.1.1* on multicultural education. The standard reads: The institution provides for multicultural education in its teacher education curricula including both the general and professional studies components (NCATE, 1982). During its existence, adherence to *Standard 2.1.1* was poor and at some universities there was little or no compliance (Gollnick, 1978).

In 1988 the standards were revised, and the multicultural standard was dropped. However, the revision included the integration of multicultural education into four of the new standards and seven criteria of compliance. (1) *The Standard on Field Experience* requires that students have field experiences with both culturally diverse and exceptional populations (NCATE, 1990, p. 49). (2) *The Standard on Students and Faculty* argues for a cultural diverse population (ibid., p. 52). (3) *The Standard on Faculty Qualifications and Assignments* requires that teaching faculty know about multicultural education and include it in their teaching and student assignments (ibid., p. 55). (4) *The Standard on Professional Studies* requires multicultural education and includes three criteria for compliance that address: (a) the preparation of teachers so that they provide knowledge about, and appropriate skills related to, cultural influences on learning, instructional strategies for exceptionalities, knowledge of different learning styles; (b) the preparation of students so that they understand and apply appropriate strategies for individual learning needs, especially for culturally diverse and exceptional population; and (c) the curriculum for professional studies includes a multicultural and global perspective (ibid., p. 48).

In her assessment of compliances of teacher-preparation programmes with the NCATE standards Gollnick (1992) posits:

> Why is that after twelve years of requiring multicultural education, institutions still have not taken seriously its incorporation into its programs and practices? . . . [N]early half of the institutions have not responded. Responses are similar: Our candidates will not teach in culturally diverse or minority schools. Those issues are taught in the sociology and anthropology courses for general education. I don't have time to add another topic to my course. The faculty has academic freedom; we can't ask them to teach this stuff unless they want to. How can the faculty learn about multicultural education on top of everything else we ask them to do? We hired someone to take care of that. (Gollnick, 1992, p. 237)

Programme Location

The geographic location of a teacher-education programme and its proximity to a research institution directly affect how it deals with multicultural education. Let's use as an example, the state of Wisconsin where I work. Wisconsin has thirteen state universities (and nineteen private colleges and universities) that have teacher-preparation programmes. The state universities are located throughout the state. Although each teacher-education programme is responsible for preparing teachers to work in any school within the state, as well as for employment opportunities in education in other states, each teacher-education programme is also designed to prepare teachers for that particular area of the state, or is designed in keeping with the research interest of the teacher-education faculty of the institution. For example, the University Wisconsin-Milwaukee teacher-education programme has an urban focus, the University Wisconsin-Platteville programme has a traditional focus (middle school), and the University of Wisconsin-Madison teacher-education programme is driven by the research interests of its faculty. The programme focus, shaped in part by programme location and faculty research interest, therefore plays a major role in determining how and to what extent issues of equity or multicultural education are dealt with. For example, one common element of all the Wisconsin teacher-education programmes is the Human Relations Code Point requirement. Each teacher-education student must satisfy eight human-relations code points before receiving his or her teaching licence. These code points describe knowledge that each teacher-education student should be exposed to and understand. As illustration, Code Point One reads:

> study in the theory and application of human relations practices including skill building activities in identifying and constructively responding to expressions or acts which devalue other persons. (University of Wisconsin-Madison, 1990, p. 2)

Also, Code Point Five describes a field experience each student should have. It reads:

a minimum of 50 documented clock hours of direct involvement with adult and pupil members of a group whose background the student does not share, including at least one of the following designated ethnic minority groups: African-American, Alaskan-Americans, American Indians, Asian-Americans, Hispanic-Americans, Pacific-Islander-American, foreign-born persons of color; and with disabled person; and with various socio-economic groups, including low income. At least 25 of the 50 clock hours of direct involvement shall be with representatives of one or more of the designated ethnic minority groups. (University of Wisconsin-Madison, 1990, p. 3)

These code points have had only a limited effect because, in part the location of the university has played a role in the nature of the field experience (Code Point 5) and the attention given to the other seven code points. Sleeter (1988) surveyed 416 Wisconsin teachers who had completed twenty-four pre-service programs and got mixed results. She discovered that, in general, most of the teachers were doing relatively little to make their curriculum multicultural. In fact, some were including people of colour in the curriculum less than once a week. She reported that teacher education programmes in urban areas were more likely to have a longer experience, and those with the longer experience were more likely to teach about racism. She comments, 'It could be that a field experience with members of another race sensitizes students to racism experienced by those with whom they work, and that the more extended this sensitization is, the more a teacher teaches about it later.' (Sleeter, 1988, p. 17) In addition, Grant and Koskela (1986) learned that, for the most part, teacher-education students at the University of Wisconsin-Madison included a multicultural perspective in their university work and school work only when it was a particular interest of their instructors.

Restructuring Teacher Education and Multicultural Education

Since the publication of *A Nation At Risk* in 1983, a report on the status of education in the United States, commissioned by the US Secretary of Education, American teacher educators have been determined to improve the efficiency of teacher preparation. *A Nation At Risk* admonished teacher educators and stated, 'that teacher preparation programs need substantial improvement.' It pointed-out that, 'the teacher preparation curriculum is weighted heavily with courses in "educational methods" at the expense of courses in subjects to be taught.'

Picking-up that gauntlet and leading the charge in the reform of teacher education is the Holmes Group. The Holmes Group was incorporated in 1986 and committed, 'to enhance the quality of schooling through research and development and the preparation of the career professional in teaching.' (The Holmes Group, 1986, p. 1). It is a consortium of nearly 100 American research universities that are committed to making their teacher-education programme more rigorous and connected — to liberal arts education, to research on learning and teaching and to wise practice in the schools. The Holmes Group has proposed five major goals (p. 4):

- to make the education of teachers intellectually more solid;
- to recognize differences in teachers' knowledge, skills and commitment in their education, certification, and work;
- to create standards of entry to the profession — examinations and educational requirements — that are professionally relevant and intellectually defensible;
- to connect its member institutions to public elementary and secondary schools; and
- to make schools better places for teachers to work and learn.

Many teacher educators agree that the Holmes Group's concern over the quality of teacher education is professionally responsible, and that its willingness to organize a consortium and provide leadership in reform effort is admirable. However, some educators question the plans and actions of the Holmes Group. Popkewitz (1987), for example, reminds us, 'To view the reform proposals as objective, disinterested plans for action is to obscure the social significance and political implication of the reports.' (Popkewitz, 1987, p. 293) Gordon (1988) makes a similar point in addressing the focus of the content and rhetoric of the Holmes Report and other statements on reform. She posits:

How is it that deviance and deficit themes are pervasive throughout the [reform] literature, while serious debate on the politics and ideology of power and control in education and in the current power configuration in this society are only tangential arguments made by a handful of so-called radical or reconceptualist scholars, few of whom are African-American or other people of color? (Gordon, 1988, p. 154)

Speaking directly to the lack of attention to minority concerns in the reform report, Oliver (1988) claims the Holmes Report needs to 'address the social realities of being a minority in this culture; structure the profession of teaching based on individual, societal and instruction factors; reconsider career theory development in structuring the teaching force and pay particular attention to minority candidates'. (Oliver, 1988, p. 165). Similarly, Smith (1988) says, 'Designers of reform, whether the Holmes Group or other policy makers, must include in their agenda positive approaches for reversing the declining number of minority teachers. The new agenda for reform must not create new policies that perpetuate old inequities.' (Smith, 1988, p. 183)

Mary Dilworth (1988) has also called attention to the Holmes Group's snubbing of the historically black colleges, that were responsible until recently for preparing 50 per cent of the nation's African-American teachers. The Holmes Group initially invited only one of the 117 historical black colleges (Howard University) to join the consortium.

Infusing Multicultural Education into Teacher Education Programmes

Over the last four years, I have twice had the task of reviewing and analyzing the educational literature that reports the attention of teacher-education programmes given to multicultural education (Grant and Secada, 1990; Grant, 1992). What I discovered is important to this discussion and merits an extensive summary here (although, I will only discuss the twenty-nine studies that report courses, programmes and field experience) because for the most part these studies were reported by researchers who are advocates of multicultural education.

I reviewed forty-four studies that reported implementing multicultural education into the pre-service teacher-education programme. I critique these studies in relationship to Grant and Sleeter's (1985) five approaches to multicultural education. These five approaches to multicultural education are:

- Teacher-education programmes operating from the *'teaching the exceptional and culturally different' approach* prepare pre-service students to fit K-12 students into the existing social structure and Eurocentric culture. Education methods suggest relating the subject matter taught to K-12 students to their life experiences and concentrating their learning on the basic skills. Pre-service students make the curriculum relevant to the K-12 students' background, learning styles, and adapt it to their skill levels. Educational programmes that prepare teachers for teaching the culturally-different student raise very few, if any, questions about the dominant culture's traditional aims. Rather, the stress is on techniques for building a bridge between K-12 students and the schools they attend, and helping the student adapt to the norms of the dominant culture. The problem of cultural discontinuity remains that of the students'.

- A *'human relations' approach* attempts to foster positive effective relationships among members of racial and cultural groups, and/or between males and females, to strengthen student self-concept, and to increase school and social harmony. A teacher-education programme stressing the 'human relations' approach has in place curriculum that teaches pre-service students how to develop lessons and activities that eliminate race, class, and gender stereotyping and that promotes individual differences and similarities. The importance of celebrating cultural holidays and highlighting heroes and heroines, and the importance of including the works of some authors of colour and women in the curriculum are pointed out. Similarly, the importance of using cooperative grouping for teaching K-12 students how to work together, and for motivating learning would be addressed. Whereas teacher education from a human-relations perspective prepares teachers to honour diverse student backgrounds and to promote harmony among students, real conflict between groups is often glossed over and a critical examination of race, class and gender oppression does not take place.

- A *'single group studies' approach* promotes social structural equality for, and immediate recognition of, an identified group. Commonly implemented in the form of ethnic studies or women's studies, these programmes assume that knowledge about particular oppressed groups should be taught separately from conventional classroom knowledge, either in separate units or separate courses. Teacher-education programmes advocating a 'single group studies' approach seek to raise consciousness concerning an identified group (e.g., Native Americans) by teaching its K-12 students about the culture and contribution of that group, as well as about how it has been oppressed by and/or has worked with the dominant groups in our society. Teacher-education programmes that place the majority of their graduates in particular geographical areas or who find that the majority of their graduates are employed in a particular community may stress this approach.

- A *'multicultural education' approach* promotes social structural equality and cultural pluralism. The curriculum is organized around the contributions and perspectives of different cultural groups, and it examines how race, class and gender inequities are played out in the various areas of society. Language arts-methods courses as well as science-methods courses see their subject matter as reflecting the concerns and culture of different ethnic groups and men as well as women. Future teachers learn how gender-biased socialization and race and social-class oppression get transmitted to their own teaching practices, and pay attention to how males and females from different ethnic backgrounds are socialized. They learn how to build on K-12 students' learning styles, adapt to their individual skill levels, and involve students actively in thinking and analyzing.

- An *'education that is multicultural and social reconstructionist (EMC-SR)' approach* extends the previous approaches (especially the last two) by teaching future teachers how to teach their K-12 students to critically analyze inequality and oppression in society, particularly in their own life circumstance. It also teaches K-12 students how to develop skills for social action. An 'education that is multicultural and social reconstructionist' teacher-education programme would promote social structural equality and cultural pluralism and prepare its graduates to work actively toward social structural equality.

Twenty-one of these studies were self-reports by professors who include multicultural education in their class. Fourteen of these courses were assigned the multicultural approach. They were designed to promote cultural pluralism, examine racial and ethnic oppression (fourteen courses), examine causes of socioeconomic divisions (twelve courses) and examine gender inequities (seven courses). Four courses were assigned to the 'human relations' approach. All of these courses focused on race and ethnic relations. For example, they attempted to prepare pre-service students for the 'culture shock' they might encounter in urban schools. Two courses were assigned to the 'single group studies' approach. These courses focused on gender equity. For example, they had students to examine their sexist attitudes and tried to help them to understand sex-role socialization. One course did not provide enough information to be assigned an approach.

Professors of these courses attempt to challenge and influence their students' understanding and beliefs about equity issues and multicultural education through discussions and assignments that include reading narratives by people of colour about the life experiences of people of colour, and using a method of instruction that requires pre-service students to analyze and critique school policy and procedures.

Nevertheless, according to the studies, a single course, regardless of the quality and quantity of multicultural curriculum and instruction does not provide enough time, nor does it have enough depth to have pre-service students with the knowledge and skills to implement multicultural education. Ladison-Billings (1991), instructor of one of the courses, acknowledges this point. She concludes, 'It would be wonderful if courses like this were some kind of magic bullet. Unfortunately they are not.' (Ladison-Billings, 1991, p. 20).

Five of the research studies were self-reports by the staff members describing the infusion of equity throughout the university-based teacher-education programmes. Most of these self-reports were high on their multicultural accomplishments; three were assigned the multicultural approach. However, these programmes were located at small institutions where only a very few staff members had responsibility for the programme, and could almost solely determine programme policy and curriculum.

Three studies reported on programmes that infused multicultural education throughout the entire pre-service experience (classroom and field), in that they had the 'student-live' and 'student-teach' in a culturally different community. These programme directors were very pleased with the knowledge and skills the student learned about multicultural teaching. For example, Mahan (1984) reports that, 'Young teachers who are immersed in the local culture do make culturally oriented adjustments in their teaching strategies and styles.' (Mahan, 1984, p. 109) Similarly, Cooper, Beare, and Thorman (1990) who placed eighteen student teachers who lived in the predominantly white area of Minnesota into a Mexican-American community in Texas observe, 'The opportunity to student-teach in Texas, with its attendant exposure to another culture, appears to generate among participants an articulated willingness to demonstrate multicultural competencies.' (Cooper *et al.*, 1990, p. 3)

Teacher Education Students

Who are the future teachers? Do their life experiences, ascribed characteristics, and future goals serve to help them teach from a multicultural perspective? Most of the students in teacher-education programmes are white, female, and would like to teach in a suburban school. Furthermore, their chance of having a number of fellow staff members of colour is continually decreasing. Based upon the review and analysis of the teacher-education programmes reported above, most of these future teachers will have a limited knowledge and understanding of multicultural education, and may experience cultural shock if assigned to teach in an urban school. Parkay (1983) describes her reaction when first going to teach in a urban school:

> [D]uring my first year at DuSable (an urban high school in Chicago) I was frequently anxious and frightened. On occasion, I even had nightmares about the place. I despaired of even understanding or accepting the students' behavior and attitudes that were so strange and threatening to me. I experienced what anthropologists and sociologists have termed 'culture shock'. (Parkay, 1983, p. 18)

Similarly, the attitude of such students toward teaching from a multicultural perspective will be benign or benevolent, because they have grown-up in a society where racism, sexism and socio-economic differences are pervasive.

Education students' attitudes have been shaped by a society that is biased along race, class and gender lines. For example, a recent Gallup Poll (1990) on racial tolerance reported that, 'while racial attitudes have changed for the better, this shift has not been accompanied by a change in opinion about the state of racial equality. And there remain sharp differences of opinion between whites and blacks about the availability of job opportunities, availability of housing for blacks and racial views in general.' (Gallup *et al.*, 1990, p. 1). Furthermore, in 1990, although the average educational attainment of Africans-Americans was only slightly below that of Whites (12.2 years and 12.6 years respectively), the median income of African families was only 60 per cent of that of white families and had improved little over a decade. Also, Hispanics with at least a high-school diploma were more than two and a half (2.5) times as likely as Whites to be living in poverty in 1988 and 1990 (US Department of Commerce, Bureau of the Census, 1991).

Although, this mostly-female teaching corps has seen an increasing number of women participating in the labour force, their attitudes have been influenced by a society where the earnings of full-time working women are only 72 per cent of the earning of full-time working white men. Even though women are making substantial inroads into some high-paying traditionally male occupations, such as law and medicine, over 60 per cent of females workers in 1991 were concentrated in low-paying 'pink collar' ghettos, such as clerical work, nursing, day care, and health services (US Department of Commerce, Bureau of Census, 1991)

Challenges to Multicultural Teacher Education Programmes

There are numerous challenges to having a teacher-education programme that actively deals with issues of race, class and gender. Access to diverse populations, finances, money to support both the necessary human and material resources needed, and leadership, are only a few of the challenges. However, for this chapter, I will delineate four challenges that I believe critical to the success of multicultural teacher-education programmes: the teacher education faculty, the meaning of multicultural education, academic ethnocentrism and elitism; and the development and production of multicultural education knowledge.

Teacher Education Faculty

A teaching staff that has an understanding of multicultural education accepts the philosophy of cultural pluralism that undergirds multicultural education, and recognizes that multicultural education is a philosophical concept and an educational process that impacts all of education, and further accepts that an important goal of multicultural education is to prepare K-12 students to take charge of their life circumstances and actively pursue positive social change. Such a teaching cadre is not in place in teacher-education programmes, nor does it seem to be close to being in place.

Nationally, 93 per cent of the professors of education are white, and of that number, 70 per cent are male. In addition, the average age for a full professor is fifty-three, an associate professor, forty-seven, and assistant professors, forty-two. With this profile, it is reasonable to assume that the great majority of education faculty has had little formal instruction in multicultural education during their formative years of professional development, and presently take a benign stance toward multicultural education. Regarding their formative professional development, I say this because, it is only recently that K-12 textbooks have begun to seriously address multicultural issues (Sleeter and Grant, 1991), and that teacher-preparation institution have offered classes in multicultural education (Grant and Koskela, 1986). Regarding their benign stance toward multicultural education Contreras (1988) explains:

> Teacher educators continue to assume that teacher education students will pick up the necessary knowledge, skills, and attitudes that will help them teach classes of socio-culturally diverse students without any direct instruction and planned experience. Moreover, teacher educators assume that most of the schools will continue to be monocultural and monosocial: therefore, there is no obligation to commit time and resources to preparing teacher to teach children who are at risk of being mis-educated and undereducated. (Contreras, 1988, p. 14)

A colleague, Gomez (1992) illuminates the lack of attention to multicultural education in a poignant reflection of her graduate-student teaching experience. She recounts:

> [David] could not identify the letters of the alphabet in September, nor could he do so in May. David's mother was a single parent and an alcoholic, she was an absent and sometimes abusive parent. While she was hospitalized the winter of my student teaching, David came to live with me and my husband ... In the Spring, when David's mother was discharged from the hospital, the state social services department required that we return David to her ... Soon afterward, my husband and I finished graduate school and moved away, leaving David in Black River Falls ... In the past few years. I have tried to untangle my uneasiness about that year, and recently I came to understand its roots. I now recognize that while on the surface we were good teachers, our practice lacked a significant dimension: Ms. Patterson and I failed to build links between the children's home and our classroom because we wanted to replace what they brought to school with what we knew and valued. *Missing were essential links to all children's school success, the critical links which bind home and school, including the recognition that all children come to school* with skills and experiences upon which we can draw, build and expand. Further, Ms Patterson and I didn't extend an invitation to the children and their families to make this school their school. [my emphasis] (Gomez, 1992, p. 133)

Meaning of Multicultural Education

Another challenge to a multicultural teacher-education programme, has to do with the meaning and the conceptualization of multicultural education by the teacher-education programme staffs. Multicultural education often means different things to different people (Banks, 1981; Gay, 1983; Grant and Sleeter, 1985), and/or sometimes multicultural education is seen as understood by everyone, and in such a way that definitions are deemed unnecessary (Grant, 1992). These points were very clear in the recent review and analysis of the forty-four studies discussed above. Very few of the studies give a clear definition of 'multicultural education,' 'diversity,' or the 'equity' when they were using the terms. Similarly, many in the study conceptualized multicultural education differently. By this, I mean some focused on race/ethnicity, some focused on race and gender, others on race and class, and a few on race and language. However, very few of the studies focused on race, class and gender collectively.

Recently, the importance of teacher-education programmes having a clear definition of multicultural education was once again made clear to me. It happened when I was invited to speak on at a university, before the entire academic faculty, on multicultural education. I was told that the faculty members, especially in the School of Education were 'really doing it, with multicultural education'. Therefore, I was told it was unnecessary to deal with the basics of multicultural education (i.e., rationale, definition, historical roots). Also I was informed to be ready for some hard questions (e.g., What is the relationship between multicultural education and science and maths? How can we do multicultural-education research? Is there a relationship between multicultural education and student achievement?).

I looked forward to my visit and the opportunity for the stimulating discourse. In order to be prepared, I asked if I could receive the syllabus from several faculty members who were 'really doing it'. When I reviewed the syllabus, I was dismayed. What I learned from the review and what was subsequently borne out by my visits was that:

- some faculty members believed that when they have prospective teachers analyze a textbook for biases, that — and mainly that — was multicultural education;
- others saw multicultural education as having their students read a single book about an ethnic group different from their own;
- others saw placing students in mixed-race schools as multicultural; and
- still other faculty members defined multicultural education as teaching about the characteristics of at-risk students, or giving their students a list of behaviours considered common to a particular ethnic group.

Academic Ethnocentrism and Elitism

In the last two or three years, multicultural education has gained some respect from traditional educators, albeit somewhat grudgingly. Acceptance and legitimation of multicultural education is important to its complete integration throughout the entire teacher-education programme. Every scholar, but especially scholars of colour and women, must know that multicultural education, if they so choose, can be their research chain of inquiry and that they will not be penalized by tenure-promotion committees for this choice. There has been and continues to be academic ethnocentrism and elitism directed toward scholars who wish to study multicultural issues and issues related to race, class and gender. Staples (1984) illuminates this point:

Black scholars are victimized by a number of the standards used on evaluating a professor's written work. First and foremost, is the suspicion that Blacks are capable and interested only in studying their own racial group. Social scientists with broader theoretical and traditional interests in their disciplines are likely to be more successful at elitist institutions than those with interest in social problem areas affecting minorities. (Staples, 1984, p. 9)

Similarly, patriarchy within academic departments often impedes women (white and of colour) from using a feminist perspective instead of the more traditional one to do their research and writing. When this happens, the work and scholarship of women professors and graduate students is often marginalized or unaccepted (Harding, 1987; Hartsock, 1987; Raymond, 1985). Ramzanoglu (1987) argues that barriers between male and female colleagues develop because academicians work in a patriarchal, competitive, and hierarchical system of education (Ramzanoglu, 1987, p. 72). She further adds that sexual harassment (insults, leers jokes, patronage) often serves as a barrier and keeps women from successfully completing their research and working with other colleagues in the production of knowledge (ibid).

Development and Production of Multicultural Education Knowledge

An area of study grows and receives respect and creditability as it attracts new scholars and as it is formally researched, studied, written about. The challenge is to continually encourage new scholars to pursue multicultural education as their academic chain of inquiry. Both undergraduate and graduate courses in multicultural education are needed. In responses to policy mandates, there is some increase in undergraduate courses in multicultural education. However, graduate courses and seminars in multicultural education are also needed. It is in graduate courses where young scholars develop and refine skills in investigations, critique and discuss the latest research findings, and debate 'old truths'. Popkewitz (1984) addressed this point when he said:

[A]s people are trained to participate in a research community, the learning involved more than the content or the field. Learning the exemplars of a field of inquiry is also to learn how to see, think about and act toward the world. An individual is taught the appropriate expectations, demands, and consistent attitudes and emotions that are involved in doing science. (Popkewitz, 1984, p. 3)

The growth of multicultural education into an established field of study, I would argue, depends in part on the development of knowledge about multicultural education and establishing community of scholars. In my review and analysis of the forty-four studies discussed above, there were very few studies that were conducted by the same researchers. It is important that new scholars are entering the area, but it is equally as important for scholars of multicultural education to develop a chain of inquiry in the area. Directly connected to this is the point that Gordon (1988) addresses when she decries the absence or marginalization of the voices of people of African-American and other people of colour. 'This is the critical time when African-American scholars must enter into these debates and discussion *en masse* so that their perspectives are articulated at the national level; our voice can no longer be obscured and muffled.' (Gordon, 1988).

Response

How do advocates of a multicultural teacher-education programme get this to happen? There are no simple responses and no sure fire solutions, for all the reasons cited above, but a few ideas that deserve serious consideration are:

- The movement toward multicultural teacher education must be assertive, firm and committed. The response must be grounded in empirical knowledge (e.g., demographic data). It must employ all of the power and direction of legislative and administrative policy mandates, and must be appealing and compelling to the sensitivities of human kind. Additionally, the effort must include the voices and faces of those who have been marginalized.
- The leadership and responsibility for implementing a multicultural teacher-education programme must be one of 'mutuality'. In other words, all who are interested must act and leadership must change in relationship to the job to be accomplished.
- Teacher educators cannot teach what they do not know. Therefore they must be re-educated from a multicultural perspective. Academic freedom and seniority will be used as reasons for some faculty members not to become involved. Nevertheless, incentives must be provided and mandates must be enforced.
- Each and every teacher-education programme must decide on a definition of multicultural education and establish accountability to make certain that the curriculum and instruction meet the intent of the definition.
- Every teacher-education student must have multicultural education. It is important to recognize that prospective teachers of colour also need multicultural education. It is probably true that one rarely encounters a person of colour who has not suffered from racism, or who has not experienced, or had first-hand knowledge of economic hardship. Also, if the person is a female, she has very probably encountered sexism, and, if a female of colour, encountered both sexism and racism.' Nevertheless, multicultural education demands both understanding schooling (its policy, curriculum, instruction, staffing, home-school relations), and the issues of race, class and gender, as well as the correspondence between the two. I have seen prospective teachers of colour who believed that, because of their ethnic background, they had it made, and would automatically be effective teaching students of colour. Similarly, female teachers may believe that they know how to relate to the girls in their class and believe that they will treat them as equal to the boys. It is not that simple. Multicultural education requires knowing about more than just your ethnic group or gender group and relying on your personal experience. It requires formal study of the intersection of race, class and gender with school life. *The*

Metropolitan Life Survey of the American Teacher (Harris, 1991) reports: 'Before beginning their teaching job, white teachers were twice as likely as Blacks or Hispanics to agree strongly that many children come to school with so many problems that it's very difficult for them to be good students. After one year of teaching experience, black and Hispanic teachers are just as likely to agree strongly with this statement'. (p. 1) The research of Gouldner (1978) and Rist (1970) reminds us of similar issues relating to coloured teachers' consideration (in this case, African-American teachers) socio-economic family background of their students'.

- Multicultural education must be infused throughout the entire pre-service programme. A multicultural workshop, or course is not sufficient for preparing teachers to teach from a multicultural perspective.
- Pre-service student teachers must be placed with cooperating teachers and university supervisors who have a thorough knowledge of multicultural education, accept multicultural education as a classroom fact of life and advocate multicultural education throughout their teaching and supervision.
- Multicultural instruction needs to take place in many forms (e.g., readings, pre-service experiences in multicultural schools, living in a multicultural community), and students need to do projects or complete assignments that require them to critically analyze race, class and gender issues.
- Programme location can impact the opportunities to have access to multicultural experiences. Nevertheless some teacher-education programmes have overcome this problem by establishing a partnership arrangement with schools in urban areas and by having a curriculum that integrate multicultural issues (Fuller *et al.*, 1987). These efforts must be increased.

Finally, the hard truth is that multicultural teacher education has not happened in the United States. Nonetheless, in spite of all the economic problems, gang violence and racial unrest, the social conditions and sufficient funds of human concern are in place for multicultural education to move from the margin to the mainstream in teacher-education programmes.

References

American Association of Colleges of Teacher Education (1972) 'No one model American . . .', Washington, D.C., AACTE.

American Association of Colleges for Teacher Education (1972) *Teaching Teachers: Facts and Figures*, Washington, D.C., American Association of Colleges for Teacher Education.

Banks, J.A. (1981) *Multiethnic education: Theory and practice*, Boston, Allyn and Bacon.

Commission on Teacher Credentialing State of California (1990) 'Standard of program quality and effectiveness and preconditions in the evaluation of professional teacher preparation programs for multiple and single subject credentials'.

Contreras, A.R. (1988) 'Multicultural attitudes and knowledge of education students at Indiana university' A paper presented at the Annual Meeting of the American Educational Research Association, New Orleans.

COOPER, A., BEARE, P. and THORMAN, J. (1990) 'Preparing teachers for diversity: A Comparison of student teaching experience in Minnesota and South Texas', *Action in Teacher Education*, 12, 3, pp. 1–4.

DILWORTH, M. (1988) 'A continuing critique of the Holmes group', *The Journal of Negro Education*, 57, pp. 199–201.

FULLER, M.L. and AHLER, J. (1987) 'Multicultural education and the monocultural student: A case study', *Action in Teacher Education*, 9, 3, pp. 33–40.

GALLUP, G. and HUGICK, L. (1990) 'Racial tolerance grows, progress on racial equality less evident', Los Angeles, The Gallup Organization.

GAY, G. (1983) 'Multiethnic education: Historical development and future prospects', *Phi Delta Kappan*, 64, 8, pp. 560–3.

GOLLNICK, D.M. (1978) *Multicultural Education in Teacher Education, The State of the science*, Washington, D.C., American Association of Colleges for Teacher Education.

GOLLNICK, D.M. (1992) 'Multicultural education: Policies and practices in teacher education', in GRANT, C.A. (Ed) *Research and multicultural: From the margins to the mainstream*, London, The Falmer Press, pp. 218–39.

GOMEZ, M.L. (1992) 'Telling Teaching Stories', *Teaching Education*, 4, 2, pp. 129–138.

GOULDNER, H. (1978) *Pets, Troublemakers, and Nobodies*, Westport, Conn., Greenwood Press.

GORDON, B.M. (1987) 'Impact of the Carnegie and Holmes reports', News Letter of the Special Interest Group: Research Focus on Black Education, American Education Research Association, *Research Focus on Black Education*, Trenton, New Jersey, pp. 5–8.

GORDON, B.M. (1988) 'Implicit assumptions of the Holmes and Carnegie reports: A view from an African-American perspective', *The Journal of Negro Education*, 57, pp. 141–58.

GRANT, C.A. (1992) (Ed) *Research and Multicultural Education: From the Margins to the Mainstream*, London, The Falmer Press.

GRANT, C.A. and SLEETER, C. (1985) 'The literature on multicultural education: Review and analysis', *Educational Review*, 37, 2, pp. 97–118.

GRANT, C. (1990) 'Barriers and facilitators to equity in the Holmes group', *Theory Into Practice*, 29, pp. 50–4.

GRANT, C. and GILLETTE, M. (1987) 'The Holmes report and minorities in education', *Social Education*, 51, pp. 517–21.

GRANT, C.A. and KOSKELA, R. (1986) 'Education that is multicultural and the relationship between preservice campus learning and field experience', *Journal of Education Research*, 79, 4, pp. 197–203.

GRANT, C.A. and SECADA, W.G. (1990) 'Preparing teachers for diversity' in HOUSTON, W.R. (Ed) *Handbook of Research on Teacher Education*, N.Y., Macmillan Publishing Co.

HARDING, S. (1987) 'Introduction: Is there a feminist method?', in HARDING, S. (Ed) *Feminism and Methodology*, Bloomington and Indianapolis, IN, Indiana University Press, pp. 1–4.

HARRIS, L. (1991) *The Metropolitan Life Survey of the American Teacher*, New York, Louis Harris.

HARTSOCK, N. (1987) 'The feminist standpoint: Developing the groundwork for a specifically feminist historical materialism', in HARDING, S. (Ed) *Feminism and Methodology*, Bloomington and Indianapolis, IN, Indiana University Press, pp. 157–80.

LADISON-BILLINGS (1991) 'Beyond multicultural illiteracy', *Journal of Negro Education*, 60, 2, pp. 147–57.

MAHAN, J.M. (1984) 'Major concerns of Anglo Student Teachers Serving in Native American Communities', *Journal of American Indian Education*, 23, 3, pp. 19–24.

NATIONAL COMMISSION ON EXCELLENCE IN EDUCATION (1983) *A nation at risk: The imperative for educational reform*, Washington, D.C., US Department of Education.

NCATE (1982) *NCATE Standards for the Accreditation of Teacher Education*, Washington, D.C., NCATE.

NCATE (1990) *NCATE Standards, Procedures and Policies for the Accreditation of Professional Education Units*, Washington, D.C., NCATE.

OLIVER, B. (1988) 'Structuring the teaching force: Will minority teachers suffer?' *Journal of Negro Education*, 57, pp. 159–65.

PARKAY, F.W. (1983) *White teacher, black school*, New York, Praeger.

POPKEWITZ, T.S. (1984) *Paradigm and Ideology in Educational Research*, London, The Falmer Press.

POPKEWITZ, T.S. (1987) 'Improving teaching and teacher education', *Social Education*, 55, 7, pp. 496–500.

RAMZANOGLU, C. (1987) 'Sex and violence in academic life or you can keep a good woman down', in HAMMER, J. and MAYNARD, M. (Eds) *Woman, violence and social conduct*, Atlantic Highland, NJ, Humanities Press, pp. 61–74.

RAYMOND, J. (1985) 'Women's studies: A knowledge of one's own', in CULLY, M. and PONTAGE, C. (Eds) *Gendered Subject: The Dynamics of Feminist Teaching*, Boston, MA, Routledge and Kegan Paul, pp. 49–63.

RIST, R.C. (1970) 'Students' social class and teacher expectations: The self-fulfilling prophecy in ghetto education', *Harvard Educational Review*, 40, pp. 411–51.

SALTZMAN, A. (1991) 'Trouble at the top', *US News and World Report*, 17 June, pp. 40–8.

SLEETER, C. (1988) 'Preservice course work and field experience in multicultural education: Impact on teacher behavior', Unpublished manuscript.

SLEETER, C.E. and GRANT, C.A. (1991) 'Race, class, gender and disability in current textbooks', in APPLE, M. and CHRISTINE-SMITH, I. (Eds) *Politics and the Textbook*, New York, Routledge and Chapman.

SMITH, B.O. (1969) *Teachers for the real world*, Washington, D.C., American Association of Colleges for Teacher Education.

SMITH, P.G. (1988) 'Tomorrow's white teachers: A response to the Holmes group', *Journal of Negro Education*, 57, pp. 178–94.

STAPLES, R. (1984) 'Racial ideology and intellectual racism: Black in academia', *The Black Scholar*, 15, 2, pp. 2–17.

THE HOLMES GROUP (1986) *Tomorrow's teacher: A report of the Holmes Group*.

UNIVERSITY OF WISCONSIN-MADISON (1990) *Recommended guideline for course listing documentation*, Madison, Wisconsin, School of Education.

US DEPARTMENT OF COMMERCE, BUREAU OF CENSUS (1991) *Workers with low earnings: 1964 to 1990*, Washington, D.C., US Government Printing Office.

Chapter 6

Beyond Tokenism: Multiculturalism and Teacher Education in Australia

---

Anne Hickling-Hudson and Marilyn McMeniman

The Significance of Multiculturalism as Australian Policy

The study of how multiculturalism emerged and developed as a national Australian policy adhered to by both major political parties, yet challenged by ideological positions on both the Left and the Right, throws light on many aspects of Australia's history, identity and experience of schooling. This chapter argues that it is essential for teachers to study multiculturalism as policy and practice in the wider society and in the educational context if they are to contribute towards intercultural understanding and challenging discrimination in a diverse society. A survey of teacher-education curricula across Australia shows that some, but not all, of the country's teacher-education institutions agree with this view.

Modern Australia is preoccupied with debates about its identity, heatedly expressed by a range of citizens through the print and electronic media, and among academics. An overarching question in the debate is how to conceive of 'Australianness': Should it remain primarily influenced by its British origins, or accept some 'dilution' of this through multiculturalism, and if the latter, to what extent? There are ongoing arguments about how far a positive acknowledgment of Aboriginal Australia should be incorporated into the national identity and whether the British monarch who still heads the Australian state should be replaced by a President of an Australian republic, which may more appropriately symbolize Australia's nationhood. Concern is often expressed, and countered, about what is seen as the increasing 'Asianization' of Australia — not only in the small but growing proportion of Asian migrants, but also by the increasing trading and diplomatic links with Asian countries. Some argue that future economic and political alliances should continue to be determined by Australia's history as part of the 'Western community of nations ... [with] liberal democratic traditions ... holding Christian values and ideals' (Abbot, 1991, p. 29), while others argue that Australia's future lies in diminishing the link with Europe and the West and taking full advantage of its Asia-Pacific geographical position and population mix. There is much debate over what kind of multicultural curriculum should be encouraged in schools: Should it be one that merely develops appreciation of other cultures or one that goes further into exploring the activist implications of antiracism, including deconstructing old prejudices, attitudes, materials and institutional structures?

58

Multiculturalism as an ideology emerged and developed gradually as an aspect of public policy largely in response to the planned mass migration from Europe after World War II and from Asia after the Vietnam war. The racist and assimilatory 'white Australia' policy which had by the 1970s become internationally embarrassing was replaced by the multiculturalist policy of both Labour and Conservative governments. This policy ended the barriers to non-white immigration, recognized ethnic minorities, including Aborigines and Torres Strait Islanders, as communities with valid concerns, positions and leaders, supported the right of these minorities to retain the expressive, social and religious aspects of their culture within a framework of shared Anglo-Australian values and institutions, and provided limited state support for multiculturalist strategies in government schools and in some media and welfare institutions.

The need for a multicultural perspective in public policy would seem to be justified by the diversity of the Australian population, which is one of the most ethnically varied in the world. Although approximately two-thirds of the 17 million have their cultural origins in the British Isles, Australia has over 100 other ethnic groups speaking some 120 immigrant languages and 150 Aboriginal languages. The vast majority of people of non-English speaking background (NESB) are from Europe. Italians, Greeks, Germans and Yugoslavs are the largest minorities, while migrants from the countries of Asia comprise about 3 or 4 per cent of the total population. Aborigines and Torres Strait Islanders comprise about 2 per cent of the population (Lewin, 1987, p. 183) but, as the indigenous inhabitants of Australia they have a unique historical significance.

The desirability of a multicultural perspective is, however, not seen to be self-evident by those who adhere to the firm belief that the Australian nation is and should remain Anglo-Australian, in language and culture, and should resist 'dilution' by ending the large intake of migrants such as Asians who are ethnically distant from these origins. This demand has been resisted by policy makers, yet the reality is reflected in the following comment: 'a predominantly Anglo-Celtic [elite of] knowledge and power managers who generate definitions and policies ... have been able to maintain their control in Australian society, defusing challenges from other ethnic groups with apparent ease' (Foster, 1988, p. 183). The radical view condemns the weakness and inadequacy of a multicultural policy which mainly emphasizes the celebration of diversity without acknowledging or tackling the pervasive institutional racism which has so far excluded many ethnic minorities from any meaningful share of political and economic power. As Jayasuriya (1990) puts it, 'Australian multicultural policies have failed to address important issues such as labour market performance, gender inequalities, racial discrimination, and full participation in the structures of society which lay more in the public than the private domain' (Jayasuriya, 1990, p. 55). There is the further issue that Aborigines refuse to be included as 'just another ethnic minority' (Castles *et al.*, 1988, p. 44) in the official policies and practices of multiculturalism, demanding separate policies and recognition based on their unique situation and role as indigenous peoples.

Two decades of multicultural policy have not been able to resolve the fact that many of Australia's inequalities have a sharp ethnic-minority profile. For example, between 30 and 40 per cent unemployment is suffered by Aborigines, Lebanese and some groups of Asians compared to a national average of up to 10 per cent. Aborigines continue to have the highest rates in the nation of poor health care, of infant mortality, of inadequate education and housing, and of status devaluation (Barsh, 1984). Aborigines and other ethnic minorities 'of colour' are often targets of racial abuse and image distortion (Hickling-Hudson, 1990).

Multiculturalism and Australian Education

Given this background, it would seem at the very least that beginning teachers would need some experience and knowledge of the characteristics, problems, strengths and aspirations of this diverse population in order to respond appropriately to it. At the policy level, the education system has accepted and affirmed cultural diversity, and its multicultural policy aims to enhance the life chances of ethnic-minority students. Policies and practices which have been implemented include limited financial support from both federal and some state governments for programmes of English as a second language and for several ethnic-minority languages (in Australia called community languages), modest curriculum development and in-service teacher education in intercultural studies, and limited support services in areas such as translation, home visits and interpretation.

Most schools, however, appear to have lagged behind policy in implementing multicultural goals (Foster, 1988, p. 158). Even after more than ten years of implementation, multicultural practice lacks coherence and visibility for many Australians and for most educational institutions. This is manifested in several ways. There persists a notion of 'them' (non-Anglo Australians, sometimes even including Aborigines and Islanders) and 'us' (typical Anglo-Australians). There is a high level of school failure for many ethnic-minority children, particularly those subconsciously assigned to the category of 'them' (Jakubowicz, 1988, pp. 51–6). In most schools the curriculum is still Anglocentric; curriculum experiences are for the most part monolingual and monocultural in orientation. Within the teaching profession there is a low incidence of ethnic-minority teachers, with the result that they are scarcely visible within the system. While the efforts of some schools to develop a multicultural approach in the curriculum must be recognized, most schools tend in these ways to reflect the social tendency to marginalize ethnic-minority groups. This contributes to depriving students of opportunities for positive social interaction with culturally different groups and for developing an understanding of the role of these groups in the broader society.

This situation is perhaps not surprising given the inadequacy of attention paid in teacher education and the inadequacy of appropriate infrastructure for preparing student teachers to meet the pedagogical challenges of a culturally diverse society (Foster, 1988, p. 151; Jakubowicz, 1988, p. 70). The monolingual and monocultural school-curriculum model is all too often reflected in the teacher-education curriculum. The data presented in this study indicate that few Australian teacher-education institutions have taken up the challenge of providing systematic and adequate courses in multicultural and antiracist education for teachers. Consequently many of these teachers are at a loss as to how to teach to meet the needs of ethnically diverse students or to achieve goals of intercultural understanding through the curriculum. They are even less able to lay a foundation which would encourage students to challenge the ethnic/racial oppression which still occurs in their society.

Our research indicates that in many universities there are only token attempts at preparing teachers for the twofold task of developing student understanding of the cultural diversity and divisions in Australian society and the implications of this for action, and responding appropriately to linguistically and culturally different students. This situation stands in contrast to the apparently greater efforts in the USA to develop multicultural education for teachers, in response to accreditation standards established by the National Council for the Accreditation of Teacher Education which include the requirement that multicultural education be integrated into teacher-education programmes (Grant and Sleeter, 1985, p. 105).

Teacher Education: Overview of Multicultural Preparation

In a series of large-scale national studies in the 1980s (Campbell and McMeniman, 1985) the researchers found that the pre-service and in-service preparation of teachers was inadequate for responding to culturally and linguistically different students. For example, as late as 1985, a student teacher could complete a professional education programme without a systematic, if any, exposure to ideas on how to foster the development of these students and to capitalize on the rich diversity that they bring to the educational setting. As a result, many general teachers had little understanding of the cultural, affective and cognitive orientations of these students. Further, such teachers are unable to encourage all students to benefit from Australia's cultural diversity in terms of language and literary resources, a sharing of different perspectives and an understanding of global issues. The cultural and linguistic diversity of students, discussed above, underscores the inappropriateness of an exclusively Anglocentric, monocultural curriculum. Education practice is notoriously resistant to change, and this is reflected in the limited improvements in teacher education a decade later.

After contacting each of the fifty-seven teacher education institutions within Australia, the authors found that of the thirty-four institutions which provided current information, seven have no specific subjects dedicated to multicultural issues, while twenty-seven provide specialist multicultural subject. Of these, fifty-nine are elective subjects taken by relatively few students, while thirty-four are compulsory. Nine universities provide subjects which fall within the category 'Education for a Multicultural Society', fifteen offer subjects which explore issues in Aboriginal education, eight provide subjects which explore multicultural teaching methods, nine offer subjects in the teaching of English as a Second Language, four offer tuition in foreign-language pedagogy, and one offers a subject in the pedagogy of Asian studies. Sixteen of the responding institutions offer contextual-education subjects which include only a small component relating to multicultural issues. There are significantly more compulsory than elective subjects from this category. The inference from these data is that specialist multicultural subjects are more likely to be offered as electives, and subjects which make only passing reference to cultural and linguistic diversity are more likely to be compulsory.

Specialist multicultural subjects appear, then, not to be valued highly enough to be included as core compulsory aspects of teacher education throughout Australia, and some institutions still do not include a multicultural component in the core units for all teacher trainees. This suggests that many teacher-education institutions have not moved beyond tokenism in educating for cultural diversity.

In these, there is little more than token acknowledgment within teacher education that schools are educating a multiethnic population for living in a multicultural society.

By way of elaboration, the most common pattern in universities is to require undergraduate-education students (in four-year Bachelor of Education and three-year Bachelor of Teaching degrees) to take one or two compulsory subjects concerning socio-cultural foundations of education. Multicultural content usually occurs as a component of these compulsory subjects, among other components which deal with social class, gender, curriculum policy, innovation etc. The extent to which a foundation subject explores multicultural issues is dependent on the particular university. Some may devote one or more lectures to this topic, while others may only devote a segment of a lecture. After studying the foundation subject(s), students may or may not encounter multicultural issues in their specialist studies — they are particularly unlikely to encounter them if they take specializations such as mathematics, the physical sciences, business or physical education.

While many undergraduate-education students have this sort of minimal exposure to multicultural education issues, postgraduate students doing fourth-year graduate diplomas of education are not guaranteed even a minimal exposure. Some universities do not require them to take even one foundation subject with multicultural component. Any experience of multicultural education is gained through elective subjects, which are likely only to be chosen by those predisposed to the aims and content of such subjects. It may be concluded then, that at present, only a small proportion of universities require student teachers to integrate multicultural education studies throughout their professional education.

In our experience as teacher educators, many student teachers, after their first encounter with teaching practice, return expressing shock at the ethnic diversity of classrooms and their lack of preparedness for dealing with this. The onus is on the institutions to provide student teachers with the requisite knowledge and skills to be able to respond appropriately to the student population, and this means ensuring that a multicultural / antiracist orientation and preparation permeate teacher-education courses.

Teacher Education Case Studies: The Integrated Multicultural Approach Versus the Token Approach

The survey conducted by the authors identified a wide range of programmes operating in Australian teacher-education institutions. At one end of a continuum occur Programmes A and B where multiculturalism permeates the whole teacher-education course and is seen as the responsibility of all lecturers. At the other end is Programme X, a token effort. Programme A is in a northern state of Australia which has a relatively large Aboriginal population. Programme B is in a southern state with a very ethnically diverse population.

Programme A

The university providing Programme A offers in the B. Ed. (Secondary) degree seven specialist multicultural subjects, three of which are compulsory and four of which are elective. For students doing the three-year Bachelor of Teaching (Primary and Early Childhood) there are four core subjects and three elective subjects all with a multicultural component. The exposure of the students to multicultural concepts is cumulative in that subsequent semesters build on conceptual understandings developed in previous ones. Initially, students are involved in values clarification relating to child socialization and education in both European and Aboriginal contexts. Then, students are invited to explore the social and cultural aspirations of Aboriginal people and are introduced to the goals of education in a multicultural context. The ethos of these subjects is that reconceptualizing the way Australian society typically perceives indigenous and non-Anglo immigrant peoples is fundamental to working for greater equality. The elective subjects provide for the classroom application of ideas and principles discussed in the core compulsory subjects. Electives offer the exploration of such topics as values teaching, resources for cross-cultural study, aspects of teaching and learning in both traditional and modern/urbanized Aboriginal societies, linguistic issues arising in a multicultural classroom and the impact of white colonization on Aboriginal society and specifically on Aboriginal education. Some electives have a particularly Aboriginal focus. 'Aboriginal Education: Historical Perspectives', for example, includes a study of sources and different interpretations of Aboriginal history, of colonialism, internal colonialism, the impact of 'scientific' theories of race and of Christian missions, particularly in relation to their education activities.

Further, even specialist subjects which traditionally devote little attention to a cultural context, such as mathematics, encourage students to explore content from the Aboriginal perspective. For example, the aims of mathematics education 3 are to: 'encourage preservice teachers to read, comprehend and apply ideas and techniques in the classroom which facilitate the acquisition of mathematical knowledge; equip preservice teachers with the knowledge which will increase their awareness of the Aboriginal system of knowledge as it applics to mathematics.'

The elective subjects with a multicultural component concentrate on field studies concerned with developing student competencies in teaching in remote Aboriginal communities, responding to difficult small-school situations, handling controversial multicultural issues, and developing resources for cross-cultural studies. It is obvious from an overview of all courses offered in this university that an overarching goal is the empowerment of Aboriginal people — apparently a rare goal indeed in universities in general (Leech, 1991).

Programme B

The focus of Programme B, the teacher-education curriculum at a newly amalgamated university in a state which has a dense population particularly of southern-European migrants, is more broadly multicultural and less oriented towards Aboriginal studies than Programme A is. Progamme B provides eight compulsory, half-year subjects. Students in the four-year B. Ed. degree are required to take the subjects 'Multicultural Studies' 1, 2, 3, and 4 over four years. Students in the three-year Diploma of Teaching are required to take Multicultural Studies 1, 2, and 3 as well as compulsory educational foundation subjects each with a multicultural component. For third-year students there is an intense concentration on multicultural studies. For example, 'Bilingual Education' and 'English as a Second Language' are compulsory third-year subjects. The subject 'Theory and Methods in Multicultural Education' includes the following topics: bilingual education and studies, community-language education, English as a second language, and NESB education.

An important point of similarity between Programmes A and B is that they introduce students to basic multicultural concepts in the first semester and, in subsequent semesters, these concepts are operationalized in the school setting. Both programmes are unusual in the extent to which a multicultural / intercultural approach permeates the entire degree. Programme B, further, runs counter to the national trend in that all the multicultural subjects offered are compulsory in the various degree structures.

Token Programme

Programme X is offered in a university in a state where Aborigines and Torres Strait lslanders comprise the largest numbers and the second largest proportion of the state population in Australia. Yet its teacher-education programme does not reflect to any great extent the goals of educating a multiethnic school population for life in a multicultural society. The one specialist multicultural subject 'Aboriginal and lslander Culture' is an elective. Student teachers are required to take several compulsory subjects, but all of these make only passing reference to multicultural education. 'Australian Studies', a subject in which multicultural education does feature more strongly, is only offered as an elective. As this university has a relatively large number of Aboriginal and Torres Strait lslander student teachers, one might expect that subjects relating to cultural and linguistic difference would have featured more strongly in the teacher-education curriculum. These and other ethnic-minority students are offered what could be regarded as a generally inappropriate curriculum for their cultural, linguistic and pedagogical needs, while Anglo-Australian students have few opportunities to broaden their cultural horizons.

Beyond Tokenism

The token approach to multicultural studies in Programme X appears to be the norm in many Australian teacher-education institutions. Yet the existence of exemplary programmes such as A and B show that the system is capable of generating approaches more responsive to the multicultural context in which they are operating. However even these latter courses may fall short of the radical position advocated by Kalantzis (1986), Singh (1987), Rizvi (1990) and others which centres on processes aimed at challenging and overcoming social and institutional structures which are built on racism and ethnocentrism.

Table 6.1 highlights major criteria against which teacher-education programmes could be evaluated for their responsiveness to issues of cultural diversity.

The focus of this study has been on the curricular response (or lack of it), primarily in terms of curriculum organization, to issues of cultural diversity in

Table 6.1: *Criteria for Evaluating the Responsiveness of Teacher Education Curricula to Cultural and Linguistic Diversity*

Criteria	Examples
1. The inclusion of core (compulsory) as well as elective subjects in Education degrees.	No teacher-education student should be able to bypass multicultural education subjects in the overall degree programme.
2. The planning of cumulative teacher-education courses in which concepts about educating for cultural diversity develop sequentially across each year of the degree programme.	In a four-year Bachelor of Education degree, core subjects such as Multicultural Studies 1, 2 and 3 in each year are accompanied by a wide range of multicultural electives.
3. The application of multicultural principles encountered theoretically to classroom and whole-school practices.	Practicum supervisors help student teachers to operationalize culturally sensitive and antiracist practices in school settings. Practicum evaluation should include categories relating to multicultural practice.
4. The incorporation in all subject content of world views and cognitions which differ from the prevailing ethnocentric framework.	In mathematics, exposure to Aboriginal systems of thinking to explain measurement, relationships etc. In social studies, exploration of differences in human relationships to the physical environment, for example, living in harmony with the environment (Aboriginal world view) compared to mastery of the environment.
5. The provision of adequate support services for cultural minority groups.	The upgrading of Aboriginal and Torres Strait Islander units and the development of support in English as a second language.

teacher-education programmes. There are several other aspects which could be considered in future studies. First the teacher-education curriculum needs to be examined in more detail, with an analysis of objectives and content. Second, there needs to be an investigation of the proportion of Aborigines and Torres Strait Islanders and NESB ethnic-minority student teachers and of how far their courses of study meet their needs, talents and interests. Third, there should be an evaluation of the extent of support and encouragement being offered by the universities to ethnic-minority student teachers. Some brief comments follow about each of these areas.

Our survey of multicultural subjects on the Australian teacher-education curriculum suggests that institutions would benefit by discussing with each other their timetabling approaches and curriculum innovations in the field, with a view to improving practice. We would like to suggest further approaches for analyzing the adequacy of an institution's programme of multicultural education. The content of the curriculum may be evaluated according to a typology of approaches which include the provision of culturally relevant education for minority student needs, the encouragement of positive interactions between students in multiethnic classrooms, developing in all students mutual respect and tolerance of other cultures, and the development of not only multicultural but also socially reconstructionist skills which teach all students to analyze critically why some groups are oppressed and to take an active role in restructuring unequal relationships. Teaching process and classroom organization may be examined for their cultural sensitivity and for the extent to which they are characterized by a top–down transmission approach or an approach which places students in the active role of analyzing, evaluating, creating and leading. The multicultural education curriculum offered could be analyzed for the extent to which it prepares student teachers for dealing with the cultural ambiguities which may occur in their teaching: for example, what constitutes the culture of a society, which differences are to be respected and supported given that some are antithetical to mainstream values, and what criteria are to be used to decide what to teach about each group? Finally, teacher-education institutions could be evaluated according to the extent to which they have developed a rationale for implementing a multicultural approach which all students will experience in a systematic way at both pre-service and in-service levels, and the extent to which they provide multicultural specializations, cross-cultural field experiences and opportunities for students to develop cross-cultural interaction skills, strategies and philosophies (Grant and Sleeter, 1985; Cave, 1983). When institutions are shown to be aware of, and working to develop within each of these categories, they could be said to be moving beyond tokenism.

Little research has been done on the proportion of, and support for, ethnic-minority student teachers in Australia. The general point may be made that although in schools NESB students attract considerable funding from the Federal government for the development of proficiency in English as a second language, there is no similar funding at the tertiary level. Not only is there a low level of representation of NESB student teachers, but there is also little funding available to support their linguistic and cultural needs. Traditionally the study of languages other than English (LOTE) has not featured strongly in the Australian curriculum. Developed in the late 1980s, Australia's National Policy on Languages (Lo Bianco, 1987, p. 6) regards the linguistic pluralism of Australia as 'a valuable economic resource in its potential for use in international trade'. As a result, large sums of money are currently being allocated to LOTE programmes in schools and to community-language initiatives. Teacher-education programmes have not yet reflected to any significant extent this change of policy relating to language education. Very few student teachers study a language other than English, thus there is likely to be a shortfall in the number of suitably qualified teachers to implement large-scale language programmes. All of these factors need to be addressed if teacher-education programmes are to move beyond a token approach to multicultural education.

Many universities have established Aboriginal and Torres Strait Islander Units funded by the Federal government. Currently there are thirty-four units which support these students academically and socially throughout the course of their tertiary studies. Increasingly the units are adding to their role wider university teaching and research (Bourke, Farrow, McConnochie and Tucker, 1991). However, the units have encountered many problems in terms of lack of recognition within the academic setting. An illustration of this is the lack of senior appointees heading the units — only two or three of them are currently headed by Associate Professors, while most are headed by appointees at the lecturer level. Funding is insufficient, with most units having to fight within their institutions for a larger share of the federally provided funding for Aboriginal and Torres Strait Islander students. A compounding factor is that most of the Aborigines studying at universities are concentrated in the teaching and social-welfare areas because support programmes for them had been located in these areas which were primarily the province of the former Colleges of Advanced Education (Leech, 1991). Since 1990 these colleges have been amalgamated into broader universities, and the newly amalgamated universities have consequently inherited Aboriginal students and support units 'by chance rather than choice'. Aborigines still need to be given more opportunity to redress under-representation in the professions and to contribute to the social and intellectual life of the universities. Regardless of the degree programme in which these students are enrolled, many are required to study subjects which are still heavily monocultural in emphasis, and which sometimes still carry the inheritance of the Eurocentric and racist ideologies of the past.

Bin-Sallik (in Leech, 1991) challenges tertiary-education administrators to 'take the lead in changing the attitudes of white Australians which universities were responsible for constructing in the first place'. She advocates that university administrators ask how they can orient policy towards changing the negative image assigned to Aborigines, how they can ensure that more Aboriginal students enter and graduate from the disciplines of anthropology, psychology and sociology, and how staff in these disciplines can counter the destructive literature which has been produced about Aborigines. Furthermore, she asks of the university administrators: 'What are you doing about teaching Aboriginal languages? What are you doing about Aboriginal staffing in those areas?' Against this background, we recommend that initial teacher education should aim to provide, besides a multicultural curriculum, carefully planned and structured opportunities for student teachers to develop their skills of operating in a multiethnic society. Students need skills in interviewing parents, in the use of interpreters, in the use of simulation situations, and in accessing services for the resolution of social problems, e.g., counselling services. Students should develop sensitivity to the expectations which different ethnic minorities may have towards 'ethnic' and ordinary schools, the role of teachers, and male and female roles. Their knowledge should include the history of migration in Australia, the ability to analyze society from the perspectives of class, ethnicity and culture, cross-cultural studies of themes such as the changing role of women, theories of language acquisition, research findings relating to attitude formation and change, stereotyping and prejudice. To avoid what Bullivant (1985, p. 20) calls the 'dangerous oversimplification' of equating culture with heritage, the teacher-education curriculum should develop in student teachers the ability to offer in schools the kind of 'survival programs' that all children need for coping with present and future demands and problems in a changing society. As well as specific pre-service programmes, teacher-education institutions should also offer an integrated in-service programme of multicultural education which should be school and community based and should respond to the perceived needs of teachers, parents and students.

In a study which attempts to tap the visions of Australia of the future held by a culturally diverse group of the country's leading thinkers (Campbell, McMeniman and Baikaloff, 1991), many participants expressed the view that 'Too many Australians feel alienated and have no sense of being part of the society . . . The society should be a compassionate one with special concern for the vulnerable and disadvantaged. In particular, justice for Aboriginal people is paramount if we are to establish ourselves as a just and mature society.' It was felt that Australia's maturity as a nation also depends on looking outward beyond its own shores. Without compromising its present ties throughout the globe, Australia should become more integrated psychologically, culturally, socially and economically into the south-east Asian and south-Pacific regions. This presents Australians with the complex challenge of maintaining its historical and cultural ties with Europe and North America as well as entering into close relationships with countries in the region. This vision goes beyond a multicultural Australia to embrace an internationally-oriented society. This is the context in which teacher-education programmes should develop, and which should provide the impetus to course developers to push beyond the tokenism of the last two decades.

References

ABBOT, K. (1991) 'Where does our future lie? In Europe or in the Asia-Pacific region?', *Journal of Australian Studies*, 29, pp. 29–37.

BARSH, R. (1984) 'Aboriginal rights, human rights and international law', *Australian Aboriginal Studies*, 2, pp. 2–11.

BOURKE, E., FARROW, R., MCCONNOCHIE, K. and TUCHER, A. (1991) *Career Development in Aboriginal Higher Education*, Canberra, Australian Government Publishing Service.

BULLIVANT, B. (1985) 'Educating the pluralist person: images of society and educational responses in Australia', in POOLE, M. and DE LACEY, P. (Eds) *Australia in Transition: Culture and Life Possibilities*, London, Harcourt, Brace, Janonovich.

CAMPBELL, J. and McMENIMAN, M. (1985) *The English as a Second Language (ESL) factors and index study*, Canberra, Commonwealth Schools Commission.

CAMPBELL, J., McMENIMAN, M. and BAIKALOFF, N. (1991) 'Towards an Education Curriculum for 2000 and Beyond', Study in progress.

CASTLES, S., KALANTZIS, M., COPE, B. and MORRISSEY, M. (1988) *Mistaken Identity: Multiculturalism and the Demise of Nationalism in Australia*, Sydney, Pluto Press.

CAVE, D. (1983) 'Teachers and Teacher Education', in FALK, B. and HARRIS, J. (Eds) *Unity in Diversity: Multicultural Education in Australia*, Victoria, The Australian College of Education.

FOSTER, L.E. (1988) *Diversity and Multicultural Education: A Sociological Perspective*. Sydney, Allen and Unwin.

GRANT, C.A. and SLEETER, C.E. (1985) 'The literature on multicultural education: review and analysis', *Educational Review*, 37, 2.

HICKLING-HUDSON, A. (1990) 'White construction of black identity in Australian films about Aborigines', *Literature/Film Quarterly*, 18, 4, pp. 263–7.

JAKUBOWICZ, A. (1988) 'The celebration of (moderate) diversity in a racist society: multiculturalism and education in Australia', *Discourse*, 8, 2.

JAYASURIYA, J. (1990) 'Rethinking Australian multiculturalism: towards a new paradigm', *The Australian Quarterly*, 62, 1, pp. 50–63.

KALANTZIS (1986) 'Racism and Pedagogy: Ethnicity and Multiculturalism', Australian Institute for Multicultural Affairs, National Research Conference, Unpublished Paper.

LEECH, R. (1991) *The Australian*, Higher Education Supplement, 14 August, p. 15. (reporting on address given by Dr. M.A. BIN SALLIK to 1991 Conference of Australian tertiary administrators)

LEWIN, F. (1987) 'The Blainey Debate in Hindsight', in JAGTENBERG, T. and D'ALTON, P. *Four Dimensional Social Space: A Reader in Australian Social Sciences*, Sydney, Harper and Row.

LO BIANCO, J. (1987) *National Policy on Languages*, Canberra, Australian Government Publishing Service.

RIZVI, F. (1990) 'Understanding and Confronting Racism in Schools', *Unicorn*, 16, 3, August.

SINGH, M.G. (1987) 'Towards a strategic redefinition of intercultural studies', *Discourse*, 7, 2, pp. 69–85.

Chapter 7

The Struggle for Change: Teacher Education in Canada

Lionel Orlikow and Jon Young

Since the publication of the National Indian Brotherhood's policy paper 'Indian Control of Indian Education' in the early 1970s, and the initial work of the City of Toronto Board of Education's Work Group on multicultural programmes, questions of 'race'/racism, ethnicity, and culture have occupied a central place within the Canadian discourse on schooling and (in)equality. The last two decades have witnessed an ongoing struggle by some to name and contest the sources of inequality built into Canadian school systems and to prescribe and effect changes within these systems. This struggle has seen a debate couched in an evolving language of various versions of 'multicultural education', 'antiracist education' and 'sovereignty and self-determination in education', and a plethora of initiatives designed to reform or transform the existing school systems.

In all of these debates the central role of teachers in the construction of school experiences and the production of school outcomes is clearly recognized. Despite this, Canadian faculties of education have contributed little to this struggle and have received little sustained attention in the multicultural or antiracist education literature in Canada. While some faculty members have taken part in the critique of school practices, and have built academic careers theorizing about such practices, our own worksites and practices have with few exceptions been virtually ignored and left beyond critique. Only twelve citations directly related to 'multicultural teacher education' appear in *The Canadian Index of Journals in Education* for the last ten years and none related to 'anti-racist teacher education'. Of the twelve articles cited, only two were more than six pages in length, only two appeared in 'scholarly journals', most were written by white, male educators, and none reported on any substantial Canadian research.

The purpose of this chapter is to first of all examine the concepts of multicultural and antiracist teacher preparation, drawing upon a literature that is for the most part non-Canadian. After this, attention will be given to reviewing Canadian developments in faculties of education. In this review a distinction will be made between 'main campus' — the mainstream programmes offered by faculties for the large majority of their students — and 'the projects' — special small-scale programmes developed during the 1960s and 1970s primarily to increase the number of First Nations/Aboriginal teachers in Canadian schools. The paper will then look specifically at one small 'project' — The Winnipeg Education Centre — which was developed at the University of Manitoba. This programme, while in many ways marginalized within the university, appears to offer much by way of illustration of what a Canadian antiracist teacher education might look like.

Teacher Education in Canada

Since the 1970s the initial preparation of teachers in Canada has operated under a system of joint direction between provincial ministries (or departments) of education — responsible for the certification of teachers — and university faculties of education within self-governing universities — responsible for the programmes of teacher education. There are currently some forty-eight faculties of education in Canada varying in size from a few faculty members to more than 200 (Andrews, 1984).

Canadian teachers entering the profession today are generally required to be university graduates with a minimum of four years of university, and many programmes are of five and six years duration. While there is considerable variation in the teacher-education programmes offered at different universities, and, in some cases, within the same institution, most programmes, leading to a Bachelor of Education degree are designed either as a 'consecutive' programme of study or a 'concurrent' programme (or a hybrid combination of the two). In a concurrent programme students usually fresh from high school enrol in a programme that combines education courses and student teaching with courses towards a Bachelor of Arts or Science degree allowing students early access to a specialized curriculum in education. The consecutive model of teacher preparation involves 'after degree' programmes in education, consisting of one or two years duration, that emphasize advanced training in a discipline prior to specialization in the education and the study of pedagogy. Combinations of these two models see some universities requiring students to complete one or more years of preliminary university work before applying for admission into a faculty of education (Teacher Education Working Group, 1986).

Multicultural Teacher Education

Baptiste and Baptiste (1980) outlining what they refer to as a 'developmental model of multicultural teacher education in the USA,' distinguish between three levels of institutional response: *a product orientation*, characterized by a lack of institutionalization, where diversity is recognized only in isolated courses and workshops taught usually by sessional instructors; *a process orientation*, in which attention is given to interrelated courses in order to provide special programmatic emphasis in multiculturalism and the development of a representative faculty and student body; and *a philosophical orientation*, where an emphasis is placed on the embodiment of 'identified multicultural competencies throughout the professional and general studies component of the total program' (Baptiste and Baptiste, 1980, p. 50), which are then delivered to an ethnically and culturally diverse student population by a similarly diverse faculty. Lynch (1986), writing from a British perspective suggests a similar but expanded typology of responses progressing from ethnocentric captivity through curricular multiculturalism to institutional and systemic multiculturalism in teacher education (see Table 7.1).

Table 7.1: A Typology of Multicultural Teacher Education

Stage 7	Systemic multiculturalism	Norms and values of system and all components attuned to core ethic of multicultural education
Stage 6	Total institutional multiculturalism	All variables and factors in total environment permeated by multicultural ethos
Stage 5	Institutional multiculturalism	For example multiethnic staff, student bodies, involvement in governance
Stage 4	Holistic policy multiculturalism	For example, policy formation at system and institutional level
Stage 3	Curricular multiculturalism	For example, new programmes
Stage 2	Ad hoc multiculturalism	For example, isolated initiatives (mainly addressing cognitive gains)
Stage 1	Ethnocentric captivity	For example, predominantly monist culture, epistemology, structure including staff, students, evaluations, and few if any, links with ethnic minorities

Source: Lynch, J. (1986) 'An Initial Typology of Perspectives on Staff Development for Multicultural Teacher Education', *Multicultural Education: The Interminable Debate*

Building on this topology while criticizing the efforts of most teacher-education institutions for being narrowly curricular in their focus; 'resting on the dubious assumption that staff have the cultural and intellectual, social and moral prerequisites already [to prepare teachers for a multiracial/cultural society]; and, for ignoring matters of structure and governance' (Lynch, 1986, p. 154), Lynch goes on to lay out an agenda for the development of institutional and systemic forms of multicultural teacher education.

Discussing six essential dimensions which he labels: cultural/contextual; moral/ affective; cognitive; pedagogical performance; consequential; and, experiential, Lynch summarizes some of the elements of each in relation to individuals, institutions and educational systems. Contextually, he argues, an indispensable element of a truly multicultural teacher-education system is a heterogeneous staff and student body accompanied by 'direct and potent' representation from ethnic-minority communities at all levels of decision-making. His moral dimension requires that teacher-training institutions formulate 'norm-encouraging' policy statements that articulate a commitment to 'the ethics of multicultural education' and develop activities that allow staff and students to examine, and where appropriate change, their race, class and sex values. Cognitively relevant components of a multicultural teacher-education programme that Lynch identifies as illustrative rather than exhaustive include: 'a knowledge of the micro-cultures of society, of ethnic minorities and their cultures, alertness to bias, ethnocentrism, stereotyping, prejudice and racism, and their educational, social and economic impact; and understanding of race relations and the impact of nationality legislation; a knowledge of the pedagogical implications of work on prejudice acquisition and reduction, cognitive styles and research on field dependence and independence, and vocational guidance; an awareness of the issues associated with testing, assessment and examinations in a multicultural society, of educability and achievement as social constructs deriving from specific cultural assumptions; the implications of cultural diversity for curriculum and teaching methods of schools; the availability of materials to support the multicultural curriculum and of criteria to evaluate them for their fidelity to that concept' (Lynch, 1986, p. 156).

Combining the categories of pedagogical performance and consequential needs, Lynch argues for the outcomes of multicultural teacher education to be demonstrable in professional action that would include: a broad intercultural competence, teaching methods and practices that would manifestly value diversity and challenge racism and prejudice, the critical evaluation of curriculum materials for their compatibility to the goals of multicultural education, the expansion of the cultural criteria used for assessment and, the ability to critically reflect upon one's own practices. Finally, he argues for the importance of both staff and students to regularly experience working within a variety of multiracial and supplementary school settings.

Antiracist Teacher Education

Within the British educational debate, considerable attention has been given to separating antiracist education from multicultural education (Sarup, 1986; Cole, 1989; Troyna, 1987) as well as other efforts to synthesize the two perspectives.

Rejecting the notion that the marginalization of black people and culture in Britain is 'an error of history [rather than] a product of power relations' (Brandt, 1986, p. 128), antiracist education starts from the premise that society is institutionally racist and that 'there exists a complex "race"/sex class hierarchy located within an exploitative male power structure and that part of the role of education in all educational institutions is to attempt to dismantle that structure both through the hidden curriculum and the active curriculum' (Cole, 1989, p. 144). Theoretically this requires that the discourse of racism be located within a broader framework of the political, social and historical production of inequality. Mullard (in Brandt, 1986) makes this point in maintaining that:

> no understanding of racism in society or in its social institutions, such as
> education, can be attained without employing a theoretical framework
> which explicitly and structurally recognizes and accounts for the connections between the oppressions, exploitations, and inequalities associated with the notions of race, class and gender. But to state that should
> be so is, of course, a lot easier and quite different from explaining how
> it is the case. (Brandt, 1986, p. 8)

The development of this framework, antiracists agree, has to be informed by black formulations based upon black experiences of racism. Politically, antiracist education requires that dismantling racism within white society is the priority and it therefore values collective action that forges links across and outside the school system as the appropriate strategy for achieving this end; racist practices are to be dismantled not through individual conversion but by reconstructed power relations that carry with them sanctions and disciplinary action against racist practices (Cole, 1989, p. 150).

In this political struggle, the significance of those institutions that regulate entry into teaching cannot but command attention. Active in taking these concerns up within 'the closed world of teacher education' in Britain has been The Anti-Racist Teacher Education Network (ARTEN) established in 1984 to 'assist in the implementation, monitoring and evaluating of anti-racist strategies at all levels of teacher education, and to seek the support of people in institutions of teacher education and the communities for this purpose' (ARTEN, 1986, p. 1). In a series of occasional papers, reporting on national seminars, the network begins the task of articulating and developing an antiracist critique of, and agenda for, teacher preparation in Britain.

Central to this critique is the virtual exclusion of a black voice within national and local governance of teacher education. The network's second occasional paper notes:

> the National Advisory Body of Public Sector Higher Education and the Council for the Accreditation of Teacher Education reflect a white social, intellectual and professional monopoly and the Department of Education and Science has proved as yet impervious to suggestions that appointments to them should reflect the multiethnic nature of British society. (ARTEN, 1986, p. 22)

Further, at the local level it concluded that things were little different and that 'while a small number [of institutions] have black representation and consult regularly with black communities, many have still to make the anti-discriminatory, equal opportunities commitment' (ARTEN, 1986, p. 23). Consistent with Cole's (1989) assertion that 'it is absolutely essential . . . that all institutions draw up and implement an anti-racist policy' and Brandt's (1986) imperative that antiracist education be enshrined within a legal system that includes critical appraisal, the third ARTEN occasional paper devotes its attention to the development of antiracist policies for teacher education institutions.

A second central tenet of the antiracist agenda in teacher training has been the recruitment of black teachers and teacher trainers into a school system within which traditionally the recruitment of a virtually exclusively white workforce has served to perpetuate white interests and authority and black subordination. Evidence to date suggests not only that relatively few black staff are being recruited into teacher-training institutions, but also that without changing existing hiring criteria and practices in teacher training as well as challenging the racism that black teachers experience within the career structure of the larger school system, efforts to change this situation will meet with little success. While ARTEN calls for the establishment of more appropriate selection criteria that facilitate the hiring of black teachers who have demonstrated a proven ability to motivate, communicate with, and relate education to a wide range of students (ARTEN, 1986, p. 53), they also recognize the need for a number of short-term strategies to bring black educators into current teacher training as paid resources. In advocating this role (as paid consultants and not free advisors), ARTEN acknowledges the potential for abuse if this approach is used as a substitute for institutional change and the hiring of black staff (ARTEN, 1986, p. 52).

Within the formal curriculum of teacher-preparation programmes the antiracist agenda requires that *all* students come to understand racism as a structural phenomenon and to recognize the forms of inequality of educational opportunity that confront black children, both in its historical and contemporary dimensions. Furthermore, students should be required, and helped, to: question their own racism; recognize the need to challenge school practices that sustain inequality; and, develop the skills to build on the range of experiences that their students bring to the classroom (ARTEN, 1988, pp. 12–13). While advocating that such requirements be articulated through an institutional code of practice, antiracist educators are critical of the concept of 'permeation' that sees 'issues' of racism introduced across the curriculum. Such an approach within the current structures of teacher education, they argue, is likely to constitute a theoretical and token treatment that 'holds anti-racism hostage to the limited levels of awareness and commitment of most staff members' (ARTEN, 1988, p. 5).

'School experience' or 'teaching practice' is a part of initial teacher preparation widely viewed by students as the most useful part of their programmes, yet it is an activity that is currently more likely to be driven by the pragmatics of finding willing sites for students than by the quality of the school experience and the existence of well-developed antiracist practices within the school. Such a situation may not only provide an inappropriate socializing experience for students but also present serious problems to those students who *have* committed themselves to antiracist principles. For student teaching to be consistent with antiracist ideals, ARTEN (1986, p. 46) suggests, requires an essentially new working relationship between teacher-training institutes, the schools and their local authorities. This relationship would include a clear statement that issues of race, class and gender are major concerns of all school experiences, that the teaching–learning model for the student be interactive, reflective and critical, and that clearly defined assessment procedures be developed that would include an element of self-assessment.

The Provision of Multicultural Education in Initial Teacher Education in Canada

The picture developed so far in this chapter of the development of multicultural and antiracist teacher education in Britain during the 1980s might be characterized by: substantial external pressure for change; a considerable amount of descriptive and prescriptive literature devoted to the issue; heated debate between advocates of multicultural and antiracist education; and some measurable change, albeit it often piecemeal and curriculum-focused. While teacher-training institutions (especially those housed in universities) have generally shown themselves to be resistant to change they have not been immobile, and individual institutions would appear to have initiated substantial changes. The picture in Canada would appear quite different, and while the call for multicultural (and, to a much lesser degree, more recently antiracist) education had been sustained within the school system, its entrance into faculties of education and into a debate around the training of teachers has been conspicuous primarily in its absence.

Consistent with the neglect of the issue of multicultural teacher education in Canada is the lack of any comprehensive description of the extent of programme offerings across the country.[1] The only national survey of multicultural teacher education was carried out by Masemann and Mock in 1986, but suffers from a disappointingly low response rate (63 per cent). The development over the last thirty years by faculties of education across Canada of a number of special First Nations/Native teacher-education programmes designed to improve the education provided to First Nations children and to increase the number of First Nations members trained as teachers constitutes the most concrete and important response to Canadian cultural diversity, and is much more fully documented (More, 1981a; Lawrence, 1985; Nyce, 1990). These sources, combined with a superficial examination of the calendars of faculty of educations across the country (Henley and Young, 1987), provide the evidence on which the description below is based.

Within the pre-service curriculum of Canadian faculties of education, specific attention to issues of 'race'/racism, ethnicity and culture have been afforded varying degrees of attention both in terms of what material is included and in terms of how, when and to whom it is presented, in part mirroring approaches already described in relation to British institutions and in part reflecting a uniquely Canadian context.

Different approaches include: the integration of materials into foundation courses; the provision of electives and/or required courses such as 'multicultural', 'cross-cultural' and 'intercultural education' or more focused courses addressing particular aspects of Canadian diversity or particular ethnic groups; the integration of material into methodology courses and field experience; the provision of minor or major areas of specialization in either the education of specific minority groups or in various general dimensions of minority education; and, the availability of special pre-service (First Nations) programmes.

An examination of Canadian university calendars, supported by the findings of the Masemann and Mock survey (1986), suggests the following generalizations. First, that the most common response in Canadian faculties of education is to include some material in foundation courses and to offer one or two elective courses that relate generally to issues of ethnic, cultural and racial diversity in Canada, such as teaching English as a second language or Native education. Masemann and Mock concluded: 'the most notable finding is the prevalence of elective courses and the dearth of compulsory courses. In only two provinces are there any compulsory courses. Moreover, many courses offered are half courses or units' (Masemann and Mock, 1986, p. 4). Second, a few universities have developed a considerable number of electives that address 'issues of diversity'. They have also developed more specialized courses dealing with either specific ethnic groups (for which Aboriginal peoples provide the most common but not exclusive focus) or issues of diversity viewed from a particular orientation: for example, 'The Education of Selected Minority Groups in Western Canada: A Historical Study (University of Alberta)'. Third, a very few faculties have developed small undergraduate programmes around multiethnic/multicultural/intercultural education. An example of this initiative would be the University of Calgary's Bachelor of Education programme in intercultural education which includes academic courses in anthropology, sociology and/or linguistics, a minor in intercultural education, teaching practice in a cross-cultural setting, and a full course in a special interest area such as English as a second language, Native studies and Latin American or Far Eastern studies. Finally, a considerable number of First Nations/Native Indian teacher-education programmes provide another significant response to ethnic diversity.

The variety of different approaches that can be documented within Canadian faculties of education should not be mistaken as an indication of any widespread recognition of the importance of culture and 'race'/racism to the task of preparing Canadian teachers. On the contrary, it is questionable whether the majority of faculties of education could justify a location other than that of 'ethnocentric captivity' within Lynch's topology outlined above or whether any could claim any developments beyond that of curriculum multiculturalism. Furthermore, it would seem that the late 1980s and beginnings of the 1990s have witnessed a stagnation in the pursuit of this kind of reform in Canadian teacher education (Henley and Young, 1990). Masemann and Mock concluded their recent survey of Canadian faculties of education with the following assessment:

> While several key institutions have some well developed programs in multicultural teacher education in place, generally speaking there is a lack of well-entrenched programs across the country. It is quite possible for students in several provinces never to encounter the concepts of multiculturalism at all in their teacher training. It is possible for almost all teachers in training in Canada to avoid taking an elective course in multiculturalism . . . The most significant finding of this first phase of the study is how little multicultural teacher education really exists in Canada. (Masemann and Mock, 1986, p. 9)

First Nations/Native Teacher Education Programmes in Canada

For advocates of multicultural teacher education the increased presence of marginalized groups within the teaching profession has become an important concern; for antiracist education it is a *sine qua non*. In Canada the development of distinctive First Nations/Native teacher-education programmes across the country has had a significant impact in increasing the numbers of First Nations teachers in Canadian schools. Because of the unique legal position of status Indians within Canadian society and the complex bureaucracy that has been established to administer their relationships with the Canadian state, group-specific data has long been available to document their conspicuous absence from the teaching force. More (1981b, p. 32), for example, noted that in 1974 there were some twenty-six Native Indian teachers in the province of British Columbia in a teaching force of 26,000, where if they were represented in proportion to their presence within the population as a whole there should be around 1,300.

In the most recent survey of First Nations teacher-education programmes Nyce (1990) identified twenty-four such programmes that began with a pilot project in 1968 in Fort Smith, Northwest Territories and which by the middle of the 1980s had produced some 328 graduates with university degrees and 725 graduates with certificates to teach (Lawrence, 1985), and has some 885 students currently enrolled in them. While these programmes continue to make a vital contribution to teacher education, the under-representation of First Nations teachers in Canadian education remains substantial. According to the Education Directorate of The Department of Indian and Inuit Affairs, in the school year 1982–3 in federal and band operated schools there were a total of 2,216 teachers of whom 684 were identified as 'Native' and 1,532 were 'non-Native' teaching 37,727 students. Within the provincial school systems (where some 50 per cent of First Nations children are educated along with 95 per cent of non-First Nations students) this advance would appear to have been significantly more slow and difficult (Saskatchewan Human Rights Commission, 1985; Winnipeg Board of Education, 1989).

Tracing the development of First Nations teacher-education programmes over the last three decades, Nyce (1990) suggests that running through the development of these programmes has been: a recognition of the importance of First Nations involvement in First Nation education; the recognition and retention of First Nations languages; the recognition of First Nations cultures; and the demand for quality programmes — that, in the words of the title of the paper, they produce 'Teachers Plus'.

More (1981b) suggests that despite the unique characteristics of each programme it is possible to recognize three broad types: *orientation and support programmes* that provide on-campus preparation and ongoing counselling for students; *significantly altered programmes*, where programmes are based largely on the regular programme but with significant alternatives such as the inclusion of Native studies/First Nations studies courses, off-campus courses, and greater amounts of student-teaching time; and *community-based programmes* where the focus of control is one or more communities and where the content of the programme is likely to be even more modified than the significantly altered programmes. All programmes tend to share several common characteristics; they are university sponsored, they are limited to First Nations students; they utilize universities mature or special admission categories; they have First Nations participation in their governance structure; and they give high priority to First Nations studies, curriculum and languages (Nyce, 1990, p. 21).

Despite perennial challenges to their legitimacy, which continue regardless of external evaluations that consistently demonstrate their effectiveness and their ability to maintain 'university standards' (Williams and Wyatt, 1987), and a continued lack of financial support for these projects, these programmes have taken root and have become a critical element of Canadian teacher education. However, their particular agenda has often seen them kept quite distinct from other teacher-education programmes and other programmes seem slow to learn from them.

In Search of a Canadian Antiracist Teacher Education Perspective

Racism (particularly institutional and systemic racism) and the role of faculties of education in confronting and challenging, as opposed to reinforcing, racist structures within society and schools is not a topic that has received a lot of attention in Canadian educational writings. Neither have faculties of education generally provided an hospitable environment in which to pursue an antiracist agenda. In looking for Canadian antiracist initiatives in teacher education, and at the same time looking for explanations for the lack of attention that these issues have received to date, it is useful to make some comparisons between the development of 'special' First Nations/Native teacher-education programmes (which while usually not rooted in a radical tradition or language of critical pedagogy surely represent the most serious efforts to address institutional racism in Canadian [teacher] education) and the 'mainstream' programmes of 'main campus'.

Community Involvement and Accountability

A central tenet of antiracist education is that oppressed groups of people need to exercise greater control over the education of their children and the systems within which they are educated (Cole, 1989; Thomas, 1987). In this sense community control — with all the ambiguities that that brings with it — has become a critical issue for proponents of antiracist education and for First Nation/Indian education in Canada over the last two decades. Stated clearly by The National Indian Brotherhood (1972): 'If we are to avoid the conflict of values which in the past has led to withdrawal and failure, Indian parents must have control of education with the responsibility for setting goals.' (National Indian Brotherhood, 1972, p. 19). Fifteen years later, The Assembly of First Nations restated this commitment as follows:

> Since 1973, under DIAND'S definition of 'Indian Control' another generation of First Nations young people have been subjected to provincial, territorial, and federal educational programs which refuse to acknowledge the importance of First Nations languages, cultures, and spiritual beliefs. First Nations have struggled to exercise jurisdiction over these programs in order to make education more relevant to their people. If First Nations truly believe that their children are their most important and precious resource, they must exercise jurisdiction over their educational programs. (Assembly of First Nations, 1988, p. 2)

In pursuit of this goal, many First Nations/Native teacher-education programmes have been able to develop First Nations involvement within their governance structures and strong ties with the communities they serve: through their community-based locations; community advisory committees (which exercise significant power over the viability of the programme); the use of community resources; and through their links with the schools where students 'practice teach' and, importantly, where they may work on graduation. Such collaboration and power-sharing, which serves to increase the accountability of the programme to the constituency that it serves is something that becomes much more problematic on 'main campus'. The claim of powerful interest groups within the university to autonomy and the privileges of tenure constitute a 'two-edged sword' which significantly reduces the ability of outside constituencies to exert a direct influence upon faculties of education.

Divorced from this influence by their relatively recent migration onto the university campus, and with considerable freedom to chart their own course, large faculties of education — with a doctorate as the entrance credential for their faculty and peer review as the basis for progress through the professorate — have tended to become distanced physically and professionally from the schools they are meant to serve. Rather than being supportive of the efforts of progressive teachers to address issues of racism, they have proven to be 'cold climates' for people and forms of knowledge that lie outside of the confines of the white, male, middle-class 'figure in dominance'.

While First Nations/Native teacher-education programmes have succeeded in employing elders as faculty members, and since the marginal status of these programmes within the university community has generally denied their faculty the rites of tenure, such programmes have generally had more open hiring practices than other programmes. However, on 'main campus' the 1970s and 1980s have not been a period of increasing the representativeness of faculty members within faculties of education. Given the lack of outside accountability, the lack of strong links to practising teachers, particularly those most involved in antiracist education, and a faculty deriving 'their cultural biography from an Anglo-centric socialization of many years duration and manifest efficiency' (Lynch, 1986, p. 154), it is probably not surprising that they have contributed to the development of the antiracist agenda.

Curriculum

Antiracist education requires that teaching be conceived as a political and moral activity before it is regarded as a technical or vocational one. As such, a task of antiracist education thus becomes the analysis of the political, historical and social processes of society which have institutionalized and work to sustain unequal power, and the ways in which schools and the people who work in them are implicated in, and may contest, those power relationships (Cole, 1989, p. 148). Such curricular agendas may increasingly be taken up in some First Nations/ Native teacher-education programmes but within faculties of education generally, such a 'foundational' perspective is oppositional to the rationalist agenda that tends to hold sway, and where priority is given to a narrowly defined vision of technical mastery in the teaching–learning environment — 'the glorification of technique at the expense of real human substance' (Henley and Young, 1989, p. 27). Within Canadian Faculties of education such attention as is afforded these issues is often crowded into a single-core course and a few poorly subscribed to elective courses, or to use Lynch's phrase quoted earlier, 'dissipated to the point of invisibility' across a fragmented and incoherent curriculum. Linkages with other faculties such as sociology, political science, economics and social work that might support these analyses are usually informal and poorly developed. Critical reflection on the role of faculties of education is not usually a part of the formal curriculum nor are substantial considerations of the political and moral role of teachers.

Nor have faculties of education generally made problematic their own craft of teaching other than in a technical manner. Liston and Zeichner (1987) argue that,

> radically orientated teacher educators must serve as living examples of
> the kind of critically orientated pedagogical practices that they seek to

have their students adopt. This means that teacher educators need to reflect critically and act strategically upon the nature of their own pedagogical practices and the institutional contexts within which they work. (Liston and Zeichner, 1987, p. 133)

While there is a developing literature on what such pedagogic practices might look like (Brookes, 1990; Kelly, 1990; Ellesworth, 1989; Troyna, 1987) such practices currently appear highly marginal to the main ethos of the faculty of education.

Students

Equally central to the antiracist agenda is the increased representation of minority teachers within the school system. First Nations/Native teacher-education programmes have clearly impacted here, as has been noted earlier. What is also worth noting here is that such programmes have well-developed admission procedures that target and actively recruit students into their programmes based upon criteria of potential such as community sponsorship, as well as a variety of support mechanisms designed to see that once admitted, students find a climate conducive to success. This is a radically different approach to the passive recruitment practices of 'main campus' with its preoccupation with 'Grade Point Average' and the bureaucratic and alienating climate (Clifton, Jenkinson, Marshall, Roberts and Webster, 1987) that students generally face on entry into teacher-education programmes. Outreach activities and affirmative action initiatives which have become common across American campuses have not become a prominent feature of Canadian universities.

The Winnipeg Education Centre: A Marginal Effort in Teacher Education at Change

The Winnipeg Education Centre (WEC) is the only multicultural, multiracial, and multiethnic teacher-education programme in Canada. Its unique nature and marginal status provides a case study illustrating the struggle for change in antiracist teacher education. WEC owes its creation to a number of piecemeal programme innovations implemented by a provincial social-democratic government in the early 1970s, that attempted to assist Aboriginal peoples through a number of economic, social and government ventures.

In 1971 the first degree-granting programme, IMPACTE, was established in south-western Manitoba under the aegis of Brandon University. Shortly afterwards a federal-provincial development agreement for northern Manitoba funded a second programme in northern communities. Both programmes, exclusively Aboriginal in student membership, delivered the programmes both in community-based settings in the north and on the main campus in Brandon. Course content and staffing remained mainstream with little attention paid to minority cultures. The same format was followed in 1973 with establishment of WEC. This new teacher-education programme essentially was different only in student composition. Only one-half of the students came from urban Aboriginals, but one-quarter were recent immigrants and the remainder, 'others', or none of the two afore-mentioned. The different composition was determined by the provincial government, the key actor in programme formation. First, the province provided total funding, the university, at best, contributed trivial resources. Second, several Jewish Cabinet ministers, sensitive to reverse discrimination because of discrimination personally experienced by themselves in their youth, sought a broader mix of students. Third, it seems bizarre that an inner-city project should be conducted by a university 130 miles distant. The key was the supportive and influential president of Brandon University who managed to roll over a host of academic concerns about programmes for non-traditional students.

And so, Manitoba had three programmes. IMPACTE died in the late 1970s when few Aboriginal graduates obtained jobs in south-western Manitoba schools. The programmes were as much instruments in economic redistribution in student financial assistance as in cultural reform. To accept university-entrance regulations and also to use the normal student-aid formulae meant that few Aboriginal candidates would have been eligible. Thus, candidates without high-school graduation certificates were enrolled. And further, a special provincial-funding package was designed, suitable to older students with dependants and other obligations. Student numbers were relatively insignificant in the context of the mainstream teacher-education programmes. Each programme enrolled fifty to eighty students, in total, a small percentage of total faculties of education enrolments. This low percentage has remained fairly consistent into the 1990s, although the Aboriginal school population is accelerating to nearly one-third of the Winnipeg public-school population.

As for WEC specifically, its essential features remained consistent over close to two decades. Programme authority did move from the University of Brandon to the University of Manitoba which is located in Winnipeg, the province's largest city with a population of some 600,000, and half of the total population. The government continued to pay total programme costs (tuition fees, instruction, rent, and so forth). The centre's location remained off-campus and close to the inner-city schools where student teaching occurred. Yet, the changes in the education environment influenced the centre. Gradually, a small but growing number of employers of the late 1980s began to recruit Aboriginal graduates. More Aboriginal agencies meant demand for Aboriginal university graduates, whether in education, or other agencies.

Virtually all WEC graduates are employed in spite of a general oversupply of teachers in western Canada. These older students know that if they drop out, there is no alternative in higher education. As more Aboriginals immigrate from northern and rural settlements into Winnipeg, the number of WEC graduates scarcely makes a pinprick upon inner-city schools, some of which are 80 to nearly 100 per cent Aboriginal. Correspondingly, graduates who are recent immigrants make little impression on the city's teaching profile (In one of the largest of the city's high schools over one-half of its students started school in a country other than Canada).

But, an unintended consequence of external change in mood about affirmative action programmes affected WEC. The attitude in the 1980s was to graduate teachers who were much better than campus graduates in a technical sense. Student teaching time was over three times longer. All students received instruction in art, physical education, music, drama, so that they handled these 'specialties' in an elementary classroom. Students were encouraged to take additional courses in science and mathematics, as both subjects were in need in minority classrooms. In short, graduates simply were prepared to be better than those on campus. Although WEC graduates usually were different in skin colour and family heritage, issues of racism and multiculturalism were treated casually through the close proximity of being classmates together for four years.

A more accepting school environment did promote structured change:

- A Summer 1991 institute on urban Aboriginal teaching strategies laid the basis for activities in the centre for all students to experience a cultural bonding.
- A proposal in 1992 to link the centre with ethnocultural associations in order to assist poor minority high-school youth promoted closer ties between WEC and the community (business, unions).
- Student are encouraged to work as volunteers in the elementary summer schools offering English as a second language.
- Various courses are taught *in schools* with a high percentage of Aboriginal and immigrant children in order to build upon multiethnic/multiracial concerns.
- Independent study permits students to assist their own communities; one such effort is 'A history of Koreans in Winnipeg'.

The list can go on. Lack of time alone denies staff the opportunity to move into other activities. Desk-top publishing, for example, would facilitate dissemination of class assignments for distribution among interested teachers. Much has changed from 1973, much remains the same in 1992.

Government continues to be the banker; the university contributes little. Although the WEC falls under university rules and regulations, its faculty are employed under sessional contracts as none are tenured. Few students move from campus to take WEC courses and the reverse does not flow. Indeed, as university access becomes more distant from poor minorities, WEC students experience more controls from campus on who is accepted.

On the other hand, WEC is moving with new confidence in terms of its programming in the 1990s. A series of external assessments confirm its solid reputation, judging by the demand of a number of employers for its graduates. Minority associations are more articulate in their requests for more graduates from their own communities. Collaboratives between WEC and inner-city schools encourage sharing resources on multiculturalism issues. A small number of faculties on campus are actively promoting policies to emphasize culture in teacher education. 'Does one swallow mean spring is coming?'

Conclusion

Canadian faculties of education in the last two decades — isolated from, and inaccessible to, those parents, children and communities whose educational needs they are supposed to be addressing — have generally proven to be either apathetic or hostile environments for those seeking to understand and challenge racism within Canadian Schools and Canadian society. Without more representation from, and accountability to, traditionally excluded groups of people, and without more faculty involvement in community action against racism, faculties of education and the professors who work within them are likely to remain ill-informed and ill-equipped for, and increasingly irrelevant to, the task of dismantling and transforming a racist school system.

For those people, within and outside faculties of education, concerned to change this situation, this chapter has attempted to elaborate something of the shape and magnitude of the task that awaits. Faculty members, as researchers, teachers and curriculum developers, and as decision makers within the committee structures that in large part run universities, have many opportunities, individually and with others, to challenge the status quo. In the specific context of individual institutions each opportunity has its own advantages to be gained and risks to be incurred.

A key challenge, we would argue, lies in upsetting the rigidity of the existing university reward systems for faculty positions, salaries, increments and position. While all universities proclaim attention is paid to teaching, research, and community service, in operational terms 'traditional research', as referred in journals, still most often remains *the* prize, rewarded above all else. In the areas of multicultural, antiracist, and First Nations' education there is a great need for solid research — little is being done. Yet, at the same time a consequence of this preferential status is to deny the significance and necessary time to applied work as well as real teaching (Smith, 1990). For many of us engaged in higher-education projects targeted at 'non-traditional' university students, we are involved in a mission that continuously runs against the present reward system: the sheer emotional energy channelled into programme maintenance often robs us of the quiet time necessary for reflection and research; teaching extra hours of classes for students whose first language is not English also takes time away from research; and, in the immediacy of the struggle to take up with classroom teachers and students practical issues of equity in school life's 'research' and 'scholarly writing' has to be seen as contributing directly to that struggle.

In the area of teaching there is much that individual faculty members can do beyond looking to the inclusiveness of their own curriculum. Universities in Canada have recently come under increasing criticism for the quality of the teaching within their faculties. For faculties of education where one might legitimately expect to see the modelling of good — if not exemplary — practices, such criticisms are particularly serious. The dominant method of teaching modelled in most Canadian faculties of education we would argue remains what Wells (1982) refers to as a 'transmission' model — an approach that assumes that it is the task of the teacher to impart knowledge to students who currently lack that knowledge, and the task of the students to make sense of the received knowledge. Such a pedagogy Cummins (1988, p. 154) argues makes a genuine multicultural orientation to teaching impossible because it entails the suppression of students' experiences and denies the validation of minority students' experience in the classroom — whether it be the university lecture theatre or the public-school classroom that student teachers are being prepared to work in. A more compatible alternative, which Cummins refers to as a 'reciprocal interaction' model requires that teachers work to empower their students and encourage them to assume greater input into, and control over, their own learning, and to collaborate among themselves as well as with the teacher in the learning process. By their collaboration with community resource persons, team-teaching activities, the assignment that they design and evaluate, and their daily interactions with students, faculty members model powerfully pedagogic practices for their students. Multicultural teacher education requires that we pay careful attention to these practices.

Within the domain of those activities generally defined as 'community service' all university faculties have opportunities to work with others to effect change within their institutions and within the wider set of professional institutions that they interact with. The key issue of entrance requirements and procedures for new student teachers, discussed earlier, serves as only one important illustration. Faculty members not only collectively establish these requirements but also individually often interpret and implement them on selection committees and interview panels. To date only a few faculties in Canada have seriously addressed this issue.[2] Most 'multicultural' programmes are segregated outside faculties, and if our model of teacher education represents our vision of education, then minority teacher education currently buttresses segregation. If we wish multiculturalism to be central within integrated communities, then access rules have to be changed and broadened for all entrants. The results would be exciting. Rather than emphasizing a 'Grade Point Average' from high school, faculties could stress a range of attributes and achievements including contributions to an ethnocultural community and second-language skills.

A further shift comes in our relations with communities. Higher education traditionally has taken 'non-traditional' students out of their communities, be that by cultural assimilation or geographic movement. A community-based orientation has to mean more than inserting a multicultural course or a first-language course in a teacher-education programme of studies. Can community leaders teach a course when they do not possess academic qualifications? How far can the curriculum reflect local needs, say in public health, or recreation, or social service, that go beyond existing teacher-education boundaries? These are central issues of power that speak to individual faculty members in their collaborative efforts in teaching and in their curriculum development activities, as well as to the wider university politics of which they are a part.

Activities such as these, we believe, are illustrative of the sort of rethinking of teacher education that needs to be undertaken — a rethinking that needs to be both institutional and personal. For anyone whose careers are built within these institutions and who seek to be a part of their transformation, Ng (1990) reminds us:

> While we begin from a recognition of the fundamental inequality between women and men, between people of different racial and ethnic groups, at the everyday level we have to recognize that we are part of those institutions. We must pay attention to the manner in which our own practices create, sustain and reinforce racism, sexism and class oppression . . . We need to re-examine our history, as well as our own beliefs and actions, on a continuous basis, so that we become able to

better understand and confront ways in which we oppress others and participate in our own oppression. (Ng, 1990, p. 19)

Notes

1 The inadequacy of an available data base upon which to base either informed debate or educational policy in the area of teacher education was emphasized in the Swann Report in the UK. The same limitations apply to the only attempt at a national survey carried out in Canada, conducted by Masemann and Mock in 1986.
2 The Faculty of Education at York University is one such faculty that has recently begun tackling this issue, and serves as an illustration of how faculty members, in association with students, have been able to initiate significant changes. See, Dippo, D., Solomon, P., Wiggan, L. (1992).

References

ANDREWS, J. (1984) 'Alternative Futures for Faculties of Education,' *Canadian Journal of Education*, 9, 3, pp. 261–75.

THE ANTI-RACIST TEACHER EDUCATION NETWORK (ARTEN) (1986) 'Anti-Racist Teacher Education', Occasional Papers 1–3, Glasgow, Jordanhill College of Education.

THE ANTI-RACIST TEACHER EDUCATION NETWORK (ARTEN) (1986) 'Anti-Racist Teacher Education; Permeation: The Road to Nowhere', Occasional Paper 4, Glasgow, Jordanhill College of Education.

ASSEMBLY OF FIRST NATIONS (1988) *Traditions and Education. Towards a Vision of the Future*, Ottawa, Assembly of First Nations.

BAPTISTE, M. and BAPTISTE, H. (1980) 'Competencies Towards Multiculturalism', *Preparing Educators to Provide Equity*, Washington, D.C., American Association of Colleges of Teacher Education.

BRANDT, G. (1986) *The Realization of Anti-Racist Teaching*, London, The Falmer Press.

BROOKES, A.-L. (1990) 'Teaching, Marginality, and Voice: A Critical Pedagogy Not Critical Enough', in HENLEY, R. and YOUNG, J. (Eds) *Canadian Perspectives on Critical Pedagogy*, Winnipeg, The Canadian Critical Pedagogy Network.

CLIFTON, R., JENKINSON, D., MARSHALL, S., ROBERTS, L. and WEBSTER, J. (1987) 'A Report of the Sub-Committee on Students', Winnipeg, Faculty of Education, The University of Manitoba.

COLE, M. (1989) *The Social Contexts of Schooling*, London, The Falmer Press.

CUMMINS, J. (1988) 'From multicultural to anti-racist education', in CUMMINS, J. and SKUTNABB-KANGAS, T. (Eds) *Minority Education: From Shame to Struggle*, Clevedon, Multilingual Matters.

DIPPO, D., SOLOMON, P. and WIGGAN, L. (1992) 'Admissions Equity in Teacher Education: York University's Access Initiative', Paper presented at the Canadian Association for Teacher Education Annual Conference, Charlottetown.

ELLESWORTH, E. (1989) 'Why Doesn't This Feel Empowering? Working Through the Repressive Myths of Critical Pedagogy', *Harvard Education Review*, 59, 3, pp. 297–324.

HENLEY, R. and YOUNG, J. (1987) 'A Clouded Vision: Faculties of Education and

Issues of Ethnicity in English-Speaking Canada', *Journal of Educational Administration and Foundations*, 2, 1, pp. 37–51.

HENLEY, R. and YOUNG, J. (1989) 'Multicultural Teacher Education: Part 3, Curriculum Content and Curriculum Structure', *Multiculturalism*, 12, 1, pp. 24–7.

HENLEY, R. and YOUNG, J. (1990) 'Indian Education in Canada: Contemporary Issues', in LAM, Y. (Ed) *The Canadian Public Education System*, Calgary, Detselig.

KELLY, U. (1990) 'On the Edge of the Eastern Ocean: Teaching, Marginality and Voice', in HENLEY, R. and YOUNG, J. (Eds) *Canadian Perspectives on Critical Pedagogy*, Winnipeg, The Canadian Critical Pedagogy Network.

LAWRENCE, D. (1985) 'Native Indian Teacher Education Programs in Canada: 1968–1985', Saskatchewan Department of Indian Education, Saskatchewan Indian Federated College.

LISTON, D. and ZEICHNER, K. (1987) 'Critical Pedagogy and Teacher Education', *Journal of Education*, Boston, 169, 3, pp. 117–37.

LYNCH, J. (1986) 'An Initial Typology of Perspectives on Staff Development for Multicultural Teacher Education', in MODGIL, S., VERMA, G.K., MALLICK, K. and MODGIL, C. (Eds) *Multicultural Education: The Interminable Debate*, London, The Falmer Press.

MASEMANN, V. and MOCK, K. (1986) 'Multicultural Teacher Education', Paper presented at the Annual Conference of the Canadian Society for the Study of Education (CSSE), June, Winnipeg.

MORE, A. (1981a) 'Native Teacher Education: A Survey of Indian and Inuit Teacher Education Programs in Canada', Canadian Indian Teacher Education Projects Conference.

MORE, A. (1981b) 'Native Indian Teacher Education in Canada', *Education Canada*, 20, pp. 32–41.

NATIONAL INDIAN BROTHERHOOD (1972) 'Indian Control of Indian Education,' Ottawa, The Brotherhood.

NG, R. (1990) 'Teaching Against the Grain: Contradictions and Possibilities', Paper presented at the Reflections and Praxis on Empowerment Conference, October, OISE Toronto.

NYCE, D. (1990) 'Teachers-Plus: First Nations Teacher Education Programs in Canada', Vancouver, First Nations' House, University of British Columbia.

SARUP, M. (1986) *The Politics of Multicultural Education*, London, Routledge and Kegan Paul.

SASKATCHEWAN HUMAN RIGHTS COMMISSION (1985) 'Education Equity', Saskatchewan, The Commission.

SMITH, S. (1990) *The Report of the Commission of Inquiry on Canadian University Education*, Ottawa, The Association of Universities and Colleges of Canada.

TEACHER EDUCATION WORKING GROUP OF THE STATE EDUCATION OF THE PEOPLE'S REPUBLIC OF CHINA (1986) 'A Report on Teacher Education in North America'.

THOMAS, B. (1987) 'Anti-Racist Education', in YOUNG, J. (Ed) *Breaking the Mosaic: Ethnic Identities and Canadian Schooling*, Toronto, Garamond Press.

TORONTO BOARD OF EDUCATION (1976) 'The Final Report of the Workgroup on Multicultural Programs', Toronto, The Board of Education for the City of Toronto.

TROYNA, B. (1987) 'Beyond Multiculturalism: Towards the Enactment of Anti-Racist Education in Policy, Provision and Pedagogy', *Oxford Review of Education*, 13, 3, pp. 307–20.

WELLS, G. (1982) 'Language, learning and the curriculum', in WELLS, G. *Language Learning and Education*, Bristol, Centre for the Study of Language and Communication, University of Bristol.

WILLIAMS, L. and WYATT, J. (1987) 'Training Indian Teachers in a Country Setting', in BANMAN, J., HEBERT, Y. and McCASKILL, D. (Eds) *Indian Education in Canada, Vol. 2: The Challenge*, Vancouver, University of British Columbia.

WINNIPEG BOARD OF EDUCATION (1989) 'Report of the Taskforce on Race Relations', Winnipeg, The Board.

Chapter 8

Social Justice and Teacher Education in the UK

Iram Siraj-Blatchford

British society has been characterized by long established and largely taken for granted inequalities of 'race', gender and class. Our national history is full of examples of exploitation of both minority groups and of the masses. The principles of stratification in today's society are grounded in our history of colonialism, imperialism, urbanization and the industrial revolution. In the twentieth century we have seen an ideological shift towards equalitarian issues, a growth of concern achieved by the Labour movement, civil rights and women's campaigns. The need for legislation to protect the rights of women and ethnic minorities has been acknowledged as a natural extension to earlier legislation providing universal suffrage.

The 1970s saw the establishment of the Commission for Racial Equality (CRE) which serves to monitor the 1976 Race Relations Act and the Equal Opportunities Commission (EOC) which promotes gender equality through the 1975 Sex Discrimination Act. However, these initiatives have provided little compensation for the deep-rooted cultural and socio-economic inequalities in the UK which are reflected in housing, employment and educational practices and which continue to disadvantage disproportionately working class, female and ethnic-minority groups.

This historical legacy of inequality is apparent in all British social institutions including teacher education and schools. Despite the progress that has been made in the past, the last decade or so has seen a conscious effort to backtrack on initiatives which promote equality in education. The New Right have attacked educational policy on equality and labelled it 'political', 'left wing' and 'loony'. This discourse has been well rehearsed elsewhere (Ball, 1990; Demaine, 1988; Crozier and Menter, 1993) but a few points are worth emphasizing at this stage to contextualize the arguments that follow.

Teacher Education and the Socio-political Scene

In recent years the New Right has flexed its muscles and attacked teacher education directly. Many of these attacks have their roots in the Centre for Policy Studies (a right-wing political think tank) and the Hillgate Group, both of which are dominated by well-known publicists of Thatcherite philosophy. The pro-nouncements from these groups have centred on attacking educational theory and in particular those theories which focus on issues of inequality which they claim are biased and irrelevant to the training of teachers (Crozier and Menter, 1993). The Hillgate group (1989) and Sheila Lawlor (1990) advocate a move towards training based upon specialist subject teaching and predominantly school-based training at the expense of theoretical and philosophical professional edu-cation in universities and other higher-education departments.

Sadly this New Right emphasis demonstrates a lack of knowledge and under-standing of the ways in which teacher education has developed in recent years and the greater collaboration with schools that now takes place. However their concern has not been only with increasing 'on the job' experience, it has also been one of protecting student teachers from theories of child development and intellectual analysis of the process of teaching itself. What is proposed is a move 'back to the basics', a return to more didactic and formal methods of teaching. This has very serious implications with respect to the education of student teach-ers and not least in the context of their understanding of the social factors that influence the learning and teaching environment in schools.

The recent political climate has thus made it increasingly difficult to promote equality issues which are not only deemed marginal; efforts have actually been made by some on the right to take them completely off the agenda. The majority of teacher-education students in Britain continue to be drawn from the suburban middle classes. If students have less time to reflect upon issues of 'race', gender and class, who are they being prepared to teach? The majority of our school population are female and/or come from working-class and/or ethnic-minority backgrounds.

Many committed individuals and some institutions in the UK have been forced to adopt a critical defensive stance to existing policies. Development of equality is only continuing through the use of those few helpful 'spaces' offered in teacher-education legislation and the National Curriculum.

What's Happening to Promote Equality in UK Teacher Education and Schools?

If we are to understand the current situation in teacher education there are a number of strands which need exploring. Teacher-education institutions in the UK supply the great majority of teachers for schools and this system has two major routes; the four-year Bachelor of Education (B.Ed.) which culminates in an honours degree and the one-year Post Graduate Certificate in Education (PGCE) which is undertaken by graduate students with an appropriate first de-gree in a National Curriculum subject. Both routes lead to 'Qualified Teacher Status' (QTS), recognized and awarded by the state Department for Education (DFE). This system also aids the reproduction of the class, gender and ethnic composition of the teaching force, which in turn serves to reproduce inequality in schools.

The continuing emphasis on schools in the debates surrounding equality has therefore only provided a partial picture. Teacher-education policies and practices need to be considered more closely in the wider context of schools and society. Inequality in education is a structural phenomenon and 'race', social class and gender have been highlighted as influential factors in the way in which both children and teachers experience education and in the ensuing underachievement of working class, female and certain ethnic-minority groups (Halsey, Heath and Ridge, 1980; Walker and Barton, 1983; Siraj-Blatchford, 1991, 1993; Sikes, 1993).

The UK 1944 and 1988 Education Acts of Parliament both make claims for promoting equality of opportunity for children, and teacher-education reforms are given particular attention. The 1988 Education Reform Act (ERA) pursues this thrust in providing an entitlement for every child to receive a National Curriculum. This entitlement is defined as a basic right to a 'broad and balanced curriculum'. Little mention is however made of how this can be realized in terms of access and relevance to the diverse educational population of our schools. Children who are developing English as their second language for example, may have the right to the same curriculum and assessment procedures as other children but if their teachers are not skilled practitioners of 'English as a Second Language' (ESL) strategies the children may be disadvantaged. Clearly this has implications for teacher education.

Another strand involves the directives sent to teacher-education departments from the DFE, the Council for the Accreditation of Teacher Education (CATE) and the Council for National Academic Awards (CNAA). In the 1980s CATE and the CNAA stated in their documents that teachers needed to be prepared to differentiate their teaching to accommodate the diverse school population. Specific mention was made to the needs of ethnic-minority pupils and for gender equality. The DFE (then the Department of Education and Science — DES) stated that student teachers should 'guard against preconceptions based on the race or sex of pupils' (DES, 1984, p. 11) and 'on completion of their course . . . should be . . . able to incorporate in their teaching cross-curricular dimensions [e.g., equal opportunities]' (DES, 1989, p. 10).

These initiatives represent 'technicist' approaches to equality. In such cases generalist statements of the intent to educate student teachers for equality and diversity are made with little support in terms of guidance for staff development, time allocation or course content. What is even more disturbing is the trend in the 1990s to align documentation to the perceived needs of 'raising educational standards' as articulated and defined by the hegemonic views of right-wing media and the New Right campaigners, and legitimized by many politicians from all political parties. The government's rhetoric to 'improve standards' by moving towards more formal methods of teaching and assessment has resulted in the relegation of equality issues further into the margins. The most recent consultative document of the reform of initial teacher education (DFE, 1992) is eloquent in its omission of *any* reference to equal opportunities at all.

In contrast the CATE criteria (DES, 1984, Circ. No. 3/84; DES, 1989, Circ. No. 24/89) have moved from some concern with issues of equality in 1984 to a predominant concern in the 'delivery' (*sic*) of the National Curriculum and subject specialisms in 1989. There has also been a shift in the representation on CATE national and local committees to bring in 'outside' groups such as 'business men' (*sic*). One may well question whose interests are best served through these changes. I don't want to argue any kind of conspiracy is operating here, merely to draw attention to the increased tension between the dominant voices in policy making and the impact on issues of equal opportunities. As I have argued elsewhere (Siraj-Blatchford, 1993), the history of state education in the UK has been motivated, measured and justified in terms of the perceived needs of society, narrowly defined according to assumed national economic and productive criteria. The question of whose perceptions these are is thus crucial. The emphasis has usually been on increasing the quantity or quality of knowledge and skills being transmitted rather than questioning the educational content and contexts themselves.

Many ITE (Initial Teacher Education) departments have made attempts at adopting a *permeation* model of provision for equal opportunities. Such a model suggests that equality issues should underpin and cascade through *all* courses and practices in ITE. As has been argued previously, such approaches tend to neglect the need for staff development and this model has thus been unviable and doomed to failure from inception. The UK Anti-Racist Teacher Education Network (ARTEN) discussed the viability of permeation and as they state, it is important to recognize that 'consensus in our society is achieved through the suppression of struggles based on "race", class and gender' (ARTEN, 1988, p. 4). It has become clear that permeation cannot succeed while it is being implemented by those who have not raised their own consciousness and understanding of issues of racism, sexism and class inequality.

In 1989 a CRE-commissioned survey of equal-opportunities policies in sixty-eight universities and polytechnics found that many institutions had a tone of moral superiority or complacency plus an ignorance of the issues (CRE, 1989). It is disturbing that compared with schools many higher-education institutions do not feel the need to promote equality policies and practice. Their complacency may be due to the fact that they do not perceive themselves as capable of unequal treatment or perhaps it is assumed that the liberal culture of higher education is in some way unable to foster and perpetuate discrimination. Either way it is clear that they are wrong. Given the numbers of ethnic-minority and working-class students and the trend to increase student numbers by the end of the century, more institutions may now be forced to review their recruitment procedures and question the reasons why certain groups are under-represented.

In recent years issues of access to higher education have become respectable, as efforts are beginning to be made to encourage an increasing number of students from non-traditional backgrounds into higher education. Particular attention has been paid to the needs of disabled, mature, female and ethnic-minority groups. Of the little known, about what happens to individuals from these groups when they enter higher education is not encouraging. The students' experiences as cited in the Autumn 1990 special issue of the British *Journal for Access Studies* (Siraj-Blatchford, 1990) suggest that the future for recruitment is bleak.

Many access students are quickly disillusioned by their experiences in higher education. They often feel that their particular needs are not given consideration. Few higher-education institutions have creches for example, few provide extra study-skills courses or inform their students about what they should do in the case of sexist or racist harassment. As a consequence many students do not complete their higher education; the entitlement is denied them.

Strategies That May Be Adopted to Promote Equality in Teacher Education

Empowerment — Providing a Platform for Students' Voices

Given the scenario described so far, it is vital that, in initial teacher education and in higher education more generally, we listen to what our black and female students articulate about their experiences. These views need to inform our policies and practices more fully. There is an emergent literature in this area with which those responsible for ITE should be cognizant (Edwards, 1990; Housee *et. al.*, 1990; Siraj-Blatchford, 1991; Blair and Maylor, 1993; Flintoff, 1993). There is also a need for further in-depth research into the experiences of students and the results; drop-out and failure rates of students from these groups need to be collected and collated. White students' perceptions of how well they are prepared to teach in a culturally diverse society are also significant. Cohen's (1989) study suggests that many are lacking in confidence and concerned about their lack of preparation.

The perceptions of existing ethnic-minority and other non-traditional students in higher education provide a good starting point for those of us motivated to provide equality and social justice. It is interesting to note that, as Breinberg (1987) has asserted, white professionals have focused predominantly on access and under-representation issues while black professionals are more concerned with course content and presentation. My own study (Siraj-Blatchford, 1990) of black students' perceptions of racism in ITE revealed that students felt that racism was widespread. More than 60 per cent of the students reported experiences of racism on their school-based practices and from white peers. Over 40 per cent identified racism from white lecturers and in course content. Others reported negative experiences during interviews, in seeking accommodation, in resources and from other higher-education support staff. As one black student put it:

> We were given inadequate preparation for teaching in a multicultural society. We were unable to challenge racism whether it was blatant or not. Lecturers think the easy way out is to ignore it, thus believing themselves to be neutral but in reality they're being racist. In the final year there was an option. It should have been compulsory. (Siraj-Blatchford, 1990, p. 179)

Rosalind Edwards (1990) in her study of mature mother-students in higher education found that gender and class experiences also impact on women, who undervalue themselves and their life experiences. Edwards cites a white working-class woman who felt that her family-life experiences were somehow inferior when in fact they may have been highly relevant:

> We felt that by bringing in sort of our home, life, what was going on, we would be sort of demeaning the conversation that was going on about a particular problem or Freud's theory or something like that. (Edwards, 1990, p. 191)

The same undervaluing of female experience may be held by some tutors. Edwards also cites another white, mature, middle-class woman who felt that her status as a mother left some lecturers in doubt as to her academic ability. She quotes the student as saying:

> One thing sticks in my mind that one particular person that I knew quite well and er, when he taught me for the first time I happened to go along to his room when he was marking one of my essays and he said, 'this is really good, you write really well,' and he sounded so surprised! And I said, 'what did you expect then?' So I think maybe sometimes people, if you are a mother, people define you as that and they don't really consider that you can do anything else! And that wasn't because he's a particularly insensitive person or whatever. But I do remember the note of surprise and I've never forgiven him for that! (Edwards, 1990, p. 192)

There are many more examples which cannot be explored fully in a mere chapter. However it is worth citing one of the studies which has attempted to link the learning experiences of mature students to gender, class and ethnicity. Edwards (1990) cites Weil (1986) whose study found that minority students were concerned about their lack of voice and thus the negation of their experience:

> Students across all departments reported 'learner identity conflicts' arising from aspects of experience related to gender, race, and/or class, being made invisible or being defined in 'tutors' terms' . . . learner identity for these students is fundamentally rooted in experiential learning about what it means to be 'working class', 'a woman' or 'black' in this society. (Weil, 1986, pp. 231–2)

It is important that *all* students and tutors are aware of these 'voices' and *hear* them in order to develop effective teaching strategies. After all, these students are to become our future teachers and if they are not given the opportunity to hear these alternative discourses in college how are they to respond effectively to the same diversity in schools? Teacher educators who ignore these voices are failing to provide the kind of relevant and student-centred courses that they generally advocate for use in schools.

Equal Opportunity Policies

Policy statements are necessary but not sufficient if they remain mere paper exercises. Policies can provide clear procedures and strategies which identify and deal with inequality. A survey by Her Majesty's Inspectorate (HMI) (DES, 1989b) of 'good practice' in sixteen ITE institutions reported that those institutions with policies had a more heightened awareness of the issues, especially where staff had been involved in the policy formulation.

It seems reasonable to assume that during the formulation of any policy an institution should involve all of those affected. A policy informed by student, community and staff concerns is much more likely to be successful in achieving its goals. Where policies lack clear planned strategies for the achievement of aims people are left frustrated and the suspicion that this fosters is alienating and retrogressive. Equal-opportunities policies should be informed by those who are concerned to promote equality and should be seen as an ongoing and developing exercise. The HMI report (DES, 1989) advised that policies should be monitored and administered by people with seniority and a commitment to the issues.

All staff and students need to be aware of any such policies, and this should be seen as a matter of individual right. Students and staff should know what their entitlement is at interview, in cases of assessment, or when they are faced with racist or sexist harassment. Students need to see that justice and equality issues are important to the institution and that they inform *all* practices and procedures. Such policies require a great deal of time and energy in formulation. Many institutions advertise themselves as equal-opportunity employers, or, as in the case of students, 'recruiters'. Most institutions fail, however, to clarify their understanding of the issues or to provide details of the procedures to be followed in the implementation of policies. Such policies often amount to little more than empty rhetoric. A survey conducted by Williams *et al.* (Williams, 1989) and commissioned by the Commission for Racial Equality found that of sixty-eight polytechnics and universities studied only twelve demonstrated any commitment to equal opportunities. In fact forty-four of the institutions had no established policy at all.

Williams *et al.* (ibid.) drew attention to the lack of commitment on the part of senior management who often marginalized and limited equal-opportunities development. Those institutions with policies which promoted 'race' and gender were limited in their impact as they were often restricted to narrow structural concerns of access and 'sameness' of provision rather than the different needs of diverse groups of students and staff. It is clear that equal-opportunities policies which do not engage with the deeper cultural aspects of the institution within an unequal society will not achieve greater equality.

Courses and Content

I have argued earlier that teacher-education departments have failed to include in their courses adequate treatment of 'race', gender and class issues. Permeation policies have proved ineffective in most courses due to poor staff commitment and lack of staff development. Courses are the main arena through which knowledge is transmitted and ideological discourses debated. Courses provide important opportunities for students to reflect on *how* children learn, to differentiate teaching styles and management, teaching and learning resource materials, all of which need to be informed by 'race' and gender considerations. Students learn quickly that approaches and content vary to cater for individual pupils, classes and between schools.

It has been the education and professional studies courses which have traditionally focused on issues of diversity. In the UK these courses have lost teaching time due to the CATE criteria (DES, 1984, 1989). Where issues of diversity were taken up in specialist subject areas it was usually in English departments or religious education. Other main-stream curriculum areas like science, mathematics and the humanities paid little attention to equality and diversity. As the Swann Report (1985) put it:

> the attempts of the teacher training system over recent years to respond
> to the multi-racial nature of society can perhaps best be seen as charac-
> terised by confusion of aims and a lack of overall coherence. (Swann,
> 1985, p. 544)

Some ITE departments have core or optional courses on 'race' and gender
while others may only offer token lectures. The implications of this are that newly
qualified teachers are often as ignorant as their older colleagues on entry to the
profession, and children continue to receive a poor preparation for life in a
culturally diverse community. What is worse, is that groups of children continue
to underachieve because of these practices. It is important to recognize that ITE
is one spoke in a deterministic cycle of inequality in education and if issues of
equality are carefully addressed that cycle could be weakened considerably.

The new UK National Curriculum has nine compulsory subjects and reference is made to cross-curricular themes of which gender and multicultural education are included alongside health, environmental education, careers, economic
and industrial education and citizenship. A few of the statutory-subject documents,
such as English, technology and physical education offer helpful avenues for
locating equality issues. Non-statutory guidance such as that for science also offers
possibilities but in all cases it is assumed that tutors and teachers have the knowledge, skills, attitudes and expertise to use these spaces creatively and effectively.
These competencies are however all too rare and there is now an urgent need to
evaluate ITE courses in this context. It is now the clear responsibility of subject
departments and institutions to facilitate staff development in this area. It is also
an area where serving teachers require in-service education.

Creating an Equality Ethos in ITE

All of the issues highlighted so far require careful consideration in their own right
but also in the context of the formulation of equal-opportunities policies. If we
are to improve the ethos of our ITE departments and institutions and contribute
to an equality culture the following issues also need to be informed by an equality
perspective:

- Admissions — Recruitment drives are needed to target minority groups.
  Prospectuses, advertising and application forms can quite easily, through
  the addition of photographs and positive statements, encourage non-
  traditional applicants. It is important that once written, these documents
  reach *all* sectors of the community through advertisements in ethnic-
  minority publications and through community group distribution. Institutions may also find it useful to take their publicity to particular schools
  and further-education colleges to positively encourage a more diverse
  population to consider their courses. Such practices also provide an ideal
  opportunity for institutions to illustrate to non-traditional groups their
  commitment to equalizing opportunities. At the same time it is worth
  noting that we cannot expect immediate results because it takes time to
  build up trust and confidence with groups that have suffered discrimination. At first these groups may well be suspicious, or even sceptical, due
  to their lived experience.

- Links with particular schools — Universities such as Oxford and Cambridge have used such methods for centuries! Links made with schools with large ethnic-minority populations show that ITE departments are serious in their endeavours to recruit from these groups. Under the CATE (DES, 1989) requirements ITE tutors must spend the equivalent of one term every five years in school; ITE staff could be encouraged to update their school experience in urban and/or multiethnic primary and secondary schools. This would provide the additional advantages of encouraging pupils to consider teaching as a profession as well as informing tutor practice back in the ITE institution.
- Interviews — All student and staff recruitment should include interview procedures which are informed by equal-opportunities practice. Interviewers should be trained for this purpose to avoid discriminatory questioning and to enable them to ask questions seeking positive commitment to the institution's policies. Clearly only those staff and students who are sympathetic and positive about promoting equality should be recruited.
- Open days — Open days which advertise both institutions and departments provide an important part of the hidden curriculum and require careful scrutiny. Such events will influence both existing and potential students' perceptions. If equal opportunities do not appear to be a priority, potential non-traditional recruits may well feel that the department or courses will be unfriendly and fail to cater for their needs.
- Validation — ITE departments should draw the attention of those who validate and accredit courses to the fact that *quality* is impossible to achieve without being informed by, and without promoting equality issues. One of the five terms of reference in CATE (DES, 1989 Circ. 24/89, par. 6) states the aim that CATE has: 'to identify and disseminate good practice in initial teacher training' (DES, 1989). Quality and performance indicators drawn up by ITE departments could illustrate this point well.
- Resources — The library and separate centres housing resources which promote equality are critical at the early stages of implementation (DES, 1989b).
- Coordination — An equal-opportunities coordinator is needed and the post should be held by someone with an appropriate level of seniority (DES, 1989b). In the early stages a working party may be necessary, with representatives drawn from all sectors of the institution including the student body and local community whose contribution will be particularly valuable in developing guidance on those areas which inhibit the promotion of equal opportunities.
- Policies — A policy is needed that addresses issues of class, gender and ethnicity. This should be made available to all students and staff and the consequences discussed. Clear guidance needs to be made available on the procedures to be followed in the event of racist or sexist harassment. The policy needs to be carefully and regularly monitored and evaluated as part of a process of continual development.

In conclusion it can be seen that we have a long way to go in the UK if we are to equalize opportunities in ITE. Progress depends very much on the time, commitment and energy which senior management wish to devote, but one thing of which we can be certain is that class, gender and ethnicity issues are *not* minority issues; they effect the majority of our population. Institutions are under pressure to increase recruitment and equality must therefore become a mainstream issue in both higher-education institutions and our schools. It is time to move these issues from the margins into a central position on our agendas for the 1990s, and beyond.

References

ANTI-RACIST TEACHER EDUCATION NETWORK (ARTEN) (1988) *Anti-racist Teacher Education, Permeation: the Road to Nowhere*, 4, Glasgow, Jordanhill College of Higher Education.

BALL, S. (1990) *Politics and Policy Making in Education*, London, Routledge.

BLAIR, M. and MAYLOR, U. (1993) 'Issues and Concerns for Black Women Teachers in Training', in SIRAJ-BLATCHFORD, I. (Ed) *'Race', Gender and the Education of Teachers*, Open University Press.

BREINBERG, P. (1987) 'The Black Perspective in Higher Education', *Multicultural Teaching*, 6, 1.

COHEN, L. (1989) 'Ignorance, not hostility: student teachers' perceptions of ethnic minorities in Britain', in VERMA, G.K. (Ed) *Education for All: A Landmark in Pluralism*, London, The Falmer Press.

CROZIER, G. and MENTER, I. (1993) 'The Heart of the Matter? Student Teachers Experiences in School', in SIRAJ-BLATCHFORD, I. (Ed) op. cit.

DEMAINE, J. (1988) 'Teachers' Work, Curriculum and the New Right', *British Journal of Sociology of Education*, 9, 3, pp. 247–64.

DEPARTMENT OF EDUCATION AND SCIENCE (DES) (1984) *Initial Teacher Training: Approval of Courses*, Cir. No. 3/84 London, Her Majesty's Stationery Office.

DEPARTMENT OF EDUCATION AND SCIENCE (DES) (1989) *Initial Teacher Training: Approval of Courses*, Circ. No. 24/89, London, Her Majesty's Stationery Office.

DEPARTMENT OF EDUCATION AND SCIENCE (DES) (1989b) *Responses to Ethnic Diversity in Teacher Training*, Circ. No. 117/89, London, Her Majesty's Stationery Office.

DEPARTMENT FOR EDUCATION (DFE) (1992) *Reform of Initial Teacher Education: A Consultative Document*, London, Her Majesty's Stationery Office.

EDWARDS, R. (1990) 'Access and Assets: the Experience of Mature Mother-Students in Higher Education', *Journal of Access Studies*, 5, 2, pp. 188–202.

FLINTOFF, A. (1993) 'One of the Boys? Gender Identities in Physical Education ITE', in SIRAJ-BLATCHFORD, I. (Ed) op. cit.

HALSEY, A., HEATH, A. and RIDGE, J. (1980) *Origins and Destinations,* London, Clarendon Press.

HER MAJESTY'S STATIONERY OFFICE (HMSO) (1975) *Sex Discrimination Act*, London, HMSO.

HER MAJESTY'S STATIONERY OFFICE (HMSO) (1976) *Race Relations Act*, London, HMSO.

HER MAJESTY'S STATIONERY OFFICE (HMSO) (1988) *Education Reform Act*, London, HMSO.

HILLGATE GROUP (1989) *Learning to Teach*, London, Claridge Press.

HOUSEE, S., WILLIAMS, J. and WILLIS, P. (1990) 'Access to What? Black Students Views of their Higher Education Experiences', *Journal of Access Studies*, 5, 2, pp. 203–13.

LAWLOR, S. (1990) *Teachers Mistaught*, London, Centre for Policy Studies.

SIKES, P. (1993) 'Gender and Teacher Education', in SIRAJ-BLATCHFORD, I. (Ed) op. cit.

Siraj-Blatchford, I. (1990) 'Access to What? Black Students' Perceptions of Initial Teacher Education, *Journal of Access Studies*, 5, 2, pp. 177–87.

Siraj-Blatchford, I. (1991) 'A Study of Black Students' Perceptions of Racism in Initial Teacher Education', *British Educational Research Journal*, 17, 1, pp. 35–50.

Siraj-Blatchford, I. (1993) *'Race', Gender and the Education of Teachers*, Open University Press.

Swann, Lord (1985) *Education for All: Report of the Committee of Inquiry into the Education of Children from Ethnic Minority Groups*, London, HMSO.

Walker, S. and Barton, L. (Eds) (1983) *Gender, Class and Education*, London, The Falmer Press.

Weil, S. (1986) 'Non-traditional Learners Within Traditional Higher Education Institutions: Discovery and Disappointment', *Studies in Higher Education*, 11, pp. 219–35.

Williams, J. *et al.* (1989) *Words or Deeds? A Review of Equal Opportunities Policies in Higher Education*, London, CRE.

Chapter 9

Access to Teacher Training and Employment

Clem Adelman

Background

If we want to develop lasting multicultural and antiracist teaching and schooling then the teacher-preparation curriculum has to complement school and national policy on racial equality. In the past decade we have seen such policies develop, for instance in the London borough of Ealing and the county of Berkshire, with little consequence for the main body of schooling. It must be said that in spite of pre-1992 criteria of the Council for the Accreditation of Teacher Education (CATE), most teacher-preparation courses have provided little or nothing to prepare white students for even cultural diversity, or black and Asian students for the racism that they encounter in schools. A minority of teacher-preparation institutions, mainly in areas with a relatively large minority ethnic population have well-developed antiracist and multicultural content in their programmes and their tutors meet regularly at conferences organized by the National Association for Multicultural Education, the National Association of Teachers in Further and Higher Education and the Commission for Racial Equality (CRE).

Her Majesty's Inspectorate (HMI) in 1980 examined Post Graduate Certificate of Education (PGCE) courses and found that they and at least one third of Bachelor of Education (B.Ed.) courses 'take no account in their preparation for teaching in a multicultural society'. What courses were provided were briefly specific but usually were said to inform and train by 'permeation'. The Committee of Inquiry chaired by the late Lord Swann cautioned

> permeation may be effective where the level of awareness and commitment amongst course tutors is high, but without specific, detailed plans for compulsory input to initial courses, backed up by specialist options for those who wish to pursue the issues in more depth and widen their expertise, it may be just a paper promise. (DES, 1985)

All PGCE and B.Ed. programmes complained that they were overcrowded with content, but some gave priority to issues of racial equality as well as gender and information technology and personal and social relationships. By 1984 the national accrediting body for the then non-university degrees, the Council for National Academic Awards (CNAA), required the polytechnic and college teacher-education courses to include antiracist and multicultural content and training. This was complemented by the accreditation criteria of CATE after its establishment in 1984, but by 1986, after heated internal controversy, the CNAA Teacher Education Board substituted 'provided without racial discrimination'. Dr Grace (now professor of Education) resigned from the board in protest. By then the Thatcher government had appointed to the CNAA governing council people from commerce who contested any policies designed seen to promote equity rather than free-market competition.

Student Composition of Teacher Education Courses

Around 15,000 new teachers are employed each year (DES, 1990). The teacher-education courses they have followed have the potential to influence their subsequent professional work and those of the colleagues in their first and subsequent schools. However, studies of teacher socialization show that new teachers are rapidly assimilated into the conventional practices of their schools. New teachers lack authority and are on probation; they seek acceptance and tutelage from their professional superiors and rarely voice criticism.

Since 1990 the ethnic origin of serving teachers has been collected by the Department of Education and Science (DES), now termed the Department for Education (DFE) and the statistics for 1990–1 are expected to be published in 1992. The 1990–1 statistics for acceptance into undergraduate ITT and education courses in the universities and eleven colleges of higher education are sixty-seven Asians, forty-five Blacks and 4,129 Whites (UCCA, 1992).[1] Of the total Asians and Blacks 101 entered ITT rather than academic education courses. Acceptance on PGCE courses for 1990–1 was 11,614 of whom 269 (177 Asians) were minority ethnic UK residents. Entrants to B.Ed. courses in polytechnics and colleges in 1990–1 were White UK 8,603; Black UK 132 and Asian UK eighty (Central Registry and Clearing House via UCCA). This gives an overall 2.3 per cent for minority ethnic acceptances to ITT. In a substantial number of other undergraduate courses minority ethnic acceptances reach 10 per cent. A glib way of summarizing this is that teaching is not a 'popular' option amongst the minority ethnic population.

Teacher preparation and education courses are underrepresented by minority ethnic students compared with their entry to many other areas of study. The statistics for minority ethnic students who gain Qualified Teacher Status (QTS) and are employed as teachers will become available when the DFE publishes its data. The regional distribution of entrants to Initial Teacher Education (ITE) should also be known more precisely; we know that entry is highest to those courses that are linked to preparatory Access courses and these are most prominent in areas where minority ethnic populations are substantial in number. At present there are 593 validated Access courses with a further 400 in the process of applying for validation. Of the 593 total, eighty-three prepare particularly for entry to B.Ed. courses. Each course has between fifteen to twenty-five places to be filled. Potentially about 1,660 Access students might apply for ITT courses per year. The proportion of these from minority ethnic backgrounds is, as yet, unknown nationally although consortia of colleges and the higher-education institutions to which they are linked have kept statistics for minority-ethnic entrants from Access courses.

The London Open College federation presently validates ten such Access courses the students on which comprise about 70 per cent minority ethnic overall. More than 50 per cent complete these Access courses, on a grant. However the national trend is to charge all students for tuition albeit on a means-related scale. Nevertheless, this is bound to discourage the least well-off and to encourage students to take the first job they are offered leading to considerable drop-out from Access courses in some areas.

Outstanding in their intake of minority ethnic students to ITT courses are the universities of North London and South Bank and Bradford and Ilkley College. The Access courses to these institutions are devised to link with further studies and practice during the ITT courses: issues of racial equality, antiracism and multicultural societies are included. Waltham Forest College in north-east London has pioneered a successful bilingual and multilingual Access course to the B.Eds of Middlesex University and the University of East London. Since the 1980s Access courses have prepared more UK resident minority-ethnic students for entry to ITT than any other route. The new CATE criteria do not recognize this change in student constituency. The CATE criteria envisage white school-leavers as the 'standard entrant'.

Employment

When minority-ethnic qualified teachers find employment as teachers they join a small minority nationally with highest proportions in inner-city secondary schools. Between 1988–1990, 691,438 white teachers were employed (98.5 per cent). The remaining 1.50 per cent of the total 702,198 comprised mainly minority ethnic teachers, about 10,000 predominantly, between the ages of thirty and fifty. In Greater London, minority ethnic teachers comprised 6.60 per cent of the total 85,768 with the West Midlands at 2.30 per cent of a total 30,445 ranking second. East Anglia and the 'rest of the west Midlands' comprised 100 per cent white schoolteachers; other regions were 1 per cent or less (Labour Force Surveys, 1988, 1989, 1990). A survey of teacher employment, which also compared the career experience of ethnic-minority against white teachers, was begun by the CRE in 1983 and published in 1988 (CRE, 1988). The survey of eight local authorities, showed that 2 per cent of the teachers were 'minority ethnic'. Of these, the greatest proportion, compared to white teachers, were in the schools with the highest proportions of ethnic-minority pupils. Although ethnic-minority teachers were spread across all types of school 75 per cent of the white teachers taught in schools with the highest proportions of white pupils (1–25 per cent). A higher proportion of ethnic-minority teachers (63 per cent of 40 per cent white) taught the 'shortage areas' of science and maths, yet amongst male teachers with similar durations of teaching employment 72 per cent of Whites compared to 54 per cent of 'minority ethnic' had posts of special responsibility and 7 per cent were head or deputy, against 16 per cent of Whites with similar career duration and experience. Yet the minority ethnic teachers were more highly qualified in terms of paper qualifications.

As Brar (1991), in a follow-up of the CRE survey in the Ealing Authority recounts, minority ethnic teachers are not favoured for promotion in the white-dominant system because they are said to be either 'too easy going' or 'too rigid' in their discipline. Pedagogic competence and appropriateness is thus defined in terms of ethnicity rather than knowledge and practice that crosses ethnic boundaries. It may be a convenient caricature to say that Catholic school teachers are 'forceful disciplinarians' with little regard for individual differences, Caribbean teachers 'too lax in discipline' and Indian teachers 'without a sense of humour'. This is racial prejudice; the same attributes are asserted by white teachers about one another but without the career consequences and structural discrepancies in rank and renumeration.

Neither the CRE (1988) nor Brar bring out the consequences of employment of the majority of minority ethnic teachers in Section 11 rather than mainstream posts. The Home Office provides 75 per cent and education authorities the remainder of salaries for Section 11 teachers. Their teaching is aimed at raising the achievement of minority ethnic pupils though the means are not specified; general guidelines are given and include teaching English as a second language and providing special support teaching for mainstream teachers in school subjects. As posts of responsibility are usually awarded on the basis of the number of staff being managed it is in Section 11 in particular that minority ethnic teachers have found promotion.

However, particularly in those areas with a substantial 'opt-out' from the education authority school budgets are devoted to staffing and resourcing the key areas of the statutory National Curriculum, which means that highest priority is given to the retention of mainstream teachers in the core subjects of the statutory stages. Where school budgets are near their limit teachers have been made redundant and even with the 75 per cent subsidy the Section 11 teacher is not in the high priority for retention category. Furthermore, Section 11 funding now has to be applied for quinquennially through project proposals based on consortia or single schools. Should the project proposal fail, then the Section 11 staff could become redundant. The work and employment of Section 11 teachers are particularly precarious in conditions of opting out, threshhold budgets and low priority to the 'multicultural dimension' of the National Curriculum.

One interpretation of the above is that even when ethnic minorities are employed as teachers they are subject to institutional apartheid; all white schools are the norm. Minority ethnic teachers are employed in white schools in shortage areas of maths and science but find it much harder to gain promotion than their white colleagues of comparable experience and minority ethnic teachers increase as the white-pupil population decreases. Whatever their qualifications and experience less than twelve minority ethnic teachers have gained the rank of head teacher and these in schools with a high proportion of minority ethnic children. The trend of this argument concludes that schools as part of the social structure are very successful in their exclusion or reduction of minority ethnic teachers.

One of the reasons why minority ethnic students turn away from education courses seems in part to avoid the compromise of acquiescence to institutional racism and, positively, to pursue studies where ability and attainment eventually 'pay off'. People do want to be judged as individuals, not as a stereotypes of an ethnic group that in itself is not homogeneous! My knowledge and experience sides with Gaine (1987) rather than Foster (1990) with regard to the capability of school to change in structure and ethos, to develop deeply founded, sustained practices of racial equality.

Whatever the rhetoric, social relations in the majority of schools do not reflect implementation of the idea of a universality of natural human rights; the practice is to grudgingly admit to the mainstream after minority ethnic have proven, usually by higher standards than the norm, that they deserve membership. Even then the wary eye is turned to any mistake, this is the regimen of the penitentiary. Such suspicion, indifference and tacit condemnation does not make for happy workplace relationships. Particularly now, when schools have been thrown into a competitive market for pupils, they are competing for preferably, the financially better-off and/or those who show promise of high grades in public examinations. Both attributes improve the profile of the school and 'success breeds success'. Black teachers are not an 'attractive image' for the white-highland schools' prospectus. Racism feeds racism. According to the UK legislation and the EC Social Charter, public-sector institutions have to practise equal-opportunity employment.

As school governors are now the employing authority since Local Management of Schools (LMS) was introduced in 1988, they, rather than education authorities, are the ones to convince that minority ethnic teachers are worth employing, indeed that an equal opportunities employment policy might be introduced, as in many regions of the USA. Head teachers as the executive officers to the governors also need convincing. As the governors are accountable to the parents it is the parents' interests and demands that have to be taken into account.

Given widespread racial prejudice the process of change will be slow; indeed most minority ethnic teachers will continue as Section 11 employees for as long as the education authorities provide a contribution to what is a reducing amount from the Home Office. Advocates for the employment of minority ethnic teachers have usually argued on the grounds that they are role models for minority ethnic pupils and thus a brake on the schools as a means of bringing about cultural assimilation; that their employment assists bilingual education and helps to match the cultural diversity of the wider society as well as the pupil constituency in some regions. These appeal to principles of social equity and justice which may not be in the minds of parents or governors seeking to maintain a competitive edge on pupil admissions. This competition may lessen in the mid 1990s when the birth-rate 'bulge' enters schools.

More widely, in the area of teacher education, recent volumes of the *European Journal of Teacher Education* repeatedly avoid the question of ethnic differences and equity with regard to the minority ethnic population, by attending to cultural differences amongst European-language speakers with asides to mother-tongue instruction of migrant workers. The USA has some of the strongest legislation with regard to equal opportunities for employment in public and many private organizations. A recent review of competencies required by beginning teachers in the USA (Reynolds, 1992) does not mention multicultural let alone antiracist knowledge and application as competencies required in a qualified teacher at the conclusion of ITT.

Similarly in the UK, the CATE specification of terminal competencies of initial teacher training mentions neither multicultural or antiracist teaching; nor even equal opportunities although cultural diversity is admitted. Section 2.6.4 of the 1992 CATE criteria states only 'an awareness of individual differences, including social, psychological, developmental and cultural dimensions'. Technically rationalized and sanitized pedagogical skills, subject knowledge and classroom management are encompassed whilst the classroom and school research which reveals the tenuousness of intercultural relationships between pupils and teacher (as in the US journals *Anthropology, Education Quarterly* and the *Harvard Review of Education*) are accommodated but not assimilated in practice, despite efforts, usually by bilingual education departments in colleges, to press for wider recognition in policy and staffing.

The detailed studies of race relations and action by Wright (1986) and Gaine (1987) provide evidence of racial discrimination by schoolteachers, whereas Foster (1990) from his study of a secondary school in the process of developing and enforcing a racial-equality policy claims that the 'problem' has so diminished as to be negligible or rather absent in practice. Connolly (1992) criticizes Foster's research for not including the perspectives of minority ethnic pupils and their parents and foregoing inquiries into discrepancy in order to build neat categories. My knowledge of teacher utterances and pupil judgments over a long period of time in two areas of south-east England concurs with Wright, Gaine and Brar.

We could read Foster as saying that effective means of retraining and re-educating a whole school had been successfully accomplished but that has not been an experience that is on record elsewhere. Reluctant, we might be, to accept that schools are not havens or autonomous in their values as this raises all sorts of issues of moral agency; the teacher cannot be neutral in beliefs and judgments and these in turn are based on those of the wider society. This has been said so many times that it is heard as a shibboleth of left politics when it is one of the few resilient understandings of social life and held by left and right, but not by religious or philosophical idealists. They believe that man kind can rise above such baseness by following moral precepts based on faith in the case of advocates of religion and scholastic aestheticism in the case of philosophers. Yet the very same also hold to original sin and determinism whilst expressing moral freewill! Fundamentalist thinking of this kind is widespread and irrespective of ethnicity.

Men and women teacher of different cultural backgrounds engage in different sorts of social interaction with male and female pupils of different cultural backgrounds; white, male teachers give a higher proportion of their positive classroom interaction to Asian boys, spend more of their interaction with Caribbean boys in disciplinary criticism, whilst women teachers give Asian girls more praise and response time than do men teachers. Like men teachers, women spend much of their interaction with Afro-Caribbean boys in discipline but give far more time to encouraging initiatives (Green, 1983). The networks of institutional factors that combine in a school as bias against black pupils (Wright, 1986) and the classroom processes that diminish the self-esteem of black girls (Fuller, 1980) are further evidence of the powerful consequences on individual lives of beliefs in racial superiority, intelligence and moral fitness held by many senior educationalists, implemented mainly by incremental omission in classrooms and schools. In the UK, incidents of racial abuse amongst pupils are commonplace, although racial prejudice amongst staff and towards pupils is more discreet and hence harder to record (CRE, 1988).

The lack of equal priority given to the multicultural dimension in the National Curriculum and the absence of even a mention of multicultural in the 1992 CATE criteria for teacher-education courses are two outstanding indications of the sustained downplaying of the multicultural, let alone any antiracist curriculum in schools and 'competencies' for trainee teachers. As Menter (1992) observes, the diminishing of multicultural and antiracist content of the ITT curriculum for long advocated by the right-wing think-tanks has met a receptive audience within the DES, particularly with the dissolution of HMI sources of opposition.

Even with the efforts of a decade, King (1992) reports the widespread ignorance of multicultural education in schools in the Cambridge region and how she and her colleagues devised, in collaboration with teachers, subject curricula that incorporated the culturally diverse contributions and perspectives on school subjects. Adelman *et al.* (1983) working with six classroom teachers who were aware of the difficulties of implementing racial equality in their classrooms attempted to change the social relationships through their own classroom action research.

The case accounts of the teachers' own attempts to bring about greater racial equality in the social relationships in their classrooms reveal the depth and complexity of the problems; the resource and task, their interpretation by different cultures; the existing social relationships of status and gender; and as background the mores of the school and the wider society. The futility of being a lone reformer is commented on by the teachers. Organizations like the Anti-Racist Teacher Education Network (ARTEN) provide the frame for joint action and, along with journals, particularly *Multicultural Teaching* and *Forum*, disseminate information, research and reflection on the educational problems and social-policy goals of antiracism and multiculturalism.

One wonders how many teaching-job applicants are now asked by school governors whether they are aware of, and have been trained to deal with, incidents of racial abuse in their classrooms let alone whether they have any considered views about the lack of cultural diversity in much of the core of the National Curriculum. Even if we ask the question, 'What are teacher-training courses doing to prepare their students for the culturally diverse classes of pupils' we only address symptoms. At issue are race prejudice, abuse and discrimination. We should start by asking ourselves an essential curriculum question, 'Is a part of the teachers' role to speak out against racism (and, it follows, other forms of bias)?' The answers are various but depend on whether the teacher has obligations and powers to act as moral agent in the classroom and school, and, furthermore, whether the moral (social) principles held by the teacher are antiracist, multicultural ones of mutual tolerance, assimilationist or antagonistic. All these are biases, but the social and educational consequences of each, the pragmatics of action along one of these moral lines have to be at least reflected upon by the citizen and by those who have contact with a large number of young people in particular.

Note

1   The author thanks the statistics offices at UCCA and the former GTTR for providing the tabulations, Philip Jones of the CNAA and Ros Wilson for information about Access courses, Myra McCulloch and Kiran Puri for their constructive comments and criticism; and remains culpable for any errors.

References

ADELMAN, C., BOXALL, W., PARSONS, I., RANSON, P., THEBAULT, Y., TREACHER, V. and RICHARDSON, R. (1983) A *Fair Hearing for All*, Reading, Bulmershe Research Publication 2.

BRAR, H.S. (1991) 'Unequal opportunities: The recruitment, selection and promotion prospects for black teachers', in GRACE, G. and LAWN, M. (Eds) *Teacher Supply and Teacher Quality*, Clevedon, Multilingual Matters.

COMMISSION FOR RACIAL EQUALITY (1988) *Ethnic Minority Schoolteachers: a supplementary survey of eight Local Education Authorities'*, RANGER, C. (Ed), London, CRE.

CONNOLLY, P. (1992) 'Playing it by the Rules: the politics of research in "race" and education' *British Educational Research Journal*, 18, 2, pp. 133–49.

DEPARTMENT OF EDUCATION AND SCIENCE (1985) *Education for All: Report of the Committee of Enquiry into the Education of Children from Ethnic Minority Groups* (The Swann Report), Cmnd. 9453, London, HMSO.

DEPARTMENT FOR EDUCATION (1990) 'Initial Teacher Training (Secondary Phase)' (CATE guidelines), Circ. No. 9/92, London, HMSO.

FOSTER, P. (1990) *Policy and Practice in multicultural and anti-racist Education*, London, Routledge.

FULLER, M. (1980) 'Black girls in a London comprehensive school', in HAMMERSLEY, M. and WOODS, P. (Eds) 1980 *Life in School: The Sociology of Pupil Culture*, Milton Keynes, Open University Press.

GAINE, C. (1987) *No Problem Here*, London, Hutchinson.

GREEN, P.A. (1983) 'Male and Female Created He Them', *Multicultural Teaching*, 2, 1, p. 47.

KING, A.S. (1992) 'Multiculturalism in the national curriculum', in *Cambridge Journal of Education*, 22, 1, pp. 17–30.

MENTER, I. (1992) 'The New right, racism and teacher education: some recent developments', *Multicultural Teaching*, 10, 2, Stoke on Trent, Trentham Books.

REYNOLDS, A. (1992) 'What is competent beginning teaching? A review of the literature', *Review of Educational Research*, 62, 1, pp. 1–35.

UNIVERSITIES CENTRAL COUNCIL ON ADMISSIONS 1990–91 statistics published in the 29th statistical supplement July 1992.

WRIGHT, C. (1986) 'School Processes: an ethnographic study', in EGGLESTON, J. (Ed) *Education for Some: the educational and vocational experience of 15–18 year old members of minority ethnic groups*, Stoke on Trent, Trentham Books.

Chapter 10

The Lost Opportunity? The Relative Failure of British Teacher Education in Tackling the Inequality of Schooling

Ivan Reid

Education, Inequality and Teachers

Perhaps the most noble theme of British educational history has been the concept of equality and, or, equality of opportunity in schooling and the efforts to achieve it. At the same time the abiding reality of British education has been the persistence of inequality and of inequality of opportunity. Throughout, this inequality has been recognized as related to the fundamental social division of society, that of social class. More recently other forms of social stratification, namely gender, ethnicity and, to a limited extent, disability have been given attention. Despite considerable effort and endeavour on a range of fronts — all the way from legislation to the work of individuals — inequalities, particularly that of social class, have remained. A very considerable body of literature exists concerned with this reality and the attempts to change or alleviate it. This chapter concentrates on a relatively neglected ingredient in this history, that of the role of the preparation of teachers. It provides an examination of how in the comparatively short history of British teacher education a unique opportunity was presented in which significant advances might have been made in equipping teachers to tackle inequality in schooling. It outlines the events surrounding the emergence of that opportunity, evaluates what was made of it and the extent to which it has been lost. It reviews the potential of the current situation for tackling the problem.

This is not to subscribe to any belief that teachers themselves, or indeed schooling and education, can have any real effect on the basic societal inequities which beset our society and underlay differential outcomes in educational achievement. The history of British education between 1960 and 1980 presented by Silver and Silver (1991) as 'An Educational War on Poverty', serves mainly to remind us of the fact of the economic basis of inequality and, consequently of relief only through the redistribution of wealth (Reid, 1992). For that to take place a fundamental shift of values is required and political will which could only be realized when poverty and inequality are properly understood and rejected. While education has a broad role to play in that realization, educational reform, however radical, can not, in itself seriously affect social inequality.

Somewhat more modest but nevertheless important claims can be made. An informed, aware, and active teaching force could have profound effects at three levels. First, as an enlightened and potentially significant aspect of the body politic — bearing in mind that there are some half a million teachers in schools in Britain and a somewhat higher number of qualified teachers outside them — they could constitute a body of opinion which could affect public and political attitudes. Second, practising teachers as a professional body have both a say and a vital role in the operation of the education system. It would be difficult to argue that teachers and their unions have been to the forefront of innovation for equality — for example, they were initially very guarded about the introduction of comprehensive schools. However, such stances serve to underline their potential as shapers, modifiers and facilitators of the undoubted rhetoric of equality of opportunity in British education towards its realization. Third, and perhaps most significantly, individual teachers have always been important in providing educational opportunity for their pupils and in alleviating aspects of inequality in classrooms and schools.

Each of these levels, together with their potentials, serves to emphasize an important aspect of teacher education — that of equipping teachers with an understanding and appreciation of the full implications of their professional role, both within and particularly beyond classroom and school. Opportunities for this can only be properly realized away from the press of actual teaching, in teacher education, either, or preferably both initial and in-service.

Teacher Education and Inequality

There can be no doubt that the most dramatic period of British teacher-education history was between 1960 and the mid-1970s. The fundamental shift appeared to be away from teacher training to teacher education. Prior to 1961 teacher training aimed to produce a craft-person competent in the classroom. The major structural changes — three-year rather than two-year courses and subsequent three and four-year degree courses, with attendant changes in curriculum content and scope — swung towards the concept of the teacher as an educated professional. These moves heralded the long-awaited all-graduate entry to the teaching profession. Alongside these developments was a considerable increase in the number undertaking teacher education; most of this expansion was in the colleges rather than the universities. This account concentrates on the college sector, since while changes did take place in Post-Graduate Certificate of Education (PGCE) courses for graduates these were severely constrained within a one-year (thirty week) time frame, at least until the mid-1980s when they were extended to thirty-six weeks.

The space created in teacher-education programmes led to the opportunity for enhancement of education (professional) and main-subject (academic) studies both in terms of scope and depth. This opportunity was taken up in a number of ways, though here we concentrate on the emergence of sociology and the sociology of education, which arguably had within their scope the potential to examine inequality and assist teachers in tackling it in classroom and schools.

The hope was that the discipline by equipping teachers with knowledge and sensitivities and, to a lesser extent, skills, would enable teachers to effect a greater degree of equality or minimise the effect of social class on educational performance. (Reid, 1980)

This is not to deny the contributions of psychology, history and philosophy to an understanding of inequality and the role of the teacher, but rather to illustrate via a discipline which had, and perhaps continues to have, a clear emphasis and contribution to make in that direction.

The origins of such a development can be clearly traced to the late 1950s and related not only to the slow emergence of sociology in British higher education, together with its initial concerns, but also to the inherently egalitarian ideals of the development of comprehensive schooling and the expansion of higher education. Peters (1977) has described, somewhat unkindly, how education studies developed from an 'undifferentiated mush' presented by a 'mother hen' single tutor to the disciplines of psychology, sociology, history and philosophy of education, taught by specialists. Of course, it is not true that issues such as inequality were completely ignored prior to this development. For example I have very clear recollection of the Vice-Principal of St. John's College, York, around 1960, delivering eclectic education lectures in which the contributions of the social-science disciplines, even on reflection, were not easy to discern. However, such was his fascination with effects of the slum conditions of Scunthorpe on the educational performance of the children of that city that his students presented him with a one-way railway ticket to that destination — though whether he used it or not remains a mystery.

The establishment of sociology as a main (or academic) course in the colleges was rapid during the 1960s, from six in 1960, to twenty-eight in 1966 and forty-six in 1968, by when it was expected that half the colleges would offer it by the mid-1970s. However it was achieved by less than a third by 1972 (Reid, 1974; ATCDE, 1972). Just as its establishment was linked with the growth of teacher-education numbers, so its halt and decline were associated with the severe contraction of numbers. Writing about the early courses, Shipman (1974) commented:

The influence of social class, the importance of factors in family life, the persistence of inequality, the meaningless of schooling for many children, the importance of education in social control and as a selective agency are now part of the folklore. A decade ago they were disturbing messages within teacher education and a revelation to students. (Shipman, 1974)

At the same time, others wrote more defensively about the contribution of sociology to classroom practice claiming that it was indirect (Craft, 1963; Taylor, 1961, 1966; Burgess, 1968). Official blessing appeared in the Newsom Report (DES, 1963) with its suggestion that sociology allowed teachers to 'put their job into its social perspective and be better prepared to understand the difficulties of pupils in certain types of area'. While Halsey (1965) made the claim that 'Without a developed sociological imagination the teacher is ill-equipped to take on the task of cultural missionary.'

One central debate in college-based (and concurrent) teacher education has been, and is, the balance between personal and professional education. In a real sense this can be viewed as a false dichotomy — as the enlightened James Report (DES, 1972) put it 'All teachers need to be well educated professionals.' However, the concern is sustained jointly by the historical fact that, in the past, teachers were not educated much beyond school (and hence their charges) and because of the assumption that in order to teach one needs to have a far greater depth of knowledge than that which is used in one's teaching. One continuing aspect of this debate has been whether a main or degree subject has to be on the schools' curriculum in order to be appropriate for teacher training. Questions surrounded the establishment of sociology as a main course in the colleges, but as will be seen, the climate was much more favourable then than now. A variety of justifications were given to, and accepted by, validating bodies. In general, these followed Musgrave's (1965) claim that sociology was as effective in educating a teacher as any other discipline. This claim was backed up to an extent by an analysis of the distribution of final teaching-practice grades in a college between 1966 and 1970, which revealed no difference between students studying sociology as a main subject and students studying a traditional teacher-training subject (Reid, 1972, 1974). There appeared to be then at least some acceptance that academic studies which supported and extended the teacher's role had a legitimacy in teacher-education courses.

The embrace of sociology in teacher education gave rise to, and provided the basis for, other innovative courses concerned with inequality. One example was the social-work main course at Edge Hill College of Education, designed to produce a teacher/social worker (Craft, 1967; Craft, Raynor and Cohen, 1967). This course commenced in 1964 and was designed to equip students with the necessary knowledge, experience and skill to bridge the gaps between school and home and the social services. It was related to considerations of the Newsom Report (DES, 1963) which observed that 'Many situations would be helped simply by schools knowing more of the home circumstances', suggested a possible specialist role and that 'this also implies a need for teachers whose training has included some realistic sociological studies.' In many ways this course anticipated some parts of the Plowden Report's (DES, 1967) suggestions and the role of teachers in the ensuing educational priority areas. The same college entered another field of inequality in 1968 with a course on the education of immigrant children. These and similar courses were also offered to teachers who were seconded from work to undertake them. In the event in-service courses involving sociology were to survive much better and longer than initial ones. The sociology of education featured in higher degrees and diplomas into the mid-1980s when secondments all but ceased, whereas dilution was fairly rapid in initial courses following the severe cut-backs in teacher education in the mid-1970s, let alone the attentions of central government via CATE in the 1980s.

What Was Taught?

It is interesting to reflect on what was offered in the courses in sociology at that time, since this is likely to be related to its reception and progress. Several analyses of syllabuses allow for a limited view, for example, Banks (1966) identified three aspects: sociology for the prospective teacher; sociology as a teaching subject; useful things for an educated person to know. He also noted that while the family was always featured, the school was not. Ellis, McCready and Morgan (1969) did not identify either classroom application or the school as an institution as a major area of study. Without any doubt this reflected the state of knowledge at the time. As Shipman (1969) detected, there was a continued dependence on, and reflection of, the university courses of the tutors. In turn, this was likely to have been reinforced by the need to convince the validating universities of the academic respectability of courses — though Shipman also found an absence of theoretical frameworks and methodology, together with the omission of conflict, power and control. In 1972 McCready's survey of social science courses' revealed syllabuses with fairly discrete approaches, capable of characterization (Reid, 1975). They ranged from purely academic/theoretical sociology to those with a strong emphasis on equipping students with the basis for teaching sociology in school and experience of understanding the local area; and from tightly prescriptive to guided student choice. Such characterization neatly encapsulates the variety of pressures on teacher-education syllabuses and the comparative freedom of the time to respond to them. Abell and Pegram's (1974) more detailed analysis found that most (76 per cent) included social stratification and more than half the sociology of education. The latter figure may seem low unless it is remembered that all students had this included in their education studies and some main-subject departments therefore ignored it. More surprising is that some syllabuses omitted stratification, though this may simply reflect the shortcomings of the brief outline syllabuses used in the analysis.

Somewhat less is known directly about the content of the sociology of education parts of education courses at this time, though it may safely be concluded that social class featured in all syllabuses. It was certainly a feature of the literature of the time, and specifically the available British textbooks. Patrick, Bernbaum and Reid (1982) questioned a large sample of PGCE students in 1979–80, 20 per cent of whom claimed to have gained a great extent of insight into social class and educational opportunity and 44 per cent some extent (percentages similar to those for mixed-ability teaching, classroom discipline and language in the classroom). However, as they record 'it is interesting to note that, despite the supposed influence of social class and educational opportunity in teacher education, that item attracts one of the highest proportions of students . . . who indicated uncertainty over the extent of insight gained.' In hindsight it is quite amazing that little or no attention was paid to forms of social stratification other than social class and, in particular, gender.

Of course both such a lack and the then growing presence of sociology and the sociology of education were products of, and constrained by, the social climate of that time. This is not the place for a full elaboration, but for the recognition of three major factors — the state of the disciplines, the social and political environment of their reception, and the previously mentioned changes in the scale of teacher education. Each of these was clearly related to the emergence and the establishment of the disciplines in teacher education, to their development and subsequent decline.

College sociology in its first phase (Reid, 1978) was almost exclusively based on structuralist (particularly functionalist) theory. Its main contributions were the clear recording of social-class inequalities in education, a challenge to views of education as an autonomous institution — it set it into a wider institutional / societal framework — a demonstration of the relationship of teachers and pupils and their activities with society and the ways in which the social structure enters and affects the social reality of the classroom, together with the exposure of the social definition and functions of education on time scales and to extents not immediately apparent to practitioners. As such, it clearly reflected those few university courses (predominantly the London School of Economics and Leicester) and the state of knowledge of the era. Such contributions were not only welcomed into teacher education but also featured in the educational policy-making of the time. Hence there were direct reflections in, for example, the Robbins Report (DES, 1963) on higher education, the Newsom Report (DES, 1963) on secondary education and the Plowden Report (DES, 1967) on primary education, which conducted sociologically informed research and included sociologists among their advisers and even on some committees.

However piecemeal and ephemeral these offerings may have been, the period saw social-class inequality treated as a subject of study in many teacher-education courses. Its failure to be fully established and developed, together with its subsequent decline, reflects Taylor's (1983) accurate caution, 'For to devise our courses exclusively in accordance with the dictates of disciplines, or in terms of what the profession states as its wants and needs, is to betray our particular task as educators of teachers.'

There were other factors at work. One was student reception and reaction to the courses, another was a shift of perspective in sociology itself from structuralist to interpretative. The erroneously called 'new sociology of education' concentrated on aspects such as the curriculum and classroom interaction which had more obvious and direct appeal within the teacher-education context and led in some cases to a neglect of more macro concerns, including, to a degree, social inequality. The decline in teacher-education numbers from the early 1970s was as dramatic as growth had been, together with what were fairly radical reorganization and changes in validation away from universities, with the inception of CNAA (Lynch, 1979).

The net result was that by the mid 1970s professional ideology had come to dominate sociology of education courses, as was shown in the survey by Burgess (1977) and there was a tendency for the disciplines to be subsumed into professional studies (Alexander and Wormald, 1979). These trends were heightened by government involvement in approving and seeking 'relevance' in teacher-education courses (HMSO, 1983; DES, 1984) and the setting up and functioning of the Council for the Accreditation of Teacher Education (CATE). For example, surviving main courses in sociology in initial courses for primary teaching presented to CATE in the mid-1980s received very careful attention in the face of its creator's — Sir Keith Joseph (then Secretary of State for Education) — display of some open hostility towards the subject. MacIntyre (1991) recounts several course considerations in which the main criteria for acceptance were the delivery of the National Curriculum and CATE criteria and during which the DES assessor indicated that the opinion of the Secretary of State was that sociology should be part of professional studies rather than a main subject. At the same time the role of the contributory disciplines in education courses was made less distinctive and the time allocated for their treatment curtailed in the face of growing demands for what was called relevance and direct utility, together with the inclusion of CATE criteria. Present demands for compentency-based courses appear set to further this trend.

There was also a marked change in the balance of training away from the B.Ed. degree and towards the PGCE. Pressure was on for a return to the thematic education courses of the 1950s in which the contributory disciplines were disguised and used in a utilitarian fashion (Reid, 1986). This situation reminds one of Broudy's (1980) caution that, 'Theories of education are rarely, if ever rejected because they have been proven false. They perish because they are outmoded, i.e., they go out of fashion.'

How Was It Received?

This is always an imponderable question in the sense of the lack of clarity about how and when to measure the reception and effect of education. Nowhere is this more so than in professional education. Is it near to the point of delivery and in answer to fairly direct questions, or to the extent to which it is reflected in practice? Most studies have, understandably, been of the former type. These reveal most student teachers to have an almost exclusive preference for the immediately utilitarian, and to reject or be dismissive of the more general or longer term (Eason and Croll, 1971; Patrick, Bernbaum and Reid, 1982). At the same time there is some evidence that teacher educators do influence the attitudes of their charges. For example, MacLeish (1970) in a very large-scale study of attitude change amongst student teachers concluded 'We must therefore assume that the colleges influence their students towards radicalism (in respect to educational values) . . . the change being also in the direction of the views of lecturers.'

In respect to social class Taylor (1969) observed 'The humbler social origins of teacher trainees and the ambiguity that surrounds the social status and financial rewards of the teacher, may help to account for the resistance that has been noted to the discussion of social class in college of education courses. Although this is gradually disappearing as sociological topics come to occupy a more assured place in the syllabus, there is still the feeling on the part of some tutors, as well as students, that the topic is "embarrassing" and best avoided.'

Reid (1980) developed a typology of teachers' responses to the teaching of social class, based on some fifteen years' experience teaching the sociology of education, and which he sees as having been sustained since. These ranged from rejection (both rational and emotional), through accommodation and neutrality, to assimilation and conversion. In his experience, accommodation and neutrality had remained the most common response, while rejection declined. On the one hand it may be argued that the teaching was relatively unsuccessful and was resisted, on the other that it slowly passed into teaching and social folklore. In either case it would be difficult to substantiate that it had any profound general effect on succeeding generations of teachers. Although it shares this with most other aspects of courses, there is a great lack of the demonstration of the effectiveness of teacher education. Generally there appears to have been an acceptance of social class as a feature of society and education, but with a resistance to its implications for schooling, teaching and self. Of course, it is precisely at this point that the sociology of education was and is at its weakest. It does not spell out adequately enough how teachers operate in reproducing inequality or how they might do otherwise. What can be claimed is that such courses at least brought inequality to attention of teachers and heightened their sensitivities towards it. Like other aspects of teacher education, the reasonable hope must be that the teachers themselves are capable of incorporating them into their practice.

A Question of Timing

A further abiding concern in teacher education is about the timing of the various ingredients of professional learning. This concern was seriously addressed by the James Report (DES, 1972) which argued that the only solution was to regard the personal education, the pre-service and induction, and the in-service education of teachers as consecutive parts of a continuing process. It proposed that these should constitute three cycles with the highest priority to be given to the expansion of the third, with all teachers being entitled to not less than one term (or equivalent) every seven years of service. Theoretical studies of education were to feature in the second cycle 'only insofar as they contribute to effective teaching, and their main development should be in the third cycle where they can be illuminated by experience' — 'building on school experience and personal maturity'. The potential of such a scheme had it been implemented was vast, particularly in respect to the concerns of this chapter. Perhaps the real challenge of attending to inequality — of social class, gender, ethnicity and disability — is more appropriate from within, rather than prior to entry into, the teaching profession. In the event opportunities for in-service education of teachers were severely curtailed, first by the virtual disappearance of secondments and later by the removal of financial and other support for part-time courses. So the present situation is much as it was, attempting to produce fully competent teachers by the end of initial training (without now a probationary year) and resulting in overloaded timetables, with the essential sometimes sacrificed to the desirable and a confusion of objectives and a tension between personal and professional education.

Permeation, Integration and Isolation

The result of the changing climate surrounding teacher education has been a marked decline in the opportunities to confront student teachers with the reality of social class and inequality. These and other aspects of sociology and the sociology of education have either disappeared or become subsumed into parts of courses which have labels of apparently greater relevance and utility. At the same time attention has shifted to other areas of social inequality. The case of special needs has been well recorded by Povey and Abbotts (1989). A survey of B.Ed. degree courses in 1979 by HMI concluded that, 'The compulsory elements of most courses did not ... bring students towards much awareness of the special needs of certain categories of children, in particular those with a cultural background different from that of the majority or those whose learning was otherwise handicapped.' (DES, 1979). The Warnock Report (DES, 1978) called for a 'special education element to be included in all courses of teacher training within the context of child development.' The 1981 Education Act incorporated this integrationalist strategy, while four-year special-education training courses were ended on the recommendation of the Advisory Committee for the Supply and Education of Teachers (ACSET, 1984). This led to the recommendation that 'An effective course of training should include those aspects of the teacher's skill which relate to . . . the recognition of children with special needs in the ordinary classroom . . . they should be part of the basic professional preparation of all teachers.' (DES, 1983).

Tomlinson (1989) recounts the considerable and protracted efforts to introduce training for multiculturalism into teacher-education courses. While Circular 3/84 (DES, 1984) called for students to be prepared for pupils' 'diversity of ability, behaviour, social background and ethnic and cultural origins', the following CATE notes on implementation did not deal directly with the issue. Like most of the new demands on teacher-education courses these issues have been incorporated not by specific treatment but by permeation. The dangers and reality of permeation are clear — it has become a catchword, can lead to trivialization, or as Gaine (1987) puts it 'things can become so well permeated that they disappear altogether.'

In any case there are inherent dangers in avoiding the recognition of the interrelationship of forms of social inequality. Not only can it lead to the compartmentalization of class, gender, ethnicity and disability, but also to a failure to understand and appreciate each. Troyna (1987) illustrates this point forcibly in writing:

> If these conceptions of reality are to be challenged effectively then it is essential to provide superior and more plausible explanation . . . This can not be done if the issues of 'race' and ethnic relations are considered in isolation; rather they need to be seen and considered as pertinent aspects of the social structure along with, say, class and gender . . . The aim is to ensure that students not only recognise the specific nature of racial inequality but the nature of the inequalities they themselves experience and share. (Troyna, 1987)

It is also salutary that in the most recent criteria for secondary-phase initial teacher training (DES, 1992) the concerns of this chapter are in the fifth rank of competencies and headed 'Further Professional Development'. The 'newly qualified should have acquired . . . the necessary foundation to develop;' (para., 2.6) 'an awareness of *individual* differences, including social, psychological, developmental and cultural dimensions (para., 2.6.4) [my emphasis]; mention is also made of special needs (para., 2.6.6), gifted pupils (para., 2.6.5) and 'an understanding of the school as an institution and its place within the community' (para., 2.6.1). There is not much obvious scope for dealing with social inequality.

Prospects

In the face of present concerns about the direct and continual involvement of central government in education it is interesting to reflect with Gosden (1984) that teacher training received such attention from its beginning. From the Committee of Council on Education in the 1840s this involvement went much further than giving grants, setting numbers and the length and structure of courses, extending until the third decade of this century to HMI setting and marking the examination papers for the certificate in education. The 'examination lesson' to examine professional competence was conducted by HMI until the end of the World War II. In many respects then, the events from the mid-1980s to the present represent an echo, but with higher levels of intervention and dictate.

As has been argued, the opportunity to fully consider inequality in teacher education was only partly seized, was of but limited success and in many ways is now lost. Yet the need for it not only remains, but has been heightened. Some 25 per cent of children in Britain in 1988/89 — 3.1 million — were in poverty, as defined by living in households receiving less than half the average income. This figure had risen from 10 per cent since 1979 and in the same period such households with the lowest 10 per cent of incomes experienced a 6 per cent cut in real income (HMSO, 1992). The very real challenge of providing educational opportunity for the variously socially disadvantaged in our society remains constant. Yet it is not only within teacher education that inequality fails to be appropriately recognized and tackled. The testing of pupils at ages 7, 11, 14 and 16 has been instituted without regard for the social-background factors known to be related to performance, or even to the child's chronological age — a vital factor particularly at age 7. Similarly, publication of league tables of school-examination performance are uncontextualized in respect to both social and educational inequality. There is even the prospect of teachers' performance related pay being established in the same manner. That these and other aspects of schooling and education reflect current political ideology and, perhaps, public opinion or relative disinterest, simply serves to further emphasize the fundamental role that teacher education could, and should, fulfil.

> Lynch and Plunkett's (1973) observations remain valid: Teacher education is a disputed territory of conflicting tendencies: ... to maintain and reproduce the pattern of traditional ways of valuing, thinking and organizing; .... to promote innovation and reform ...The aims of teacher education are problematic insofar as society and the role on which they are focused reflect contradictory tendencies. (Lynch and Plunkett, 1973)

To an extent we missed the opportunity provided to tackle inequality and presently face perhaps unprecedented circumstances and constraints. But now, probably more than ever before, there is a vital need to continue to confront student and practising teachers with the reality of inequality in our society and its education system. It is difficult to escape Borrowman's (1956) stricture, 'Teacher educators vary in their sensitivity to underlying forces which move society. Yet inevitably they reflect these forces, and their thoughts [and actions] must be judged accordingly.' As Ginsburg (1988) has pointed out, we must provide students with the necessary analytical skills and conceptual tools to critically reflect and enquire about their own and broader experiences of school and society. Teacher-education courses must make use of these to examine issues relevant to social class, gender, ethnicity and all forms of inequality. Teacher education must provide not only relevant classroom skills, but also the focus of critical examination. One thing is for sure, ignoring inequality will not make it go away.

References

ABELL, B. and PEGRAM, M. (1974) 'An analysis of sociology course syllabuses', in REID, I. and WORMALD, E. (Eds) *Sociology and Teacher Education*, London, ATCDE.

ACSET (1984) *Teacher Training and Special Educational Needs*, London, DES.

ALEXANDER, R.J., CRAFT, M. and LYNCH, J. (1984) *Change in Teacher Education*, London, Holt, Rinehart and Winston.

ALEXANDER, R.J. and WORMALD, E. (1979) *Professional Studies for Teaching*, London, SHRE.

ATCDE (1969) *Sociology in the Education of Teachers*, (Sociology Section Report), London, ATCDE.

ATCDE (1972) *Handbook of Colleges and Departments of Education*, London, ATCDE.

BANKS, J.A. (1966) 'An examination of syllabuses', An address to a conference of the British Sociological Association and ASA, London.

BARTON, L. and MEIGHAN, R. (1987) *Sociological Interpretations of Schooling and Classrooms: A Reappraisal*, Driffield, Nafferton.

BORROWMAN, M. (1956) *The Liberal and the Technical in Teacher Education*, Westport, Greenwood Press.

BROUDY, H.S. (1980) 'What do professors of education profess?', *Education Forum*, 44, 4 May.

BURGESS, R.G. (1968) 'Sociology as a main course', *Cambridge Institute of Education Bulletin*, 3, 7.

BURGESS, R.G. (1977) 'Sociology of education courses for the intending teacher; an empirical study', *Research in Education*, 17.

CRAFT, M. (1963) 'Why sociology for teachers?', *Education for Teaching*, 62 (reproduced in REID, I. and WORMALD, E., 1974).

CRAFT, M. (1967) 'The Teacher/Social Worker', in CRAFT, M., RAYNOR, J. and COHEN, L. (Eds), *Linking Home and School*, London, Longman.

CRAFT, M., RAYNOR, J. and COHEN, L. (1967) *Linking Home and School*, London, Longman.

DES (1963) *Half Our Future* (The Newsom Report), London, HMSO.

DES (1963) *Higher Education* (The Robbins Report), London, HMSO.

DES (1967) *Children and Their Primary Schools* (The Plowden Report), London, HMSO.

DES (1972) *Teacher Education and Training* (The James Report), London, HMSO.

DES (1978) *Special Educational Needs* (The Warnock Report), London, HMSO.

DES (1979) *Developments in the BEd Degree Course*, London, HMSO.

DES (1983) *Training in Schools: The Content of Initial Training*, London, HMSO.

DES (1984) *Initial Teacher Training: Approval of Courses*, Circ. No. 3/84 London, HMSO.

DES (1992) *Initial Teacher training [Secondary Phase]*, Circ. No. 9/92 London, HMSO.

EASON, T.W. and CROLL, E.J. (1971) *Staff and Student attitudes in colleges of education*, Slough, NFER.

ELLIS, D., McCREADY, D. and MORGAN, C. (1969) *Sociology in the Education of Teachers*, London, ATCDE.

GAINE, C. (1987) *No Problem Here — A practical approach to Education and Race in White Schools*, London, Hutchinson.

GINSBURG, M.B. (1988) *Contradictions in Teacher Education and Society: A Critical Analysis*, London, The Falmer Press.

GOSDEN, P.H.J.H. (1984) 'The role of central government and its agencies, 1963–82', in ALEXANDER, R.J., CRAFT, M. and LYNCH, J. (Eds) *Change in Teacher Education*, London, Holt, Rinehart and Winston.

HALSEY, A.H. (1965) 'Sociology for teachers', *New Society* 30 September, in REID, I. and WORMALD, E. (Eds) *Sociology and Teacher Education*, London, ATCDE.

HMSO (1983) *Teacher Quality*, (Cmnd. 8836, London, HMSO.

HMSO (1992) *Households Below Average Income: A Statistical Analysis 1979–1988/ 9*, London, HMSO,

LYNCH, J. (1979) *The Reform of Teacher Education in the United Kingdom*, Guildford, University of Surrey, SHRE.

LYNCH, J. and PLUNKETT, H. (1973) *Teacher education and cultural change: England, France and West Germany*, London, Allen and Unwin.

MACINTYRE, G. (1991) *Accreditation of Teacher Education: The Story of CATE, 1984– 1989*, London, The Falmer Press.

MACLEISH, J. (1970) *Student Attitudes and College Environments*, Cambridge, Cambridge Institute of Education.

MCCLELLAND, V.A. and VARMA, V.P. (1989) *Advances in Teacher Education*, London, Routledge and Kegan Paul.

MCCREADY, D. (1972) *Guide to Social Science Courses*, London, ATCDE.

MUSGRAVE, P.W. (1965) 'Syllabuses and teaching methods for sociology in colleges of education', *Education for Teaching*, 68 (reproduced in REID, I. and WORMALD, E. (Eds) 1974).

PATRICK, H., BERNBAUM, G. and REID, K. (1982) *The Structure and Process of Initial Teacher Education Within Universities in England and Wales*, Leicester, University of Leicester School of Education.

PETERS, R.S. (1977) *Education and the Education of Teachers*, London, Routledge and Kegan Paul.

POVEY, R. and ABBOTTS, P. (1989) 'Training for special needs', in MCCLELLAND, V.A. and VARMA, V.P. (Eds) *Advances in Teacher Education*, London, Routledge and Kegan Paul.

REID, I. (1972) 'Social science and teaching performance', *Educational Research*, 15, 1.

REID, I. (1974) 'Sociology and teaching performance', in REID, I. and WORMALD, E. (Eds), *Sociology and Teacher Education*, London, ATCDE.

REID, I. (1975) 'Some reflections on sociology in colleges of education', *Educational Studies*, 1, 1.

REID, I. (1978) 'Past and present trends in the sociology of education', in BARTON, L. and MEIGHAN, R. (Eds) *Sociological Interpretations of Schooling and Classrooms: A Re-appraisal*, Driffield, Nafferton.

REID, I. (1980) 'Teachers and social class', *Westminster Studies in Education*, 3.

REID, I. (1986) 'Hoops, roundabouts and swings in teacher education: a critical review of the CATE criteria', *Journal of Higher and Further Education*, 10, 2.

REID, I. (1992) 'War, skirmish or feint? Education against poverty 1960 to 1980', *British Journal of Sociology of Education*, 13, 4.

REID, I. and WORMALD, E. (1974) *Sociology and Teacher Education*, London, ATCDE.

SHIPMAN, M.D. (1969) *Sociology in the Education of Teachers*, London, ATCDE.

SHIPMAN, M.D. (1974) 'Reflections on early courses', in REID, I. and WORMALD, E. (Eds) 1974.

SILVER, H. and SILVER, P. (1991) *An Educational War On Poverty: American and British Policy Making 1960–1980*, Cambridge, Cambridge University Press.

TAYLOR, W. (1961) 'The sociology of education in the training college', *'Education for Teaching*, 54, in REID, I. and WORMALD, E. (Eds) *Sociology and Teacher Education*, London, ATCDE.

TAYLOR, W. (1966) 'The sociology of education', in TIBBLE, J.W. (Ed) *The Study of Education*, London, Routledge and Kegan Paul.

TAYLOR, W. (1969) *Society and the Education of Teachers*, London, Faber and Faber.

TAYLOR, W. (1983) 'The crisis of confidence in teacher education: an international perspective', *Oxford Review of Education*, 9, 1.

TIBBLE, J.W. (1966) *The Study of Education*, London, Routledge and Kegan Paul.

TOMLINSON, S. (1989) 'Training for multiculturalism', in MCCLELLAND, V.A. and VARMA, V.P. (Eds) *Advances in Teacher Education*, London, Routledge and Kegan Paul.

TROYNA, B. (1987) 'Beyond multiculturalism: towards the enactment of antiracist education in policy, provision and pedagogy', *Oxford Review of Education*, 13.

Chapter 11

Multicultural Education and Dutch Primary School Teacher Training Institutes

Hans de Frankrijker

From 1980 the Dutch government acknowledged that the ethnic-minority groups who arrived in the decades after World War II were here to stay permanently. Since then, a formal minority policy has developed for the groups of 'guest labourers', immigrants from Dutch colonies (Surinam and The Antilles), travelling people and refugees from Asia, Africa and eastern Europe. This educational minority policy was formulated in the context of equal educational opportunities. It represented a turning point in the approach to ethnic and cultural diversity by the Dutch government. Actually it could be said that the approach in The Netherlands developed along similar lines to that in Great Britain, Canada and the United States one or two decades earlier. The policy of assimilation was dropped in favour of a policy of integration. When it became obvious that the ethnic and cultural minority groups were here to stay the insight grew that it would be an illusion to think simply that all these groups would or should be absorbed in the cultural heritage of the dominant majority.

In the Netherlands this turning point found its expression in the educational concept of intercultural education which can be seen as a logical consequence of this policy of integration (Sietaram, 1984). In the Dutch context intercultural education is defined as the promotion of interaction and communication between people of different cultural backgrounds. The main goal is that all aspects of the institutions, such as the curriculum, the media and the organization, work towards this end. The characteristics of intercultural education are that all those involved are affected, pupils, students and teachers alike, regardless of class, ethnicity, sex or nationality. Actually in the debate about equal educational opportunities for all ethnic and cultural groups in society the concept of intercultural education takes in a central position. The (third) OECD examiners' report on Dutch national policy for education concludes that 'Dutch policy on how to deal with ethnic minorities and immigrants has, over the past 15 years, been among the most vigorous and constructive in Western Europe. It has also evolved in very different directions during the recent past' (OECD, 1991, p. 59).

From a formal policy point of view the Primary Education Act 1985 (Section 8, Subsection 3) specifies that education should take account of the fact that all children in the Netherlands grow up in a multicultural society. In the report of the ARBO committee (1988, p. 13), a governmental advisory committee, intercultural education is deemed imperative for the entire field of Dutch education: ... 'also in schools with few or no pupils from ethnic minority groups'. This view is also supported by the report of the Scientific Committee for the Government's Policies (WRR, 1989). In this WRR report the scientific committee points to the crucial importance of teachers' behaviour, knowledge and attitudes to the school career of ethnic-minority pupils. It indicated that many teachers lack adequate knowledge and skills to teach in multicultural groups. Quite remarkable is that in another report of the ARBO committee *Progressie in professie* Progress in the Profession, (ARBO, 1988) intercultural education is not mentioned at all, neither in regular teacher-training courses nor in postgraduate courses. Yet the ARBO resolution of 26 September 1983 lists as the fifth of its ten objectives for PABOs (Dutch teacher-training institutes for primary education): 'Appreciation of other cultures and concern for cultural minorities'. This objective is developed by outlining how PABO trainees should be able to stimulate their pupils to appreciate each other's differences. Language acquisition and positive aspects of different cultures should receive special attention. There should also be attention for the problems this entails for the school's organization.

Considering developments on a conceptual level in countries like Great Britain, Canada and the USA, the integration approach has evolved from theories of cultural pluralism. This pluralist approach can be considered as a reaction to the harmonious approach of integration that seems to be aimed at a harmless melting process of distinctive ethnic and cultural groups (Baptiste, 1986; Verma, 1988). In fact the integration view ignores the existence of minority and majority positions and conflicting interests between and within groups. The integrative melting-pot theory suggests that inequalities in the distribution of power, education, labour-market positions, status and income do not exist, or at least do not disturb the integration process. The approach of cultural pluralism includes a philosophy of equal valuation of distinctive contributions of diverse cultural and ethnic groups. Equality of (educational) opportunities and retention and maintenance of ethnic and cultural identity are important values and policy aims. Yet different conceptions of multicultural education are used in the USA and in Great Britain. Grant and Secada (1990) distinguish five different conceptions of multicultural education:

- teaching the different child;
- human relations;
- single-group studies;
- multicultural approaches and education that is multicultural; and
- social reconstructionism.

In the debate about intercultural education in the Netherlands similar distinctive conceptions can be found. There are three main different approaches to intercultural education: promoting mutual understanding and interaction between distinctive cultural and ethnic groups; knowledge exchange; and antiracist education and emancipation. Nevertheless according to the comparative findings of Lynch (1986, p. 33), the development of educational policies for cultural pluralism in western Europe still rests at a very immature stage. It is still the case that beyond the educational policies of many countries there is the real hope that 'they' will become like 'us' (OECD, 1991, p. 97).

The term 'multicultural education' will be used later in this chapter but one has to realize that in the Dutch context it is conceptualized in terms of intercultural education, in a predominantly integrative perspective. The differences in conceptualization between and within several countries will not be further analyzed here. This chapter will focus on how Dutch teacher-training institutes for primary education (PABOs) deal with multicultural education and on how they are implementing teaching programmes.

Research into Multicultural Aspects in Teacher Education

Since the mid-1980s a growing amount of educational research into multicultural education has been conducted. Fase and van den Berg (1985) conducted one of the first research studies into multicultural education in Dutch primary education. They found a relationship between the number of ethnic-minority pupils and the degree of multicultural activities at a given school. It was shown that only schools with more than 25 per cent ethnic-minority pupils developed any multicultural education activities. Almost half of the schools in the study gave some attention to multicultural education. A follow-up study (Fase *et al.*, 1987); Education Inspectorate Report, 1989) showed that about 10 per cent of all primary schools actually put this attention into practice. 30 to 40 per cent of the primary schools only have made plans to give attention to multicultural activities (Fase *et al.*, 1990).

Kloosterman (1990) gave an informative account of developments in training and retraining in intercultural education during the past decade. His paper was concerned primarily with the policies and results of intercultural education, not with findings about and activities in PABOs. Consultation of several archives, including those of the Ministry of Education and Science, yielded only a few relevant but greatly different publications about multicultural education in practice in PABOs. (Van der Heijden *et al.*, 1983; PICOO, 1984; De Kler, 1984; Giesbertz and Remijnse, 1983; 1984). The first three referenced publications are from the field of education, the other two are an M.A. thesis and a thesis for a secondary teacher's certificate.

In 1983 the journal *Over Vernieuwing* (About Innovation) issued a special on multicultural project courses at teacher-training colleges. In its introduction the periodical called for incorporating multicultural education as a structural component of the curriculum. The journal went on to provide an overview of intercultural activities at four PABOs and ideas of the teachers. The report of van der Heijden *et al.* (1983) primarily contains teaching suggestions and references to literature for the use of teacher training. The report assembles the findings of a project group that conducted a survey at a number of teacher-training colleges in Groningen. It was published as part of the '*Modelonderwijsleerplan*' (the ideal curriculum model) conceived by LOBO (a project group for the development of curricula for trainee teachers in primary education). In 1984, PICOO (project for multicultural education at teacher-training colleges) funded by the Ministry of Education, published five reports. These relate how several colleges worked on the execution of one particular subject in the period 1982–84. The subjects were: child care in infant schools, cultural orientation, child care in primary schools, teacher training for the multicultural education of young children, and courses to stimulate multicultural education. It is noteworthy that the project had no follow-up. De Kler (1984) in her M.A. thesis reported interviews with lecturers from five teacher-training colleges in Rotterdam, which had been involved with the development of an overall curriculum for cultural minorities in the Rijnmond area from 1981. She examined how far the colleges had progressed in incorporating multicultural education. This project had no follow-up either. De Kler concluded that the colleges with culturally mixed populations gave more attention to multicultural education. She recommended that, if multicultural education was to be successfully incorporated into the curriculum, the lecturers who were most motivated should receive special facilities. In their M.A. thesis Giesbertz and Remijnse (1983) reported on multicultural education at teacher-training colleges. They interviewed one lecturer from twenty-five training colleges and sent questionnaires to sixty-six colleges, twenty-seven of which were returned. In an edited version of the thesis (1984) they classified their findings into four categories: the extent to which multicultural education formed a structural component of the curriculum; the involvement of teachers; the degree of implicit and explicit attention for multicultural education; and the degree of incidental versus integrated attention for intercultural education. Each category had an initial phase and a goal (final) phase. The colleges were rated according to the phase they were in for each category. Only a few of the colleges were found to have reached the desired final phase. At none of the colleges was the entire team involved with incorporating multicultural education into the curriculum. At some of the colleges (exact numbers are not given) all of the work was carried out by individuals or groups of lecturers, usually from one department and only rarely from more. A 'rather large group' of colleges was found to be concerned only implicitly with multicultural education. On the other hand there was also a considerable group that is concerned with it explicitly. A limited number of colleges was concerned with multicultural education only incidentally. Most of the colleges dealt with it in special projects, separate courses, block-release courses or a series of classes. The researchers did not find a single college where intercultural education was an integral part of the total curriculum.

Teacher Training and the Dutch Educational System

The historical development of the Dutch educational system has resulted in a structural diversification of institutes for the training of teachers for distinctive educational levels. In the nineteenth century it was usual for prospective teachers to be recruited from the schools they attended. The training of primary-school teachers was directly connected with and practised by the headmaster of the school that they had attended as a pupil. This resulted in a situation whereby every type of school trained its own teaching staff. It is this historical background which explains why there still are different types of teacher institutes, training teachers for one specific type of school or particular school level. In the Netherlands there are currently four main types of teacher training for different school levels:

- forty-one teacher-training institutes for primary education (PABOs); (3–5 institutes for special education are at the planning stage);

- nine new-style teacher-training courses (NLOs) established since 1970; offering a qualification in one subject in the second grade sector: secondary education;
- fourteen institutes for second-grade and first-grade (MOs); offering a qualification for one subject in secondary or higher vocational and (pre) university education; and
- thirteen postgraduate university teaching-training courses (ULOs); offering a qualification in the first-grade sector: higher vocational and (pre) university education.

There are also a few teacher-training courses, many of them run on a part-time basis or in-service, in health care, agriculture, gymnastics and others. The Dutch education system is presented as it is today in Figure 11.1. As can be seen, the PABO is positioned in the 'higher vocational education' block. The current form of the colleges for primary teacher training (PABOs) was established in 1984. At that time the courses for primary and nursery teachers were integrated. One year later primary schools and nursery schools were integrated into schools for primary education. Qualified teachers for primary education are considered to be able to teach any subject to children of any age from four to twelve. The courses last for four years and lead to such a broad qualification that every primary-school teacher must be able to teach every subject taught in primary schools.

Multicultural Activities in Dutch PABOs

The OECD examiners noted that efforts were just beginning to create a teaching programme for a multicultural future. They concluded that multicultural training was becoming part of the teacher-training curriculum but still in a very abstract way (OECD, 1991, p. 97) This confirms our earlier observation that in hardly any institute multicultural education forms an integral part of the teaching programme.

An inventory was made of the multicultural activities in teacher-training courses as formally defined in the curricula and actually put into practice. The description below is based on results from a telephone survey conducted at fifty-five PABOs (including individual course sites).

Composition of Student Population and Teaching Staff of the PABOs

The labelling of 'black and white schools' does not simply depend on percentages but also has to be analyzed in a broader social context. Research shows that Dutch primary schools are labelled as 'black' by the community when the percentage of pupils from ethnic-minority groups goes beyond 40 per cent of the total school population. In the four big cities of the Netherlands the number of schools with more than 50 per cent pupils from ethnic-minority groups increases quite rapidly. Almost one third of the primary schools in the big cities are attended by more than 50 per cent ethnic-minority pupils (Teunissen, 1992). 'Black' schools in the rest of the country are still rare. But it appears that some schools with more than 60 per cent pupils from ethnic-minority groups are not labelled as 'black' by the area. It turned out that these were schools with a broad interethnic

Hans de Frankrijker

Figure 11.1: The Dutch Education System Today (1992)

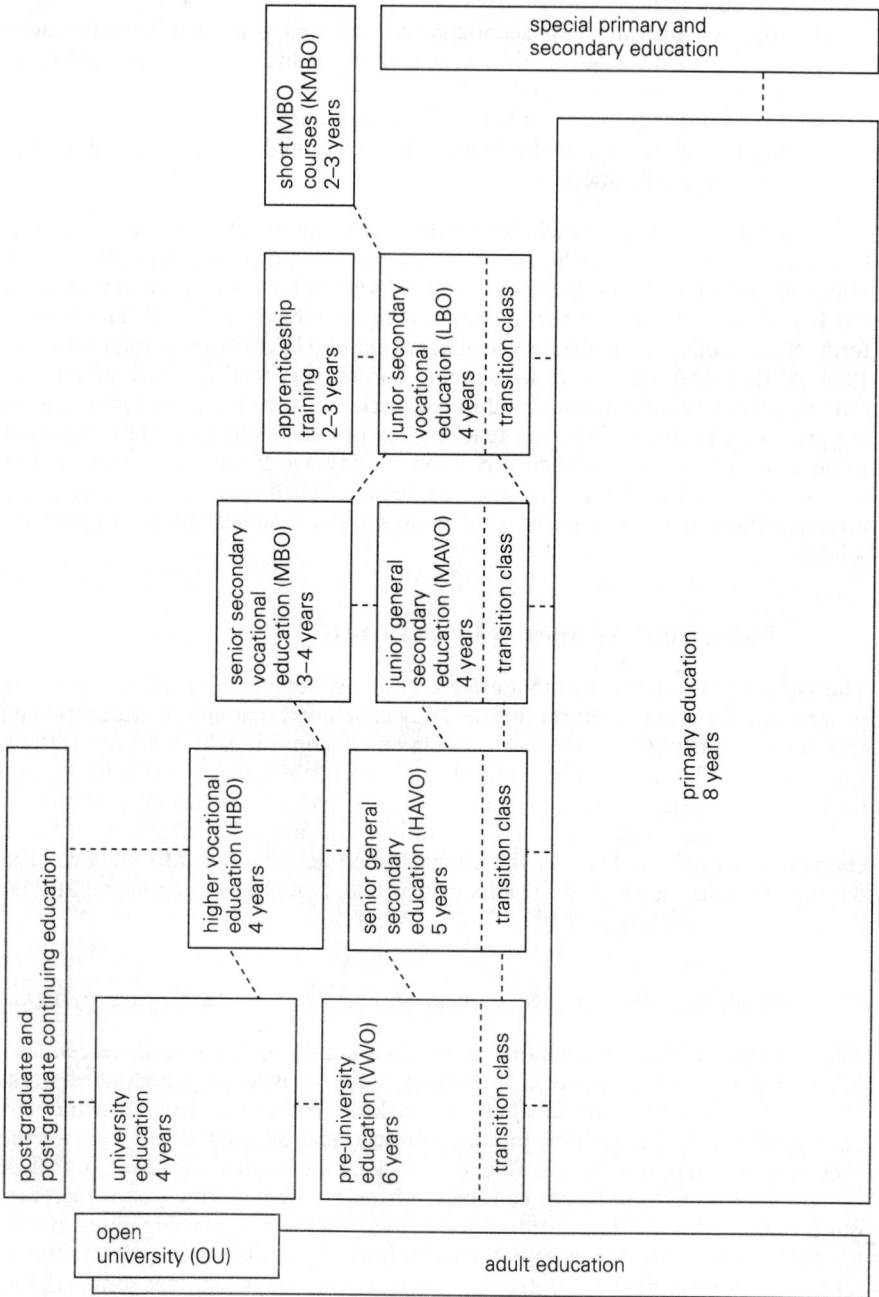

Source: Netherlands, Ministry of Education and Science.

Table 11.1: Numbers of Dutch Students and Students from Ethnic-minority Groups at PABOs in the Four Large Cities

	Amsterdam Dutch Ethn		Rotterdam Dutch Ethn		The Hague Dutch Ethn		Utrecht Dutch Ethn		Total Dutch Ethn		N=
State sch.	320	5	200	10	240	21	421	10	1,181	46	4
Roman Catholic	—	—	200	5	195	4	320	4	715	13	3
Protestant	—	—	295	3	150	3	443	0	888	6	3
Other	248	5	—	—	—	—	—	—	248	5	1
Total	568	10	695	18	585	28	1,184	14	3,032	70	11

variation of pupils without any numerically dominant ethnic-minority group (Dekker, 1992).

In 1989 the number of students at the fifty-five PABOs totalled 11,892, 151 of which were of mixed cultural, non-Dutch backgrounds, i.e., 1.20 per cent of the total. The number of ethnic-minority students, i.e., students from non-Dutch or ethnic-minority groups, per college, varied between one and ten. Most of the ethnic students originated from Surinam, the Antilles and Turkey. Nine colleges did not have any at all. One college, located in one of the large cities, formed an exception with twenty-one ethnic-minority students, nearly 10 per cent of its total student population. This PABO is known as a 'black PABO' or 'Turkish PABO', which is seen by staff and students as a negative image. This situation has given rise to an internal discussion about how to survive by avoiding a 'flight of white students'.

Table 11.1 shows that seventy (46 per cent) of all 151 ethnic-minority students were at eleven PABOs serving four large cities (Amsterdam, Rotterdam, The Hague and Utrecht). Considering the numbers of the teaching staff at the PABOs there are only a few teacher trainers belonging to, or considered to be a member of, a cultural and ethnic-minority group. The population of primary-school teachers in the Netherlands, as is the case in many other western countries, is becoming more and more homogenized. The teaching force for primary education is made up of an overwhelming percentage of white females which is still increasing. There is a common belief that diversity of the teaching staff is important especially in classrooms and schools with diverse learners. Grant and Secada (1990) posed the relevant question as to why diversity of the teaching staff is so important. At the moment there is insufficient empirical evidence to validate the widely held view that a diverse teaching force will positively affect the achievement scores and well-being of all pupils and students, regardless of their cultural and ethnic background.

Only a few ethnic-minority students opt to study for the teaching profession and hardly any of them finish the teacher-training programme and qualify. Table 11.2 shows that there are only six PABOs attended by more than five ethnic-minority students. Seen from that angle no relevant pressure can be expected on training colleges for action on multiculturalism and pluralism. And as we mentioned above it is known from research on multicultural education in primary education that the number of minority pupils in a school is a good predictor for the intensity of multicultural activities (Fase and van den Berg, 1985; Fase *et al.*, 1990; Education Inspectorate Report, 1989).

Table 11.2: Forms of Multicultural Activities in Dutch PABOs Relative to the Number of Ethnic-minority Students

Number of ethnic- minority students*	0	1–5	>5
Number of PABOs	N=9	N=40	N=6
Lectures	8	32	4
Guest lectures	3	1	—
Excursions	1	1	—
Block courses	—	5	—
Projects**	6	20	1
Compulsory practical training	—	10	4
Other	1	2	—

* Figures of 1990; based on response from fifty-five PABOs.
** Projects comprise project days and weeks, and week and month block courses.

As is shown in table 11.2, multicultural education takes many shapes. Three PABOs have made the choice not to incorporate specific multicultural activities. Almost all the other institutes give some attention to it within the various components of the curriculum, such as culture and society, pedagogy and didactics, and other skill-related subjects. Special lectures, guest lectures and excursions are the means by which the multicultural aspects are imparted. Five colleges require their students to take one or more block courses in multicultural education. A more extended approach, that goes somewhat beyond incidental educational components, is found at twenty-six PABOs. They have organized project weeks and days. At least fourteen colleges require their students to acquire practical experience at multiethnic primary schools.

The data from table 11.2 may serve as an indication that the number of students from ethnic and cultural minority groups is not a proper predictor of the scale of activities a given PABO devotes to multicultural education. The relation between the number of ethnic-minority students and the scale of multicultural education in the curriculum signalled by Fase and van den Berg (1985) at primary schools proves not to hold for PABOs. A comparison between PABOs and primary schools is difficult as the average percentage of ethnic-minority pupils at primary schools exceeds that of PABOs many times. Among primary schools the percentage varies from 0 to 100 per cent, whereas at PABOs none exceeds 5 per cent, except for one. For this reason, generally speaking, the number of ethnic-minority students carries too small a weight to be a positive factor in bringing multicultural education to the teaching programme.

Positive and Negative Factors Affecting Intercultural Education in PABOs

What teacher trainers see as the main positive and negative factors in the preparation of teachers for ethnic diversity is shown in the tables 11.3 and 11.4. These factors are classified into three main areas: government policy, the PABO itself and the educational environment (the primary schools in particular). Tables 11.3 and 11.4 show the (absolute) frequency in which factors were named, classified into the three areas.

Table 11.3: Primary Negative Factors Influencing Multicultural Education at PABOs

Government	PABO	Environment
Mergers 9	Lecturer's lack of skills 13	Insufficient shools with ethnic students for teaching practice 7
Cuts in spendings 7	Overcrowded programme 11	No demand from education field 6
Insufficient facilities 3	Lack of time 11	
	Lecturer's lack of motivation 7	
	Insufficient ethnic students 5	

Table 11.4: Primary Positive Factors Influencing Multicultural Education in Dutch PABOs

Government	PABO	Environment
Retraining 6	Stimulus of lecturer and student 11	Contacts with SBD* and ethnic groups 8
Plenty of course material 5	Teaching practice in primary school with many ethnic-minority students 9	Demand from primary schools 6

Note: * SBD=Educational guidance and counselling service to primary schools

Other negative factors, cited less than five times, include racism and prejudice among students and lecturers, mentality and attitude of lecturers at PABOs and teachers at primary schools where students do teaching experience. The teaching programme is also cited which does not correspond to the demands of primary schools with many ethnic-minority pupils, work pressure and part-time jobs. Most of the negative factors mentioned are related to the PABOs themselves. It is certainly not the case that negative factors are only seen as external. The teaching staff is aware that the negative and positive factors arise from a complex of internal and external factors.

The results shown in table 11.4 indicate that teaching staff see positive factors as being internal as well as external. The interaction between students and teachers is seen as an important internal positive factor. This underlines the importance of a positive school climate on the PABO. Noticeable is the attention given to teaching practice in multicultural classrooms. Only nine respondents claimed the importance of teaching practice in this perspective of multicultural education. Also remarkable is reference to the retraining of lecturers of training colleges. Retraining is seen as a stimulus to incorporate multicultural education in the curricula.

Conclusion

In an international survey Watson (1985) pointed out that most colleges of education in western countries have made little progress in preparing their students properly for teaching in a multicultural and multiethnic society. Baptiste (1986) concluded, that the internationalization of multiculturalism in education in America is moving slowly. Using Baptiste's (Baptiste and Baptiste, 1980; Baptiste, 1986) conceptual levels of multiculturalism (from multicultural education as a (single) product to a combination of product and process through to integrated philosophy and practice) it has to be concluded that the Dutch training programmes do not reach beyond the first lowest level.

Apart from governmental action in merging institutes the PABO lecturers' lack of skills are most frequently cited as the negative factors in incorporating multicultural education. The 1980s kept most PABOs under the strain of mergers and scale enlargement that led to institutional and curricular reorganizations. This has to be seen as a significant factor in why action on multicultural education in PABOs has stagnated. The 1984 merger of two different types of colleges (for nursery-school and primary-school teachers) entailed a great deal of time and effort to blend the differences in educational vision and college-bound culture into a new harmony. But these circumstances cannot be used to excuse or legitimize the underdevelopment of a multicultural teaching programme.

The PABO teaching force expects retraining through in-service training of teacher trainers to act as an important stimulus to incorporate multicultural education into the curricula (see table 11.4). But who will retrain the teacher trainers? What can be expected from primary schoolteachers as long as they are inadequately prepared by teacher trainers lacking sufficient levels of multicultural competence? If the new educational policy of the state, named 'steering from a distance', becomes effective in the mid-1990s it will have far-reaching consequences. From 1995, INSET will be organized on the basis of the free-market principle which means that schools will get their own INSET funding and are free to choose the support they want. Foreign experts reviewing the future support policy in the Netherlands point to the short-term solutions that will be produced by a free-market approach (APS, 1992). Without a mixed model of a free and controlled market for educational support and guidance it may happen that the need for support in realizing multicultural education will be inadequate. In other words, a free market can have a counter-productive impact on the preparation of experienced teachers for multicultural education. Teacher trainers have also been offered special in-service courses and conferences on multicultural education. Courses of Racism Awareness Training (RAT) are developed by the three Dutch national-education support institutes but the response rates have been low. As Burtonwood (1990) describes in his overview of INSET in Britain, the Netherlands have also seen a more recent trend to focus on an organization development perspective. It seems that the successfulness of multicultural changes in schools depends very much on the support of senior-staff management.

PABOs have the important task to supply expertise to primary schools. This role has not been played by the PABOs in the field of multicultural education. In a number of regions teachers of primary schools have learned multicultural teaching the hard way, forced by practical circumstances in which they were confronted with a high percentage of pupils from ethnic-minority groups. The

PABOs could and should make much more structural use of the practical expertise of primary and secondary-school teachers. The latter already act as tutors for trainee teachers, but they should also be invited to contribute to other parts of the teaching programme. In the coming years, the need for competent and well-prepared teachers for teaching diverse ethnic learners will grow in the Netherlands and in the other west-European countries as well!

References

ARBO, Adviesraad voor het basisonderwijs, het speciaal onderwijs en het voortgezet speciaal onderwijs (1988) *Progressie in professie. Advies over de ontwikkeling van de PABO*, (Progression in Profession. Advice on the development of the PABO) Zeist, December.

APS, Algemeen Pedagogisch Studiecentrum (General Pedagogic Centre) (1992) 'De onderwijsverzorging in de toekomst' *Het moet niet alleen kloppen, maar ook werken! Commentaar van buitenlandse experts op het WRR-advies* (It needs not only to be right but it must also be effective!) Comments of foreign experts on the recommendations of the Advisory Council (WRR) 'The educational support in the future', Amsterdam, APS.

BAPTISTE, M. and BAPTISTE, H. JR. (1980) 'Competencies toward multiculturalism', *Multicultural Teacher Education: Preparing Educators to Provide Educational Equity*, 1, Washington, D.C., AACTE, pp. 44–73.

BAPTISTE, J. JR. (1986) 'Multicultural education and urban schools from a socio-historical perspective: internalizing multiculturalism', *Journal of Educational Equity and Leadership*, 6, 4, pp. 295–312.

BURTONWOOD, N. (1990) 'INSET and education for multicultural society: a review of the literature', *British Educational Research Journal*, 14, 6, pp. 321–34.

DEKKER, R. (1992) 'Educating children in a Dutch caravanserai: Local educational policy in a multicultural city', in FRANKRIJKER, H. DE and KIEVIET, F. (Eds) *Education in a multicultural, multi-ethnic society*, De Lier, Academic Book Center.

EDUCATION INSPECTORATE REPORT (1989) *Gelijkwaardig en gezamenlijk: Onderzoek naar de ontwikkeling van het intercultureel onderwijs in het Nederlands basisonderwijs* (Equal and together: Research to the development of intercultural education in Dutch primary education), Zoetermeer, Inspectorate of Education.

FASE, W. and VAN DEN BERG, G. (1985) *Theorie en praktijk van intercultureel onderwijs* (Theory and practice of intercultural education), Gravenhage, SVO.

FASE, W. *et al.* (1987) 'Overheidsbeleid faalt. Nog geen 10 per cent van de basisscholen doet iets aan intercultureel onderwijs' (The government fails. Less than 10 per cent of the primary schools devotes attention to intercultural education), in *Stimulans*, 5, 10, pp. 3–8.

FASE, W. *et al.* (1990) *Vorm geven aan intercultureel onderwijs* (Constructing intercultural education), De Lier, ABC.

FRANKRIJKER, H. DE (1991) 'De aandacht en de waardering voor intercultureel onderwijs in de PABO' (The attention to, and appraisal for, intercultural education in the PABO), *Tijdschrift voor Lerarenopleiders VELON* (Journal for teacher trainers VELON), 2, 12, pp. 22–8.

GIESBERTZ, W. and REMIJNSE, A. (1983) *Etnische minderheden in het basisonderwijs als programma binnen een opleiding voor onderwijsgevenden* (Ethnic minorities in primary education as a programme within a course for teachers), M.A. thesis, University of Utrecht, Utrecht.

GIESBERTZ, W. and REMIJNSE, A. (1984) 'Ontwikkeling en invoering van een nieuw opleidings-programma. Een onderzoek naar de invoering van een PABO-programma "etnische minderheden in het basisonderwijs'", (Development and implementation of a new programme. A study of the implementation of a PABO programme for 'ethnic minority groups in primary education'), in *ID, Tijdschrift voor Lerarenopleiders* (Journal for Teacher Trainers), 5, 4, pp. 223–31.

GRANT, C. and SECADA, W. (1990) 'Preparing teachers for diversity', in HOUSTON, W.R. (Ed) *Handbook of Research on Teacher Education*, New York Macmillan Publishing Company, pp. 403–23.

HEIJDEN, J. VAN DER *et al.* (1983) *Intercultureel onderwijs in de opleiding* (Intercultural education in education) B-deel modelonderwijsleerplan PABO, Enschede, SLO.

KLER, E. DE (1984) *Intercultureel onderwijs binnen de opleiding van onderwijsgevenden*, (Intercultural education in teacher training courses), Tilburg (thesis for a secondary teacher's certificate).

KLOOSTERMAN, A. (1990) 'Opleiden voor intercultureel onderwijs: een overzicht van ontwikkelingen gedurende ruim tien jaar' (Teaching intercultural education: a survey of the developments of the last decade), in *IDEE, Tijdschrift voor Lerarenopleiders* (IDEE, Journal for Teacher Trainers), 11, 3, pp. 127–36.

LYNCH, J. (1986) *Multicultural Education: Principles and Practice*, London, Routledge and Kegan Paul.

NANHEKHAN, F. (1990) 'Een landelijk onderzoek naar de plaats en waardering van Intercultureel onderwijs binnen de lerarenopleiding basisonderwijs' *Intercultureel onderwijs binnen de Lerarenopleiding basisonderwijs*, (Intercultural education within teacher training for primary education: A national study into the place and appreciation of intercultural education within teacher training for primary education), Leiden, M.A. thesis, University of Leiden.

PROJEKT INTERCULTUREEL ONDERWIJS VOOR DE OPLEIDINGEN (PICOO) (1984) (Intercultural Education for Teacher Training Institutes).

OECD (1991) *Reviews of national policies for education, Netherlands*, Paris, Author.

OPVANG IN HET KLEUTERONDERWIJS (1984) (Child care at infant schools) PICOO/OVB, 34, Hoevelaken.

CULTUUR EN ORIËNTATIE (1984) (Culture and orientation) PICOO/OVB, 35, Hoevelaken.

OPVANG IN HET LAGER ONDERWIJS (1984) (Child care in primary education) PICOO/OVB, 36, Hoevelaken.

OPLEIDEN TOT INTERCULTUREEL ONDERWIJS VOOR JONGE KINDEREN (1984) (Teacher training for intercultural education for young children) PICOO/OVB, 37, Hoevelaken.

STIMULERINGSSCHOLEN (1984) (Schools for motivation) PICOO/OVB, 53, Hoevelaken.

SIETARAM, K. (1984) *Intercultureel onderwijs. Een samenleving van vele culturen vraagt opvoeding tot nieuw culturbesef via intercultureel onderwijs* (Intercultural education. A society of many cultures needs education for a new culture awareness via intercultural education), Culemborg, Educaboek.

TEUNISSEN, J. (1992) 'School segregation in the Netherlands: black and white schools', in FRANKRIJKER H. DE and KIEVIET, F. (Eds) *Education in a multicultural, multiethnic society*, De Lier, Academic Book Center.

VERMA, G.K. (1988) 'Issues in Multicultural Education', in VERMA, G.K. and PUMFREY, P.D. *Educational Attainments: Issues and Outcomes in Multicultural Education*, London, The Falmer Press.

WATSON, K. (1985) 'Educational policy and provision for a multi-cultural society', in WATSON, K. (Ed) *Key issues in education — comparative perspectives or They do it differently abroad*, London, Routledge and Kegan Paul, pp. 64–87.

WETENSCHAPPELIJKE RAAD VOOR HET REGERINGSBELEID (WRR) (1989) *Allochtonenbeleid* (Policy regarding ethnic-minority groups) Gravenhage, SDU.

Chapter 12

Interculturalism and Dutch Teacher Education

H. Wilfred Campbell

In present society the school, as a major institution, cannot restrict itself merely to the transfer of a well-established body of knowledge and traditionally based norms and values. Advanced technology has given rise to changes in society which the school has to recognize if it is to prepare its pupils to function in an adequate manner in the new technological world. This technological world and the people who had to function in it could, a number of decades ago, be approached in western Europe from the point of view of the norms and values of a more or less monocultural society. In the last decades, however, the school has become faced with the challenge of reacting to the changes in the composition of a society based on substantial ethnic and cultural differences. In addition to the question of how to teach the children from migrant groups within the context of its institutional practice, it is faced with the problem of preparing all pupils including indigenous ones to function in a society which is characterized by people with different ethnic and cultural backgrounds. The meeting of this challenge depends very much on the kind of society the government is striving to create. The response of the school to the racial, ethnic and cultural diversities in society will be different when the norms and values of the dominant group are to be followed (monocultural approach) as opposed to norms and values reflecting the different racial ethnic and cultural groups in society (multicultural approach). This difference does not only have a bearing on the nature of the curriculum but also on the kind of teacher (knowledge, attitude and teaching skills) needed in the classroom. That is to say, the development of a multiethnic and/or multicultural society through a multicultural approach to education, requires a teacher-training programme that produces teachers equipped to use and develop that approach. The teachers need to acquire the necessary cross-cultural expertise.

Multiethnicity and Inequality

Dutch society, like others in western Europe, has shown the effects, in terms of the composition of its population, of the mass immigration of people from different parts of the world. This immigration was, especially in the 1960s and early 1970s, related to shortages in the labour market of unskilled and partly-skilled workers (Penninx, 1988). The influx of people from former Dutch colonies

(Surinam and Dutch Antilles) as well as from the Mediterranean (especially Morocco and Turkey) was the direct result of the need for labourers. There were also other reasons for people from the former Dutch colonies to come to the Netherlands. People migrate to the Netherlands for educational purposes and do not return to their native country. In the case of the Moluccans, immigration was related to the military order given to the Moluccan soldiers who fought in the late 1940s and early 1950s for the Dutch government against the freedom fighters in Indonesia (Schumacher, 1987).

The plurality of groups of people with different cultural backgrounds in Dutch society became a reality in the late 1970s and early 1980s. By then it was clear to the Dutch government that the majority of immigrants and their children would not return to their native countries, but would settle and form separate minority communities. Since these people had limited schooling, limited skills and limited knowledge of the Dutch language the individual member of these groups had practically no possibilities to change socio-economic position through a better job and higher income than other group members. Belonging to a migrant group became almost synonymous with having a low socio-economic status, limited chances to change this situation and, because of being from a different ethnic and cultural background, hardly any kind of participation in the existing social, economic and political networks in the wider Dutch society. They were more or less restricted to their own minority community.

Two different categories of reasons were given to account for this restricted participation. First of all it was stated, that because of the process of group formation in terms of ethnic cultural characteristics, people from a specific ethnic-minority group formed their own social networks and self-help organizations, and in so doing were able to defend themselves against the demands imposed upon them by Dutch society (Penninx, 1988). Recognition of separate ethnic identity was considered a way of separation at group level which in the long run would harm some people. Since this process of group formation was especially noticeable among people with a low social-economic status, it was hypothesized, that one of the characteristics of an ethnic group is the low socio-economic status of its members (Van Amersfoort, 1974). People with the same ethnic/cultural backgrounds but with a higher socio-economic status were not considered members of the particular ethnic-minority group, but as people who were assimilated in the traditional (existing) Dutch society. So, by the same token assimilation was considered the way by which the immigrant could enhance his socio-economic status in society. By trying to assimilate, he should of course shake off all his ethnic specific characteristics and substitute them by those related to a new identity, that of the dominant majority group.

The other reason is related to a process of segregation by the dominant majority. In using specific ethnic characteristics, including the language, cultural traditions and skin colour of members of the ethnic groups, these group members were categorized as different from those of the dominant majority. Processes related to ethnocentrism (uniqueness and better characteristics of one's own group) and social comparison of groups (Tajfel, 1978; Turner, 1975) within the majority led to ideas of the superiority of one's own group and the inferiority of ethnic-minority groups. Observations in school, at work and in the neighbourhood concerning prejudice, discrimination and racism were enough evidence to prove the existing negative interethnic relations between the white majority and the ethnic minorities in everyday life. Limited knowledge of the Dutch language, low levels of schooling and limited occupational training among members of the ethnic-minority groups and the difference in cultural backgrounds were used as an excuse to restrict the participation of ethnic minorities in the field of education. In fact, segregation as a perspective on society places the white majority in a position of complete control in terms of *social structures* (the political, economic and social structures of the dominant group), *values* (dominant values in institutional settings, school, work, etc.), *culture* (culture of the dominant group forms the criterion for correct behaviour) and *power* (the dominant group has power). Members of the ethnic minorities are under those circumstances considered passive, powerless, lookers-on, followers, misfits and victims. For members of ethnic minorities, acceptance of complete assimilation, i.e., acceptance of the structures, values, culture and power of the majority, could be a way out of experiencing the negative effects of segregation as a perspective of the majority on the multiethnic society. At the same time, however, they would have to accept the notion of superiority of the white part of society and the inferiority of Blacks whenever confrontation in terms of race took place (Chesler, 1976; Rex, 1986).

The perspective on multiethnicity in the 1960s and 1970s led to a response in educational policy-making and educational practice which can be characterized as 'preparation for assimilation'. Since it was assumed that members of the ethnic-minority groups would eventually return to their respective native countries, no substantial changes in educational policy and practice were created with respect to learning of the Dutch language in order to fit in as quickly as possible into mainstream education. The same line of thinking underlies the special (compensatory) support that was given to ethnic pupils who did not have the proper knowledge and skills that were expected of them on the basis of their age. In this sense no specific attention was paid to the ethnic identity of the child.

Former training colleges developed a curriculum for teaching children who in the future would have to function in a (Dutch) society that had no multiethnic orientation. The important issues of that period were related to changes in modern technological society. Education was given the task to prepare the child to contribute to the industrial developments that lay ahead of them. The period of post-war rebuilding would then have been completed. Teachers in both primary and secondary schools were not trained to teach children from ethnic-minority groups. In the case of 'education in the vernacular language and culture' special teachers from the respective ethnic-minority groups were recruited (in a few cases directly from Turkey or Morocco) to teach this kind of supplementary subject.

Education As an Agent for Change

General governmental policy in the 1980s with respect to the multiethnic nature of Dutch society, has had a major impact on the perspective on education. Educational policy-making as well as the educational practice were used to implement the aim of preparing the child to function in a multiethnic society. In 1981–3 governmental policy with respect to the multiethnic nature of the Dutch society was the result of the growing awareness that members of the ethnic communities would not return to their respective native countries (WRR, 1989), that separate ethnic identities had to be recognized and that negative interethnic relations would have damaging effects on the image and character of the whole Dutch society. The government decided then that members of ethnic-minority groups should be considered citizens of this country and should have the same status in society as the non-immigrants. The perspective on ethnic-minority groups became one according to which members of separate ethnic-minority groups should 'integrate while keeping their own identity' (Home Office, 1992). The concept of 'integration' was then loosely used as a substitute for 'assimilation'. By introducing the complement 'while keeping their own identity' the acceptance of multiethnicity in the Dutch society was stated *'de jure'*. The phrase 'integration while keeping their own identity' was changed into 'mutual adaptation in a multicultural society' (Home Office, 1983).

The acceptance by the government of a policy that was based on a multiethnic, multicultural society had its direct effect on education. From 1979 to 1981 this effect was informed by the concept 'acculturation'. Specific projects were developed and implemented in schools with the objective to 'learn to know, accept and value each other and to be open for the culture of the other or elements of it'. In a transitional Law on Primary Education (1982) it was stated that 'education [as an institution] should assume that pupils are developing in a multi-cultural society'. That is to say, all the subjects in the curriculum should reflect the view that multiculturalism was a fact in the Dutch society. This can be shown in subjects as 'history', language use, geography and natural history. Intercultural education (ICO in Dutch) was considered a relevant instrument to realize the aim of 'acculturation' in a policy paper (Ministry of Education, 1986).

Intercultural Education

A governmental policy paper 'Intercultural Education' was presented in 1984, (Lijenhorst van, 1984) with the specific objective to increase the intercultural nature of education. The direct aim of 'education as an agent for change' was no longer 'acculturation' but to 'Teach pupils how to deal with similarities and differences which are related to ethnic and cultural backgrounds'. This should be considered from the point of view of functioning on equal footing in Dutch society. In the policy paper in 1986 (Ministry of Education, 1986) the 'knowledge component' of intercultural education was *stressed*. It was stated that pupils should know one another's backgrounds, circumstances and cultures, with respect to both majority group and ethnic-minority groups, and acquire mutual insight into the way values, norms, habits and circumstances determine the behaviour of people. Certain directives were given for the period 1986 to 1991. These were, among others, the distribution of information, leaflets, specific evaluation by school inspectors on the basis of reports and projects in primary education.

Given the governmental backing, through its policy papers, of intercultural education one might assume that the school would have no difficulties to implement it, with the ultimate objective of realizing the aim of the government concerning the multiethnicity of the Dutch society. As has been stated this aim was 'mutual adjustment in a multi-cultural society'. Fase, Kole, Paridon and Vlug (1990) have however indicated in their research report that the implementation of intercultural education was based on a specific interpretation by the school of the policy and pedagogic idealism which it had been trying to follow. They found, that of every ten schools in the Netherlands five or six of them did not make any attempt to implement intercultural education. Most of the schools which had implemented, or made preparations to implement, intercultural education had a school population of which more than 25 per cent of the pupils were from ethnic-minority groups. Moreover many of these pupils belonged to working-class families and lived in parts of the cities where living conditions were poor. It seems therefore, that intercultural education will be implemented when the school population has a certain level of multiethnicity and because of the low socio-economic status problems were anticipated. In primary education the aim of intercultural education is the 'integration of pupils from the majority and minority groups'. Knowledge of, and insight by pupils into, the backgrounds of other pupils are considered the best means to obtain this integration. However, whereas pupils from the majority group are receiving a lot of information about the backgrounds of pupils from the minority groups, which also provide this information, the pupils from minority groups do not receive (a similar amount of) information about the pupils from the majority group. It seems that in practice the main aim has been to try to eliminate negative attitudes (racism) of the pupils from the majority group. In the secondary school the 'increase in school achievement' seems to take precedence over relationships. Different kinds of 'remedial teaching and pupil guidance' form parts of intercultural education. The activities related to intercultural education are characterized by short-term projects in connection with language, history, geography and social world orientation. Specific themes (racism, prejudice and living together) may also be realized through projects. The conclusion is that the introduction of intercultural education has not led to radical changes in the curriculum. The failure to obtain a widespread implementation of the basic aim of intercultural education as well as a radical change of the curriculum might be considered the failure of the teacher-training institution. It is therefore necessary to see in what way governmental policy for teacher training has included aspects of the general policy with respect to a multiethnic society.

Teacher Training: Need for Cross-cultural Expertise

If the teacher has to implement 'intercultural education' (which is considered an instrument for change towards a multiethnic society) then it should be stated very clearly what the expectations are with respect to the teacher knowledge, attitudes and skills in relation to this kind of education. Given the policy papers in 1984 (Lijenhorst, 1984) and 1986 (Ministry of Education, 1986) concerning 'intercultural education', it should be expected that teachers ought to be well-equipped with cross-cultural expertise with respect to both the curriculum and the interaction with all the pupils they have to deal.

What is cross-cultural expertise? One can distinguish the following four components of cross-cultural expertise (Campbell and Moreno, 1990):

- Knowledge: knowledge of the cultural and social backgrounds of the members of each of the ethnic-minority groups involved. In the Netherlands this means that one should know the backgrounds relating to at least five ethnic-minority groups.

- Perspective: cultural/pluralistic insight which follows from lengthy personal contact and experience with referential contexts of other cultures.
- Attitude: an attitude which signals knowledge and perspective concerning ethnic minorities and which generates trust.
- Acting: the way one acts reflects the necessary insight and skills to teach in an effective way (language use, flexibility and presentation of subjects of curriculum).

Since cross-cultural expertise may require some degree of familiarity with five or more cultural groups, it is important to be aware of aspects of these cultures which are universal as opposed to those which are cultural-specific. Information based on cross-cultural research or from people who have a great amount of cross-cultural experience can help to distinguish universal from specific cultural aspects (i.e., behavioural characteristics). Cross-cultural expertise can be learnt.

If teachers are expected to teach children to take notice of, and appreciate, cultural differences among themselves then these teachers should receive a proper training in cross-cultural expertise. This kind of teacher expertise is necessary to ensure the implementation of a curriculum that is in accordance with the aims of intercultural education. Moreover, it is necessary to create a classroom climate which results in positive relations among pupils from different ethnic backgrounds. In order to enable teachers to obtain this 'cross-cultural expertise' the training college should provide student teachers with a curriculum that stresses, on the one hand, knowledge and experience of different cultural groups and, on the other, the ability to teach a subject (for example, history or geography) in such a way that the information presented relates to different cultures and nationalities (especially those of the ethnic-minority groups) i.e., a multiethnic approach to the subject. In short, the curriculum and organization of teacher education should reflect these expectations of teacher–classroom behaviour.

Current Practice in Training Colleges

De Frankrijker (1991) presents an overview of intercultural education in a particular category of teacher-training colleges. Central to these discussions are findings based on a Dutch telephone survey conducted in 1989 by F. Nanhekhan. These findings, which are reactions to four questions, give an idea of what is going on in training colleges in relation to intercultural education. The four questions concern the number of ethnic-minority students attending the colleges, the manner in which attention is paid to intercultural education (which components of the curriculum and how), their opinion about the degree to which attention is paid to intercultural education and their opinion on the negative and positive factors with regard to the introduction of intercultural education.

Only 1.2 per cent of the students of fifty-five training colleges (total of 11,892 students) belong to the ethnic-minority groups (De Frankrijker, 1991). Nine of these training colleges did not have any students from ethnic-minority groups and in the others the number varied from one to ten students. Different reasons can be given for the low percentage of ethnic-minority students. First, the number of ethnic-minority pupils with the proper qualifications at secondary-school level to be admitted to training college is low. Only about 20 per cent of all youngsters (13–18 years) from ethnic-minority groups attend the type of secondary school leading to the necessary qualifications compared to 52 per cent of youngsters (13–18 years) from the majority group (WRR, 1989). Moreover, the motivation to become a teacher might be lower for ethnic-minority youngsters. They might anticipate problems, among others, related to getting employment in a school located in an area they prefer or gaining promotion within the school. Problems concerning the promotion of ethnic minorities to higher ranks in a labour organization are well-known (ibid.).

Slightly more than half the training colleges (52 per cent) indicated that insufficient attention was paid to intercultural education. No significant correlation was found between the degree of attention paid to intercultural education and the number of students from ethnic-minority groups. Intercultural education is mostly presented in the form of lectures, presentation of papers (guest lecturers) and projects (specific theme day — week or month, specific courses and project weeks). It has been indicated that during the period 1984–90 no significant changes took place in the manner in which attention had been paid to intercultural education. It seems that students who finished their teacher training in the period 1984–90 were not exposed to a totally intercultural perspective on education. These teachers will not be able to implement intercultural education as is required.

According to de Franrijker (1991), most of the factors considered as having a negative effect on the implementation of intercultural education could be categorized in the area 'training colleges': lack of lecturer expertise at the college, overloaded programmes, shortage of time. 'Governmental actions' were the next category with the highest number of responses: merging of institutions, cutbacks in expenditure and insufficient facilities. Relevant factors with respect to 'the school environment' were few schools with many ethnic-minority pupils available for trainees and no requests from the schools. It seems that there is insufficient expertise in the teacher-training institutions to pay adequate attention to intercultural education. Because of overloaded programmes and shortage of time there will be no possibility to acquire (develop) the expertise within the context of the teacher-training institution. Therefore this expertise, which should be cross-cultural, needs to be developed outside the teacher-training institution and made available to it.

Positive factors mentioned also fell most frequently under the category 'training college'. These were: stimulation of teacher and student, and possibility for trainee at primary schools. 'School environment' was another category within which positive factors mentioned could be categorized: contacts with 'school-guidance service' and requests from primary schools. Factors related to 'governmental actions' as a category included in-service training and training material. It seems therefore that if there is at least one lecturer with expertise in intercultural education as well as interest among students, more activities with respect to intercultural education will take place. Moreover, possibilities for teaching experience for students with ethnic-minority pupils in primary schools, and contacts with the school-guidance service will facilitate the implementation of intercultural education in the teacher-training institution.

Intervention Programmes and Cross-cultural Expertise

Since training colleges, as a consequence of negative factors, do not pay enough attention to 'intercultural education', teachers entering the primary or secondary school will not be able to implement 'intercultural education' in the required manner. They will lack the appropriate cross-cultural expertise necessary for the selection and presentation of suitable materials and the creation of a classroom climate reflecting a multiethnic perspective. Therefore an intervention programme by an external agency must be implemented in training colleges in order to increase the cross-cultural expertise of students. A brief discussion follows of two intervention programmes which are already developed, but not yet used in training colleges. These are a project for the development of teaching materials and a project called 'OMEP' developed for educational guidance services.

To produce intercultural education material for use in teacher-training colleges a project (ICO-NLO) was developed (Hendriks *et al.*, 1991). The project, financed by the Ministry of Education, sought to produce books covering all subject areas of the teacher-training college curriculum, giving an intercultural approach to the teaching of each subject. The output of the project consists of a series of books (published in 1992), one for each of twenty-four subjects which are covered in teacher-training institutions. Each volume consists of information and exercises related to the particular subject. The training-college lecturers can follow guidelines presented in a teacher's book. The volumes in the series include *General aspects of Intercultural Education* (basic book), *Intercultural Pupil Guidance, Intercultural Problems?, An introduction for Future Teachers of English, History and Intercultural Education* and *Physics and Technique*. Each volume was written by a group of subject specialists. The editorial team provided the authors with guidelines in order to give uniformity to the series. The same aim of intercultural education (the equivalent joint functioning in the Dutch society) had to underlie each volume. In order to reach this aim education had to focus correctly on the promotion of good interethnic relationships and on the improvement of chances of pupils from ethnic-minority groups by, among other things, combatting prejudice and racism. Similar general structural and contents-oriented features can be recognized in each volume. These include the wider cultural and historic context of the subject, the enlargement of the historic and social awareness, (power) relations in terms of ethnicity, race, class and gender as well as ethnocentrism with regard to choice, vernacular language and culture-specific referential knowledge. Besides, suggestions are given on the way in which the lecturer might organize and present the information related to the subject.

The OMEP project (Derveld *et al.*, 1991) is a joint project involving AFS (Anne Frank Foundation), APS (General Pedagogic Study Centre) and ABC (Amsterdam Guidance Centre). OMEP (a Multiethnic perspective of educational guidance) started in 1989, financed by the Ministry of Education. The aim of the project is to stimulate 'educational guidance services' (the OBD) to promote effective multiethnic education. The OBD is an in-service guidance facility for teachers and pupils in primary and secondary education. It also has a working relationship with teacher-training institutions (pre-service training). The project has offered courses, training and policy advice to about twenty OBD areas.

The OMEP project was accepted by the OBDs as a significant intervention.

They have admitted that they have too little specific expertise with respect to multiethnic education. Since the OBDs have a working relationship with training colleges, the influence OMEP has on the OBDs (as in-service training agent) will have an effect on these training colleges (pre-service training). Besides, the materials developed in OMEP will also be available to training colleges. OBDs will be influenced by the activities in OMEP in terms of policy-making, policy implementation and policy evaluation. In this sense the aim of the project (obtaining effective multiethnic education) will be achieved.

The influence on the policy-making of OBD is concerned with the awareness question. This question has been framed as: 'which kind of innovation is necessary to increase the school achievement of pupils from ethnic minorities and to create less one-sided education for all white pupils'. The OMEP project seeks to find an answer on this question based on the assumption that school success for all pupils requires fundamental revision of teaching material, of teachers' styles and school policy. Monoethnic education should give way to multiethnic education. Furthermore, the disadvantaged position of ethnic-minority pupils in school is stressed in terms of different ethnic background, multilingualism, etc. instead of any kind of deficit model when they are compared to pupils from the majority group. By taking the view that the Dutch society should be considered a multiethnic society the project seeks to support intercultural interethnic education.

Policy implementation will be realized by giving all the people involved in the educational guidance service (OBD) a professional training, which will lead to:

- insight in the concepts related to intercultural and antiracist education and the skill to apply this insight with respect to teaching situations and teaching materials;
- a positive attitude towards multiethnicity; and
- knowledge and skills necessary to give teachers the help they are most in need of in the multiethnic classroom.

Policy evaluation within the OMEP project will be demonstrated by effective innovation. This will be obtained by formulating concrete guidelines for organizational development and policy-making. Moreover, together with a developed 'project-package' concrete materials are available for managers and staff. The OMEP product-package consists of a general script for managers, a book providing a basic course and four books, each of which is concerned with a specific topic (i.e., language, pupil guidance, world orientation and focus on all pupils).

Although this OMEP project was not especially developed as an intervention programme to realize multiethnic education in training colleges, it can be used in these colleges to increase the cross-cultural expertise of both lecturers and students. These students may then become fully oriented towards the kind of perspective and action strategies they will need as teachers.

Conclusion

In the Netherlands members of ethnic minorities need to integrate in the Dutch society in order to function fully. They need to agree with the Dutch government that this integration should mean 'full-fledged participation in society' (Home Office, 1992). However, that integration needs a multiethnic and multicultural society. Teacher training must be organized in such a way that training college students will have the opportunity to acquire the necessary cross-cultural expertise to enable them to flourish as teachers to adopt a multiethnic approach. This should be adopted regardless of the ethnic composition of the school or classroom.

The differences in the ethnic class and/or gender of pupils in the classroom should be recognized. The introduction of intercultural education, aimed at 'equivalent joint functioning in the Dutch society', will support (as an instrument for change) the aim of integrating as 'full-fledged participation in society'. Therefore, teacher training should promote 'intercultural education' in such a way, that the students are not only confronted with an intercultural approach at a theoretical level through (lectures, seminars etc.) but also in a real teaching situation in a classroom (during teaching practice).

Students in training colleges need to become aware that they will have to function as teachers in a multiethnic society. In the training college, meeting fellow students who differ in ethnicity, class and gender should increase their awareness (in the context of intercultural education) of the effects of selection processes in society. The comparatively small number of fellow students from ethnic-minority groups should be considered the result of selection processes that are the product and evidence of the current inequality in ethnicity, class and gender.

References[1]

AMERSFOORT, J.M.M. VAN (1974) *Immigratie en minderheidsvorming: een analyse van de Nederlandse situatie 1943–1973*, Samson, Alphen a/d Rijn.
CAMPBELL, H.W. and MORENO, L. (1990) *Hulpverlening door Allochtonen*, Utrecht/ Bunnik, SSI/BVGB.
CHESLER, M.A. (1976) 'Contemporary Sociological theories of racism', in Katz, Ph.A. *Towards the elimination of racism*, New York, Pergamon Press Inc.
DERVELD, P.H., KRAMER, M., VLERK, K. VAN DER (1991) *Basisfilosofie en product beschrijving van het OMEP-project*, Amsterdam, Anne Frank Stichting.
FASE, W., KOLE, S.C.A., PARIDON, C.A.G.M. VAN and VLUG, V. (1990) *Vorm geven aan intercultureel onderwijs*, De Lier, Academies Boeken Centrum.
FRANKRIJKER, H. DE (1991) 'De aandacht en de waardering voor intercultureel onderwijs' in de PABO, VELONT Tijdschrift, 12, 21, pp. 22–8.
HENDRIKS, F., HILTE, J. and WIERDSMA, T.J. (1991) 'Naar een meer intercultureel gericht onderwijs op de Nieuwe Leraren Opleidingen' (project ICO-NLO), Leeuwarden, Educatief Centrum Noord bij de Noordelijke Hogeschool Leeuwarden.
HOME OFFICE (1983) *Minderhedennota*, Den Haag, Staatsuitgeverij.
HOME OFFICE (1992) *Nation wide debate Integration*, The Hague.
LAW ON PRIMARY EDUCATION (1982) Overgangswet, Kamerstuk 117628, The Hague, 7 October.
LIJENHORST, G. VAN (1984) 'Intercultural Education', Letter from Junior Minister of Education to Parliament, The Hague, 1 November.

---

[1] All titles of publications related to a governmental office have been translated in English by the author.

MINISTRY OF EDUCATION (1986) *Cultural Minorities in Education*, The Hague.
PENNINX, R. (1988) *Minderheidsvorming en emancipatie*, Alphen a/d Rijn, Samson.
REX, J. (1986) *Race and Ethnicity*, Milton Keynes, Open University Press.
SCHUMACHER, P. (1987) *De Minderheden*, Amsterdam, Van Gennip.
TAJFEL, H. (1978) *Differentiation between social groups*, London, Academic Press Inc.
TURNER, J.C. (1975) 'Social Comparison and Social Identity: Some prospects for intergroup behaviour', *European Journal of Social Psychology*, 5, pp. 5–35.
WRR, WETENSCHAPPELIJKE RAAD VOOR HET REGERINGSBELEID (1989) Allochtonenbeleid, Den Haag, Staatsuitgeverij.

Chapter 13

Teachers and the Contradictions of Culturalism

Fazal Rizvi and Vicki Crowley

Much of the recent rhetoric of Aboriginal reconciliation and multiculturalism in Australia maintains that teachers have a special responsibility in tackling the problems of racism. No matter how systematic and coherent the goals of these discourses, it suggests, these goals cannot be fully realized unless teachers have an adequate understanding of the role of education in sustaining and ameliorating racism. Thus, most reports on Aboriginal and multicultural education in Australia view teachers as key agents of reform. For example, the report of the National Aboriginal Education Committee (1986) suggests that teachers have a major role to play in developing effective strategies for promoting a socially just attitude in Australian society. The recent *Report of the National Inquiry into Racist Violence in Australia* (Human Rights and Equal Opportunities Commission, 1991, p. 351) wants teachers and teacher unions to work with government and non-government education authorities, as well as students, parents and community groups affected by racism, to develop antiracist education policies and practices. Bullivant (1981, p. 84) put it more bluntly a decade ago when he argued that despite all the curricular and organizational reforms, 'we cannot escape the inevitable fact that the success or failure of poly-ethnic education is fairly and squarely in the hands of the teachers. The "curriculum buck" stops there'.

In Britain, too, advocates of both multicultural and antiracist education have underlined the importance of teachers. The Swann Report (1985), for example, requires of all teachers that they convey to *all* children a more intelligent appreciation of diversity in British society. But beyond this liberal-pluralist appeal, antiracist educators such as Brandt (1986, p. 129) have also suggested that teachers develop an oppositional pedagogy, 'both for the deconstruction of racism and the reconstruction of non-racism through anti-racism'. Teachers are thus placed at the heart of the reform process. Given the importance attached to the role of teachers, it is therefore surprising how little there has been in the way of systematic investigation of the way teachers actually think about racism and develop measures to combat it in schools. Even the radical antiracist educators who accord teachers an important transformative task seldom provide any evidence for their confidence in the capacity of teachers to be able to undertake this task. Similarly, most statements of policy stress the importance of the work of teachers but do not explore the way teachers construct their views of cultural difference, interpret the nature and scope of racism in schools and society and conceptualize relations of pedagogy and curriculum.

Drawing on the findings of two separate research projects carried out in Australia over the past three years, this chapter describes some of the ways in which teachers think about cultural difference and its implications for multicultural and antiracist pedagogy. We report that while most teachers in the schools we researched are supportive of the policies of multiculturalism and antiracism, the frames within which they interpret and understand these policies are frequently informed by a popular theory of racism viewed as individual prejudice and antiracism as an educational project designed to minimize social conflict. This theory of racism sustains pedagogic practices of multiculturalism and antiracism constructed and implemented in ways which reflect a reliance on culturalist assumptions. These assumptions involve the formation of categories of cultural difference which are separate from the social, educational and political contexts in which they are embedded. They treat cultures as hermetically sealed off from one another, giving rise to what Gilroy (1987, p. 12) has referred to as 'cultural insiderism'. Cultures are treated as *the given* upon which pedagogy must be constructed. Within the framework of this set of assumptions, teachers treat issues of difference more as a fact to be taken into account than as constitutive of curricular and pedagogic relations. They often assume a position of neutrality in the formation of such relations, as somehow external to the more general processes of cultural articulation in society. Thus, while multiculturalism is viewed as intrinsically oppositional in nature, all cultural practices are thought to be valid within their own terms. These culturalist presuppositions support a rationalist pedagogy that is both ahistorical and depoliticized — ahistorical because culture is treated as something fixed, finished or final, and depoliticized because it obscures the inherently political character of the term.

The version of multiculturalism accepted by most teachers embraces notions of culture within an anthropological sense of 'way of life' (Sachs, 1989). Yet in most pedagogic practice 'way of life' is reduced to a cultural form made visible in language, arts, habits and customs. This reduction both appeals to, and lends itself to, essentialism; and by ignoring and obscuring its historical and political construction, it reifies culture, according it autonomous status. The version of multicultural education it supports thus involves learning about 'other' cultures as a way of breaking down stereotypes and thus promoting greater tolerance of diversity in society. A major problem with this approach is that it does not define the 'other' as relational, in a way that might refer to the speaking position. Rather, it naturalizes the 'other' in representations that are assumed to be objective. The issues of disadvantage and discrimination are thus obscured, as are the politics of ethnic formation. Teachers believe sincerely that they are working towards an agenda of racial justice, but the contradictions of their culturalist assumptions mean that the hegemonic racist representations and practices are often reinforced in schools.

These culturalist assumptions have become a part of the hegemonic common sense around which conceptions of racism and racial justice are now defined in Australian society. As the great majority of teachers are Anglo-Australians and as there is no requirement for teachers to examine these issues during their initial teacher training, common-sense understandings inevitably prevail. However, we believe that initial teacher training and in-service professional development are still important sites where this hegemonic common sense can be deconstructed and opposed. Without serious interventions at that level, we want to argue, we will continue to have often well-meaning and committed antiracist teachers thwarted in their efforts.

The Research Sites

The discussion in this chapter is based on two complementary research projects. Both projects utilized ethnographic methods to explore the ways in which school processes and structures *racialized* every-day experience of schooling. One of these projects was conducted in a multiracial school in Adelaide, and sought to examine the manner in which the school's taken-for-granted assumptions about the appropriate ways of structuring pedagogic and social relations articulated with the constructions of minority categories, and in particular those involving Aboriginal students.[1] The other project sought to identify the part, if any, racism played in defining interracial discourse, social relationships and organizational practices of four multiracial schools in Melbourne.[2] And while neither project focused initially on teachers, the need to have a comprehensive picture of the various ways teachers constructed their ideas of racial difference, and the manner in which they used these ideas to develop multicultural and anitracist educational practices, soon became evident.

The Adelaide project was conducted in Ealing High School,[3] which is an inner-city state school with 560 students. Ealing is a mixed housing area which contains some houses with large and leafy gardens but is mostly made up of government housing and flats. The area is ethnically diverse, with a number of migrant hostels and a significant Aboriginal population. 61 per cent of the student at Ealing High School come from families where a language other than English is spoken at home. It is an area of massive unemployment, with 53 per cent of the students receiving some form of government financial assistance.

The Melbourne project was conducted in four schools with widely differing demographic profiles. The first of these was St. Peters Primary School, an inner-city parish school with 140 students. The school is next to a block of flats. 65 per cent of the children attending the school live in these flats which are occupied mostly by recent immigrants from South-East Asia. More than 90 per cent of the children at the school speak a language other than English at home, including, Arabic, Turkish, Polish, Spanish and Hindi. According to the principal, more than 60 per cent of the parents at the school are either unemployed or are on some form of welfare benefit. The second school, Morley High School, is similarly diverse, though the students of non-English speaking background who attend the school were mostly born in Australia of parents who immigrated to this country from eastern Europe. 22 per cent of the students speak Macedonian at home, with the next largest numbers coming from Croatian and Polish-speaking backgrounds. The number of students from Asia is increasing and is currently around 4 per cent. The Morley area has in recent years been badly affected by a downturn in the motor-car industry, raising its unemployment to 40 per cent. Morley is perhaps one of the most economically deprived areas in the state of Victoria. The third school, Birmingham Primary School is, in contrast, a wealthy public school in a beach-side suburb. The school has excellent playing facilities, maintained mostly by volunteer parents, most of whom are in professional employment and belong to the dominant Anglo-Celtic group in Australia. The fourth school, St. Joseph's College, is also a 'ruling class' school (Connell, Ashenden, Dowsett and Kessler, 1982), though unlike Birmingham, it is a private school. The parents of its 820 students pay large fees in order to ensure that their children mix with an elite section of the Australian community. In a sense, this meritocratic aspiration sits uneasily with the College's commitment to a religious education informed by the principles of the order of the Christian Brothers.

While the five schools in which we conducted our research varied in the composition of their student populations, it should be noted that the teacher profile in each of the schools was broadly similar. At the most representative end, Ealing High School had fifteen teachers (out of total of sixty-seven) who did not belong to the dominant Anglo-Celtic group. Of these, all except three taught in such subjects as English as a second language, a community language, home economics or art. This confirmed their minority status within the school because they were allied with subject areas most associated with common-sense understandings of ethnicity and with subjects least likely to lead to significant life opportunities. At St. Peter's, apart from an elderly Vietnamese-speaking teacher's aide, all other teachers belonged to the dominant Anglo-Celtic group. Birmingham had no minority teachers. At St. Joseph's, there were five teachers who did not belong to the dominant group, while at Morley, the figure was ten. At Morley, there was an Indian-born teacher of English, a fact that the principal of the school clearly found ironic. Significantly, none of these teachers from a non-English speaking background were in a position of responsibility, although the name of the principal of Morley High School suggested a Dutch background. Proudly he stressed that he was 'a third-generation migrant from Holland', but simultaneously thought this to be irrelevant to the pedagogic and administrative practices of the school.

These statistics are broadly in line with an Australia-wide survey Logan *et al.* completed in 1989. The Logan Report (1989) indicated that only 12 per cent of teachers in Australia spoke a language other than English at home, but, more alarmingly, that this 'per cent' figure had increased by only 2 per cent in the last decade. Logan found that only 9 per cent of the teachers were born overseas. The report concluded, 'there is little evidence from the survey results of the recruitment of teachers from non-English speaking ethnic background, despite the increasing multicultural mix of the Australian population' (Logan *et al.*, 1989, p. 6).

Significantly, however, all five schools expressed a strong commitment to an education that tackled issues of ethnic disadvantage, though in ways that varied. For example, Ealing High School expressed this commitment through its policies of social justice and inclusive curriculum. It aspired to compensate students for the 'social and physical disadvantage [by] providing physical amenities, stability and a sense of identity and belonging', not only to the school but also to the ethnic groups to which they belonged. The school was also committed to provide an environment where students could 'experience success by enhancing their self-concept and morale'. Having a significant number of Aboriginal students, Ealing was provided through government funding with an Aboriginal education team, which defined its role in terms of helping the mainstream teachers 'to feel good about teaching Aboriginal students', 'resolving conflicts' and 'allowing the student to value themselves'. All of these factors were seen to contribute to strengthening the Aboriginal sense of identity.

The Melbourne schools, on the other hand, did not directly address the issue of Aboriginality, assuming it to be irrelevant to schools which did not have a large number of Aboriginal students. At both Morley and St. Peter's, the emphasis was on a multiculturalism conceptualized in terms of a notion of ethnic disadvantage. Working with a cultural deficit view, St. Peter's sought to provide students with an environment in which they 'can feel safe from the pressures of the outside society'. The school believed this security could partly be achieved through an emphasis on the maintenance of cultural traditions, but also through the teaching of the values of intercultural tolerance and harmony.

In contrast, St. Joseph's and Birmingham expressed their commitment to multiculturalism in a celebratory mode. Birmingham Primary School, for example, organized an international day in which both students and parents were encouraged to attend wearing costumes that represented ethnic diversity in Australia. But significantly, the costumes were mostly exotic and traditional, bearing little resemblance to the way people actually dress, either in Australia or indeed elsewhere. St. Joseph's commitment to multiculturalism was limited to two sentences in its school policy, though its principal did insist that any version of multiculturalism the school could 'tolerate will have to be compatible with the principles of a Catholic school and mainstream Australian society'.

In a different way, Ealing High School was also 'afraid of multiculturalism', suspecting it might lead to interethnic violence. While the school provided its Greek students with the opportunity to take Bouzouki and Greek dancing lessons during lunchtime, the term 'multiculturalism' was largely avoided. However, the school more happily supported out-of-school expressions of multiculturalism, and, through its newsletter, advertised community events and celebrations, such as an Italian fashion parade and a Greek food festival. In this sense, the school accepted the culturalist assumptions that constituted the dominant manner in which the idea of ethnic difference and the dynamics of ethnic relations were conceptualized by teachers.

The Ideology of Culturalism

We use the notion of culturalism to refer to an ideology that informs the way most teachers think about cultural difference. It relates to the manner in which they use the idea of culture to explain social relations and construct relations of pedagogy and curriculum. In this sense, culturalism does not so much refer to the totality of ideas, beliefs and generalizations teachers have about various cultural forms as to methods of thinking and reasoning about cultural relations and processes. As an ideology, culturalism represents a distinctive and discernible way of approaching social and educational problems. It represents a set of discursive practices that foreclose discussion and legitimate processes and structures. In this sense, they are not only 'ideological' but have a materiality expressed in pedagogic and organizational practices. The ideology of culturalism is linked to the discourse of ethnicity, based on an understanding that was once anthropological, concerned with documenting differences between societies, and which has more recently become appropriated by sociologists and policy makers to study intergroup behaviour. According to Smith (1981), the current interest in ethnicity has emerged as a result of a recognition that the earlier cosmopolitan ideal that cultural differences would simply disappear in modern societies has proved to be wrong, and that the current 'ethnic revival' has shown ethnicity to be a permanent feature of human organization.

For policy makers in Australia, this conclusion has led them to abandon earlier assimilationist and integrationist policies in favour of a policy stance which places ethnicity at the heart of the issues concerning the distribution of social, political and economic goods. The most liberal version of this ideology suggests that all groups in a society should enjoy the same rights and privileges, including the right to maintain their cultures. The most obvious official expression of this sentiment in Australia may be found in the policy of multiculturalism, which rejects the idea of cultural homogeneity as either possible or indeed desirable.

Most policy documents and reports in Australia have thus emphasized the contribution multiculturalism can make in defusing social conflict. The Galbally Report (1978, pp. 11–12) for example exhorts teachers to foster 'the retention of the cultural heritage of different ethnic groups and promote intercultural understanding'. The New South Wales multicultural education policy (New South Wales Department of Education, 1983) seeks the 'development of skills and attitudes necessary to interact effectively in a multicultural society'. More recently, the New South Wales Education Department has been developing an antiracist policy (1991), but this policy too rests on similar culturalist assumptions. It is thus predicated on the belief that an environment which affirms students' cultural identity is central to the achievement of racially harmonious schools and society.

It is indeed remarkable how quickly multiculturalism, and the culturalist assumptions upon which its various expressions are based, has become a part of the hegemonic common sense of teachers. It was only less than twenty years ago that Australian teachers regarded assimilation as the only progressive educational policy not only for migrants but also for the indigenous population of this country. Migrant and Aboriginal children were then asked to accept the opportunities education offered to assimilate into the dominant Anglo-Celtic cultural landscape of Australia in order to have a realistic chance of achieving its rewards.

Teachers now work with a very different rhetoric. While they admit that the experiences of Aboriginal and migrant children are differentially related to the dominant structure, they nevertheless assume that greater equality can only be achieved through positive ethnic identification. The discourse of ethnicity thus highlights the subjective dimension of people's lives (Pettman, 1992). The culturalism to which it gives rise is however a much broader ideology, constituted by a further cluster of assumptions.

First, it is assumed that while identification of groups of people into 'races' is clearly flawed, since 'race' not does refer to any objective biological reality, people can nevertheless be differentiated into various cultural groups. Ethnic groups are thus thought to have distinctive historic culture and ancestry which express themselves in various traditions, beliefs and values. As Wallman (1986) argues, a racial category is the consequence of categorization by the dominant group focusing on physical criteria, while an ethnic group is the consequence of self-categorization using the criteria of culture and traditions. Racial boundaries are imposed while an ethnic boundary is self-defined and self-maintained by the group.

Second, it is thought that ethnic groups have a natural inclination to reproduce their language, religion, rituals and other customs in order to define themselves as distinctive. While the view that ethnic groups are biologically self-perpetuating is not accepted, it is nevertheless believed that ethnic groups share common cultural values, realized in overt unity through a variety of boundary maintenance strategies. As Barth (1969) has suggested, boundaries between ethnic groups are self-ascribed and represent the collective act of a group of people to recognize and maintain in their interaction with others and their distinctiveness in various cultural, symbolic and linguistic terms.

Third, it is assumed that ethnicity is a major factor in terms of which members of a group relate to other groups. Ethnicity thus represents a form of corporate organization on the basis of beliefs, attitudes and values that are sufficiently similar to permit the collective pursuit of common objectives. According to Glazer and Moynihan (1970), ethnicity is a persistent form of social identification through which people make political claims on the state and express their interests.

Fourth, it is assumed that ethnicity is an independent social variable. Glazer and Moynihan (1970, p. 169) suggest that as a social and explanatory category, it is quite distinct from class; and that in modern societies, it is more salient than class 'because it can combine an interest with an affective tie'. Similarly, just as gender is not reducible to class, neither is ethnicity. Thus, while it is not denied that various patterns of relations exist between class, gender and ethnicity, it is nevertheless maintained that, in analytical terms, ethnicity is *sui generis*.

Fifth, linked to earlier assumptions, it is believed that since ethnicity is an inevitable and significant factor influencing the lives of people, it ought to play an important role in the structuring of social and political life in Australia. Ethnic diversity should be celebrated, and every effort should be made to provide every person the opportunity to maintain their cultural traditions, and it is through this provision that greater equality of opportunity can be obtained. Schools, it is argued, can help children develop a truly multicultural attitude by fostering the retention of the cultural heritage of different ethnic groups and promoting intercultural understanding. As Smolicz (1984) has suggested, students who value their own ethnicity are, because they have positive self-esteem, more likely to understand and respect cultural heritages other than their own. Multiculturalism is thus viewed as a major instrument for tackling problems of racism through activating a minority child's normative identification with his or her heritage.

In what follows, we attempt to show how these assumptions now represent a powerful ideology that has become dominant in Australian educational discourse (Rizvi, 1991). It now informs the way teachers view the social world of their schools, as well as the educational theories around which to organize curriculum, pedagogy and organizational arrangements. We argue, however, that these culturalist assumptions are fundamentally contradictory, often producing outcomes that are contrary to the aspirations and life chances of most minority students.

Teachers and the Assumptions of Culturalism

We do not wish to suggest, however, that the manner in which teachers express these culturalist assumptions does not vary. We found considerable diversity in the way teachers approached the issues of ethnic diversity and racism. Yet it should be noted that an overwhelming majority of teachers regarded these issues to be irrelevant to their work, especially in those schools like Birmingham and St. Joseph's where the number of students of non-English background was small. Even in these schools, however, there were exceptions. For example, Jenny Jones at St. Joseph's believed that the school could not afford to be complacent about racism. For her, there was not only evidence of racism outside her school but within it. She maintained that 'for a Christian school, we are not doing enough to address the issue of social justice'. More typically, however, while teachers at St. Joseph's and Birmingham regarded the teaching of cultures as important, they could not see how their pedagogy was itself culturally defined. For most of them, multiculturalism meant providing non-English speaking students with an op-portunity to affirm their cultural identity. Interestingly, culturalist assumptions also informed the views of teachers who were either ambivalent or hostile to multiculturalism. For example, Rhonda, a teacher at Morley High School, main-tained that 'multiculturalism had gone too far. It forces you to treat students from some backgrounds with kid gloves'. According to Rhonda, taking cognizance of such 'racial difference is illegitimate and is likely to lead to discrimination against the minority group or reverse discrimination in its favour. Neither of these is desirable'. As she added:

> I don't really notice what background students come from. Children are children, not Japanese or Chinese or Australian. I think multiculturalism puts barriers in front of people, makes them defensive. I can't be critical of Aboriginal kids for the fear of being branded a racist. Sooner we teach them all to get along, and not see each other in terms of colour or class or sex, the better...

This 'colour-blind' (Gaertner and Dovidio, 1986) perspective represents a hegemonic discourse among many teachers. But the liberal individualism it re-presents ignores the fact that many everyday practices of schools are already racialized. An example may help to illustrate how this is so.

At Birmingham Primary School, we attended a grade 1 art lesson, around the theme of crime, which required children to draw, using coloured pencils, a scene that depicted a crime being committed. Not surprisingly, the representational images students produced relied heavily on the stereotypes of 'cops and robbers' stories. The images demonstrated clearly how their imagination was socially or-ganized, since almost half of the students drew robbers as black, while none of the police, nor the people robbed, were so represented. At the end of the lesson we pointed this out to the teacher, Hilary, who was initially shocked, but later suggested that there was little she could do about such representations. The romantic expressive theory of art education she held allowed the reproduction of racist images to go unchallenged. Her presumed neutrality nevertheless supported the racialized representations that students had learned through other message systems of society. It should be noted however that Hilary was disturbed by the contradiction generated by the philosophy of art education she espoused, on the one hand, and the commitment she expressed to the liberal ideology of 'colour blindness', on the other.

This example, and many others like it, reveal that the ideological biases of Australian schools often operate to produce a representation of reality that tends to reinforce existing social and political structures of inequality, even in cases where the ostensive intention of teachers is to question and perhaps undermine various expressions of racism. The problem here is that their culturalist assumptions prevent teachers from realizing that the structures of curriculum and pedagogy, and the organizational arrangements of school, may already be racialized. They find it hard to see how racism could structure their pedagogy without the actual presence of minority students in their classrooms.

Thus, we have the kind of contradictory views that Peter McConnell, a senior teacher at St. Joseph's, holds. Peter believed, on the one hand, that the problem of racism could not exist at St. Joseph's because it had so few minority students. On the other hand, when questioned further, Peter insisted that by discussing these problems we would run the risk of somehow making them appear:

> sure there are some kids who are prejudiced, but we can't do everything. We are lucky we don't have the problem of racism here. If we did we would have to do something about it, but why open the pandora's box here.

Peter was also concerned about the tentative moves that St. Joseph's was making to attract fee-paying Asian students to the College. According to Peter, 'this might generate problems of racism, as there inevitably will be some kind of competition between Asians and Australian kids'. When asked to explain, he simply said, 'it's kind of natural, isn't it . . . just look around [at] the problems they have at Islington High', referring to a nearby school in Melbourne with a high proportion of Asian immigrants.

Peter's comments reveal a view of 'racial' difference that is widely held among teachers and educational administrators. While many teachers now reject biological conceptions of 'race' and 'race' relations, they are quite happy to accept its cultural variants. So, while by and large, teachers reject biological classifications of people into racial groups, and also the theories of racial superiority and inferiority that gave rise to the nineteenth-century eugenics movement, they nevertheless accept the validity of naturalized cultural differentiation. Cultural categories are thus often used to explain forms of social variations, and to develop pedagogic, curriculum and administrative policies.

For example, at St. Peter's Primary School, we discussed a broad range of subjects with the principal. Our interest was in finding out how a Catholic school determined its attitude towards students who were not Catholic. The principal began by reassuring us of the school's commitment to multiculturalism, and by insisting that there was no philosophical conflict between its principles and Catholicism. They shared a common commitment to social justice, fairness and equality and the right of people to maintain their culture. As a result, a large number of non-Catholic Asian students were enrolled at St. Peter's. However, when it came to Moslem students, the school drew a line. The school discouraged applications from Moslem families, while encouraging Buddhist and Jewish applicants. The principal explained this discrepancy by drawing a distinction between those cultures the school considered *non-Christian* and those it regarded as *anti-Christian*. Moslem families were unacceptable because 'they were anti-Christian'. Although nowhere stated in these precise terms, this ideological assumption had been converted into policy, as, on another occasion, the parish priest said much the same thing. Neither the principal nor the parish priest believed their views about Moslems were in any way discriminatory or prejudiced. In other conversations, both indicated a strong affinity with the victims of past injustices and supported effects to promote racial equality. At the same time, however, their culturalist assumptions led them to insist that there were a number of irreconcilable differences between Moslems and Christians which made any harmonious relation between the two groups highly unlikely. The cultural boundaries they drew between the two groups were thus naturalized, treated as self-evident and inevitable. The historical character of the formation of this difference and the political nature of its maintenance were simply ignored. What was also assumed was that some instances of cultural interaction are necessarily competitive, and that a form of cultural separatism is a permanent feature of human life.

Perhaps one more example might help to illustrate the way these culturalist assumptions work. It relates to an incident we observed at St. Peter's. One of the researchers and a teacher were walking around the playground during lunch when the teacher, Sue Owen, pointed to two girls holding hands together. Nothing special about that, except that the teacher felt it necessary to remark that one of the girls was white while the other was clearly of an Asian background. However, just as Sue was stressing the fact that this was a common occurrence at the school, an older child, David, in grade 6, came running in to disturb this example of intercultural harmony. David forced them apart. Later in an interview, David explained his action in terms of his belief that 'Asians and Australian people shouldn't be friendly like ... they are different, and should keep to their own'. David expressed a sentiment that had become a part of the way he acted upon the world (Billig, 1988).

What was the response of the teacher? Understandably, Sue was embarrassed and appropriately scolded David for his unacceptable behaviour. And to the researcher, she dismissed David's actions as those of a bully who had 'often been in trouble picking on younger *Chinese girls*'. She added further, that 'Asian boys had often ganged up on him'. When asked whether she regarded David's behaviour as racist, Sue agreed that this was in fact the case, as he had never been seen 'picking' on white students. But significantly the terms in which Sue spoke of this behaviour as racist were narrow and reflected a popular theory of racism as constitutive of an individual's irrational and deviant-belief-system, resulting from either an inadequate personality or his or her lack of appreciation of other cultures' mores or costumes (Henriques, 1984). She viewed racism as an expression of an individual's negative attitude of prejudice which was directed against another individual or a group of individuals on the basis of some presumed physical or cultural differentiation. Consistent with this view, Sue interpreted David's racism as an example of his deviant behaviour, not as something that resulted from the racist representations of both the experienced and imagined 'other' (Miles, 1989) with which he interpreted and acted upon the world. From the school's point of view, the solution to the problem of racism was better intercultural understanding. As Sue went on to explain, 'the school was doing everything possible to teach children about other cultures so we don't have the kind of thing we saw at lunchtime.'

In a sense, however, Sue constructed her representations of ethnic boundaries in much the same way as David. The way she talked about the Asians, the Chinese and the Australians reflected the way she had homogenized cultures, treating them as if their social characteristics were uniform and their boundaries unproblematic. Sue spoke freely of the Chinese as 'hardworking, clean and only interested in getting on with their lives — they do not like creating waves'. She contrasted this view of the Chinese with the generalizations she had developed about the Australians. Australians, she said, 'avoided work, didn't work hard enough and were only out for a good time'.

There is much in common between Sue's views and Bullivant's (1987) analysis of the way English-speaking Australians and non-English-speaking migrant children in Australia relate differentially to schooling. In explaining the success of non-English-speaking migrants in schools, Bullivant argues that it is due in large part to what he calls the 'ethnic work ethic', which he contrasts with the lack of drive that many Anglo-Australians display towards educational work. He suggests the latter group has become the new 'self-deprived' who have a 'shirk-work ethic'.

Bullivant has rightly been criticized for the assumptions upon which his analysis is based (Troyna, 1988). It has been pointed out, for example, that Bullivant treats various groups in an homogeneous manner, and mistakenly considers ethnicity to be a variable that is somehow separable from other social categories such as class and gender. Non-English-Speaking Background (NESB) students represent far too broad a category about which to formulate generalizations. As Kalantzis and Cope (1989) argue, the category of NESB needs to be disaggregated in order to assess how specific practices in schools disadvantage particular people. While these criticisms are indeed valid, Bullivant's analysis nevertheless alerts us to the fact that many teachers may have expectations of the minority students that are based more on their culturalist assumptions than on the students' actual aspirations, ability and performance.

In our research, there were numerous examples of teachers underestimating the capacity of minority children to take on more advanced academic work on the basis of their assumptions concerning 'ethnic disadvantage'. For just as Sue Owen had a number of stereotypes about the Chinese, she also regarded the Lebanese as 'basically lazy, unable to concentrate on material they are given'. Similarly, Tom Moore, a social-studies teacher at Morley High School, believed that 'Croatians are aggressive people, confrontational, always ready for a fight'. He had accordingly included pedagogic activities in his class that were designed to minimize conflict and promote 'positive attitudes', 'they needed to feel good about themselves, and about being Croatians', he maintained. Tom believed that the aggressive disposition of the Croatian students had a marked impact on their academic results, though our examination of the results could not discern any such pattern of underachievement. Nor could we, on the basis of our field research, concur with his stereotype of Croatians as any more aggressive and troublesome than any other group. It seems that Tom, like so many other teachers, had tacitly accepted the popular representations of Croatians, and of other minority groups in Australia. Tom had a homogenized representation of a group of people, with whom his relations were contradictory. For, on the one hand, he espoused a number of negative evaluations about their capacity, behaviour and achievement, while, on the other hand, he felt compelled to ensure that they maintained their cultural identity. Nowhere is this contradiction more clear than in the way many teachers construct their view of the Aboriginal students and their educational needs.

Teachers, Culturalism and Aboriginal Students

As we have already noted, the four schools in the Melbourne project had few Aboriginal students and saw little need to confront issues of Aboriginal Education. At Ealing High School, however, these issues could not be overlooked, as the politics of Aboriginality impinged upon it in a much more direct sense. In Australia, policies and programmes of multiculturalism have historically been constructed in relation to migrant and ethnic groups separate from policies and programmes in relation to Aborigines or Torres Strait Islanders. This is in part a response to indigenous politics which argue that the trajectory of racism experienced by Aborigines and Torres Strait Islanders has little, if any, convergence with the migrant experience, and that multiculturalism has not been able to accommodate the sovereign rights of Aborigines and Torres Strait Islanders. It is also in part a response to historical events which only recognized Aborigines and Torres Strait Islanders as citizens in 1967. Policies and programmes for Aborigines and migrant and ethnic groups have thus been developed as separate domains and constructed in relation to demands and understandings about the particular needs of their subject groups. Aboriginal people have thus argued for a different set of social and educational policy provisions. Ealing High School acknowledges this difference, as do all departments of education throughout Australia, and the school has constructed different educational programmes for Aboriginal and ethnic students.

The notion of separate domains, however, has purchase on both common sense and radical activism and, as our research suggests, the discourse of diversity, Aboriginality and multiculturalism is exercised through a discourse of containment. What is remarkable at Ealing High School is that despite the recognition of difference, both multicultural and Aboriginal programmes stress the more overt expression of culture. Indeed the culturalist assumptions of social cohesion, cultural identity, tolerance and sensitivity to different cultural backgrounds within multiculturalism, have come to inform representations and understandings of Aboriginality and Aboriginal education. A reductive focus on culture as 'primordial, static and innocent and essentially pre-colonial' (Pettman, 1992, p. 108) and culture as made present in art, dance, habits and customs represents a translation of ethnicity across social sites. In this sense, Aboriginality and Aboriginal education have become *ethnicized*. Importantly, this ethnicization has served to defuse uncomfortable questions about trajectories of racism and their different histories.

The teaching of Aboriginal students at Ealing is thus often restricted to performing traditional dances and learning about pre-invasion lifeways, and does not involve examining issues concerning the socio-economic structure of Australian society, thus confining many Aboriginal people to its fringes.[4] We are not suggesting that such cultural leanings are unimportant; rather that they are overwhelmingly divorced from more contemporary concerns. Not only this, but issues to do with Aboriginality are often regarded as applicable only to people from that background. The emphasis on cultural learning is often justified in terms of such notions as self-esteem and, as one teacher put it, 'making them happy in themselves'. This ideology permeates almost all of Ealing High school's policies and practices. The school's social-justice project and its commitment to the idea of inclusive curriculum, its policies concerning the placement of Aboriginal children in Year 8 classes and its programme of Aboriginal studies are premised on the assumptions of culturalism. The manner in which predominantly Anglo-Celtic teachers at the school relate to Aboriginal students and the way they think about issues of racism in the school and society similarly reflect culturalist understandings.

At the level of policy, Ealing High School is committed to the ideas of social justice and inclusive curriculum. With government funding, it has appointed a priority-projects officer, Tina Smith, specifically to work with teachers to help them think through issues of social justice. The way she views the idea of inclusive curriculum is therefore crucial. Tina argued that 'the practice of inclusivity involves the idea that you draw on the kids' experience and knowledge so that they can be included in it'. She suggested that social justice means that we:

> draw on and include the knowledge and experience of a wide variety of cultures, e.g., myths, folk tales, art, medicine, literature, including that of ethnic minority writers, music, crafts, dance, cooking, games, etc., value and draw on the knowledge and experience students bring with them to school, e.g., another language, stories, games, dances, food, family structure, values, attitudes.

What is clear from this account is that Tina, and the school, interpret the idea of social justice largely in culturalist terms, devoid of any reference to its social construction and its political relevance.

Ealing High School has attempted to implement its commitment to social justice in a variety of ways. As far as the Aboriginal students are concerned, it has developed an informal policy of placing incoming Aboriginal students with other Aborigines in their first year of high school. The Year 8 coordinator explained that this practice was based on Aboriginal students' 'need to be with other Aboriginal kids'. This was consistent with the school's concern to make the transition between primary and secondary school less difficult and alienating, but the Year 8 coordinator was also concerned about the special needs of Aboriginal students. The placement practice took on additional significance for Aborigines, as it resonated with popular ideologies in Aboriginal education which emphasize characteristics of extended family, kinship obligations, a cultural preference for cooperative work and an ethic of sharing (Coombs, Brandl and Snowdon, 1983). The placement practice was seen as a process of supporting Aboriginality but the support was contingent upon Aboriginal students being viewed as inextricably bound by cultural practices in which their previous educational experience, contemporary and complex out-of-school life ways do not figure. A major consequence of this approach is that almost all incoming Aboriginal students are placed in the 'basic' class where behaviour problems are prevalent and where an emphasis on identity and self-esteem, not coincidentally, are priorities.

Similar understandings about extended families, family orientation and co-operation, were popularly held about Asian, Greek and Italian students. The form of cultural support and priority accorded to Aborigines, however was not extended to other student groups at Ealing. Indeed other presumed cultural characteristics were brought to the fore and culturalist ways of seeing Asian students, for instance, led to their placement in the Year 10 'advanced' English stream. The English teacher, Bridget Kitson, saw her practice as contradictory and explained the placement as:

a bit of an anachronism, really, because quite a lot of them (Asian students) aren't Advanced English students. They're only there because if they were put in to one of the other English classes they couldn't learn very much because so much time is concentrated on discipline.

Her explanation echoes views held at St. Peter's about the work ethic and passivity of Asian students and resonates with culturalist understandings that construct all Asian students as neither presenting discipline or behavioural problems nor as unsuited to 'advanced' school work.

For both the Year 8 coordinator and Bridget, culturalist explanations naturalized the placement of students in class. On the one hand, the culturalist practices and explanations achieve coherence through an appeal to cultural relativism. On the other hand, and in contradiction to aims of antiracism, the same relativism not only sustains stereotypic understandings about particular groups but the form of education that accompanied the culturally suitable class placement, profoundly affected the life chances of student groups.

Ealing High School provides a further example of the contradictory ways in which culturalism works. While Aboriginal studies had the dual objectives of cultural maintenance and renewal for Aboriginal students and cultural awareness for non-Aboriginal students, it was also a programme to overcome 'the polarisation of ethnic groups and lack of tolerance'. As Beverley, the teacher in charge of the programme, explained, 'one of the reasons for introducing Aboriginal Studies was to try to make it a general approach to teaching kids more tolerance about racial areas generally, not just the Aborigine'. Much of the content of the Aboriginal-studies course focused on understanding Aborigines through the local Kaurna people, with emphasis on such things as a 'Kaurna Dreaming Trail' (Tjilbruke) and activities involving a handful of Kaurna words for naming body parts, places and fauna. Beverley insisted that some information is essential for the development of appropriate attitudes. Accordingly, she designed the programme in a sequence where:

Year 8 . . . is fairly much a general (year) and I guess I tend to concentrate on the content more than a lot of attitudes. Year 9, I'm much happier about because I'm concentrating more on attitudes because the kids are that much more mature. Year 8, they're unable to cope with it.

However, she argued that many Year 8 students are able to cope with exposure to notions of diversity, tolerance and difference. To this end, Beverley introduced Aboriginal studies to a Year 8 class in the following manner:

Beverley: One of the things that is very important is getting along with people who are different to ourselves. Some Aboriginal people are different to ourselves in a very obvious way — Who can tell me?
Student: They're black.
Beverley: Yes, but some of them don't look Aboriginal . . . We've got people of all different backgrounds . . . [looking at a student] . . . Your great, great, great grandfather would have been English, now Tony, your grandfather would have been

(questioning) Greek? Italian! Jonathan, English? Ivan, what country? Your parents were born in Yugoslavia? You were too? You don't have an accent, you must have been small when you came out (goes around class to all) . . . So you see, we've got very different backgrounds. There's lots of other ways we're different. What's your favourite food [gets responses, none of which are ethnically particular]. Some of us like different food, different sports, different television, different music . . . we need to learn to get on with people who are different from us.

An analysis of the above exchange reveals that tolerance is constructed within a framework of difference as self-evident and concomitant with diversity. Biological racism is unchallenged and difference remains unproblematic and immutable. Within this construction difference is depoliticized. But the tolerance presented here, through languaging of the 'obvious', 'ourselves' and 'them', cements Aborigines as always the marginal 'other' (Spivak, 1990).

Other aspects of the Aboriginal-studies programme frequently emphasized traditional and pre-invasion life ways in such a way as to present a naturalized, romantic and unproblematic past. Contemporary situations and the often immediate realities of racism in Australia and the school were ignored. This meant that the Anglo-Celtic teachers were mostly 'better' informed than the Aboriginal students thus denying them authenticity and marginalizing their experience. As a result Beverley could, for example, claim that while Aboriginal students were 'an absolute part' of Aboriginal studies 'they didn't show any special knowledge of anything', although 'occasionally' they 'knew more about what it was all about but not a lot'. Through a narrow construction of Aboriginality and a minimizing of Aboriginal students' knowledge, the teacher remains firmly the expert on Aboriginality and Aboriginal life ways.

In contrast, Mary Johnstone, another teacher, regarded Aboriginal students as 'obviously' knowledgeable 'when it was things they had heard about, legends and stuff and names of tribes and they'd be, they'd like to show off their knowledge obviously'. However, she also noted contradictions in the emphasis on 'listening to stories' and considered the 'dreamtime stories' as 'inappropriate because of urban kids'. Despite the supposed contradiction, Mary was unwilling to include contemporary Aboriginal literature in her programme. While she saw problems in seeming to be 'too Anglo' she nonetheless argued that 'as far as finding stories that would involve different races I'm a bit wary of selecting things purely on that basis. I'd rather look for stuff that I see as valuable for their language development stuff obviously'. In different ways both Mary and Beverley saw a natural connection between Aborigines and the traditional but their understandings denied the contemporary relations of groups they ostensibly wish to include.

Contemporary Aboriginal issues were not entirely absent from the Aboriginal-studies course but the course structure and its sequential overreliance on the ancestral past, archaeology and pre-invasion history undermined the school's effort to develop an inclusive curriculum and be relevant to the 'lives of Aboriginal people living in our local community'. It undermined it in two ways. Firstly, culturalism exteriorized culture by constructing it as remote, the past and the exotic, making culture unlikely to be analyzed as the present, the ordinary and the lived realities of a deeply racialized social world mediated by the politics of gender, ethnicity and class (Hall, 1986). Secondly, it did not take into account the pervasiveness of the historical, social and economic construction of 'race' and thus constructed the experience of particular groups in Australia as if they were unparalleled, entirely unique and a separate set of circumstances apart from the social relations in which they were embedded. It is through the seemingly concrete forms of the particular that culturalism achieves its predominance as explanation. Its denials of the social construction of 'race' provided coherence and centrality to culturalism. Culturalism was also contradictory in the way teachers related to particular Aboriginal students. Beverley, for example, found herself in a bit of a quandary regarding some Aboriginal students, as she believed it important to support Aboriginal identity but didn't like several of the Aboriginal boys in her English class. While she felt, along with the specialist Aboriginal education worker and Aboriginal-education resource teacher, 'partly committed to help the Aboriginal students . . . maintain their own identity', she nonetheless found this 'very difficult' when she had 'Leon Brinkwell and some of them'.

An Aboriginal-studies programme which collapses the distinction between teaching Aboriginal students and teaching the subject 'Aboriginal studies', goes some way towards explaining Beverley's dilemma. Her commitment to the preservation of a particular form of cultural identity created no space for the discontinuities of complex and uneven identities — a space that might provide more explanatory options than the resignations of letting the boys 'get to her, too much' and wondering 'whether I am prejudiced'. A course in which Aboriginal identity is constructed as intrinsically attached to ancient cultural roots similarly provides little space for contextualizing student resistance and dissatisfaction with schooling or to engage with students in an examination of their experiences of racism.

Teachers at Ealing High School persistently offered contradictory explanations for racism. In effect what counts as a just intervention and interpretation for one group does not for another. Aboriginal students were almost always constructed as being at the heart of a problem they were seen to create rather than confront (Troyna and Williams, 1986). Beverley sought to explain the presence of racism at Ealing High School:

> There are still racist attitudes within the school . . . but I think that they're sort of . . . a bit generalized in that they are racist to anyone who is different from them. The Greeks can be racist about anyone who's not Greek. Here comes a nice racist statement, you'll find the Yugoslavs as a group are some of the most racist and prejudiced lot I've come across . . . And of course there's still quite a deal of feeling against Asian, Indo-Chinese kids, at varying levels, but it's there . . . not so much the staff, because of the point of view that the Indo-Chinese generally kids work very hard, and do the right thing

Beverley's explanation involves understandings of racism as an intolerance of difference made natural through the assertion of racism as a generalized attitude, common to all groups. Her own assessment and experience of 'Yugoslavs' verified her understanding of racist attitudes and cancelled the racism of her 'nice racist statement'. Culturalist presuppositions of totalized groups assume universalized systems of meaning devoid and thus Beverley's understandings were able to explain race relations and racism in terms of racial or ethnic factors (Anthias, 1990) which disguised processes and structures of oppression and subordination. Her explanation legitimates, within culturalist terms, both her own racism and the way she, and many other teachers, could simply assert that a group of Aboriginal boys were themselves the problem.

Understandings about Aboriginal students as cooperative and sharing were readily abandoned when teachers came to explaining overt racism. Indeed, Aboriginal students were frequently constructed as being responsible for the racism they confronted. As Beverley indicated in her dislike of some of the Year 10 Aboriginal boys, it is their behaviours that makes things difficult for teachers. Even more directly, however, Jenny Dawson laid the blame squarely with the victims themselves and in so doing accorded differential significance to racism at both the individual and group level. She explained that Milly did not experience racism:

> not since she showed what a tough enemy she could be. I mean, occa-
> sionally Colin or one or two others, I think, would throw in the boong
> and black bitch type stuff if she was being particularly nasty. They didn't
> really start it off, I don't think, because I don't think any of them take
> racism that seriously, but I know that as soon as she showed any, she
> does it herself, you know. She'll call Ivan a Yugoslav git and that sort of
> thing, and we come down pretty heavy on that. But to start with there
> would be that, yeah, because she wasn't particular popular. But I think
> now that she's much more accepted and a lot calmer in herself, I don't
> think I hear any sort of colour and race at all much.

Alarmingly, but as we have repeatedly demonstrated in this chapter, teachers continue to recognize and privilege some forms of racism over and above others. Jenny's explanation suggests that sexist racism is unlikely to qualify in the recognition stakes. The way in which culturalism is continuously relativized through both the particular and the general makes individualized and group explanations plausible within in its own terms. This relativism provides the threads of cohesiveness to culturalism. As Jenny Dawson's explanation demonstrates, contradictions do not of themselves interrupt the logics of culturalism. Jenny, like so many other teachers, was able to uncritically match behaviours and characteristics to the racist abuse experienced by Milly. The artificial divides of culturalism meant that Ivan's experience of racism was worthy of recognition and intervention where Milly's was not.

Conclusion

In this chapter, we have argued that most teachers in Australia, and we suspect elsewhere as well, approach issues of cultural difference and antiracist curriculum and pedagogy within the framework of what we have referred to as an ideology of culturalism. This has the consequence of 'domesticating' the potential of antiracist reforms. We have shown through a variety of examples how culturalist frameworks direct and constrain pedagogic programmes of reform, reproducing understandings about the nature of racism in Australia (discrete, dichotomous, ahistorical) and denying contradictions that lie at the heart of social relations in schools and society.

The ideology of culturalism is, we have argued, founded on a construction of 'culture' that implies a consensus often about unspecified or loosely identified attributes which deny the structural influences of class and gender. It presumes a totalized view of cultural groups representing a universal system of meaning devoid, for example, of political factions. It romanticizes and reifies the past. It locates social inequality within a domain of 'culture clash' and social conflict. It ignores the complexity of intersections between the dominant and subordinate groups except as examples of domination and oppression, giving rise to simplistic views of racism as prejudice and discrimination. It thus denies the possibility of past and future intersection, or commonalities, with other groups' experience of oppression. Culturalism thus impels pedagogic solutions within a framework of 'understanding' and 'respecting each others' customs' which is seen to be a major instrument for reducing social conflict and ethnocentrism. Such a construction however fails to take account of the historical and contemporary political, economic and social influences which suggest that while there are group and individual experiences, these are not singular but rather are multidimensional and intersect with, and arise amid, structural inequalities.

Culturalism works through a hegemonic common sense that has become all too popular in education. Such a common sense avoids addressing contradictory articulations of racism with issues of class and gender. But it is through these contradictions that common sense is both maintained and reproduced. Yet culturalism appears to provide a non-contradictory unity through a common sense appeal to imagined and universalized principles. For instance, it is, to borrow from Errol Lawrence (1982), 'just plain common sense' to be proud of one's heritage and background. At a universal level, this was unproblematic for the principal of Morley High, who was proud of his Dutch heritage. Similarly, at the universal level, Beverley willingly acknowledged the salience of identity and heritage for Aboriginal students. Neither Beverley nor the principal of Morley High, however, were able to translate this commitment or belief to the machinations of everyday schooling or the particularity of students' lives. The irrelevance of cultural heritage and background to the administrative and pedagogic practices at Morley High is not only an assertion of the idea of discrete domains and forms of cultural salience but it is also a denial, among other things, of historical contingencies which might question how it is that he has a taken-for-granted pride in his 'migrant background' where other groups do not, and how it is that such taken-for-grantedness is a site of enormous political struggle for Aborigines. In contrast, yet not dissimilarly, Beverley made no connections between her commitment to helping Aboriginal students maintain their identity and her difficulties at the particularized level of behaviours, likes and dislikes. On the one hand, the unitary culturalist illusion remains intact and, on the other, it is unable to provide explanatory tools or pedagogic strategies for exploring administrative, pedagogic or classroom dilemmas.

These examples clearly indicate that while culturalist notions may appear to be attending and giving voice to subjectivities, they frequently mask the contradictory trajectories of racial formations. Like Omi and Winant (1986, p. 71), we argue that it is imperative to examine how these subjectivities are linked to operations of the racial state because schools are a major site of the state where these are negotiated. Subjectivities are not arrived at individually or momentarily. They draw on unexpected sources and are informed by ideologies and historical patterns of inclusion and exclusion. Teachers are of course implicated in these processes. They cannot assume a position of neutrality in the formation of social relations in schools. Their own social experiences have a crucial bearing on the way educational encounters are culturally defined. Their methods of thinking and reasoning about cultural relations and processes often have the consequence of differentially weighting culturalist ideas, which in turn work academically and socially in contradictory ways, for and against, student groups constructed as the ethnic or racial 'other'. Furthermore, racism works relationally through the operations of schools in which the authority of teachers is legitimated by the structural conditions that define their work. The culturalist assumption that it is possible for them to accord all minority groups an equal voice conflicts therefore with the realization that schools reproduce the unequal gender, ethnic and class orders of the wider society.

These considerations highlight the need to re-examine the nature of pre-service and in-service education of teachers, because teacher education is one of the major sites where teachers develop their common sense ideas about cultural difference and racism, often without the recognition that they are inherently contradictory. In our view, teacher education should consist less in giving teachers a range of facts about cultural traditions and values, and more in developing their conceptual critical skills with which to decode and deconstruct racist representations (Cohen, 1987), and with which to understand and work with the contradictions of cultural life. Much more opportunity needs to be provided for teachers to make sense of their own histories — how their own subjectivities and interests are shaped by their experiences of class, race, gender and other socially defined categories in ways that are often contradictory.

Examples such as those discussed in this chapter show curriculum and pedagogy to contain numerous contradictory elements. Such contradictions need to be viewed as much more than the paradox of logical inconsistency. Contradictions are spaces of dissimilarity, disclamation, echo, and countercharge (McCarthy, 1990). Not only does the presence of contradiction indicate evidence of contestation but it also represents political opportunities through which the overlapping axes of oppression and the concrete reflection of the lives of students and teachers can be actively engaged in antiracism programmes. It is only with an ability to work effectively with contradictions that teachers can transcend the narrow parameters of culturalism in order to develop more socially just practices of representation.

Notes

1 This project was conducted over 1988–90, and is reported more fully in Crowley, V. (1990) 'Educational Inequality: A Cast-study of Aborigines in Secondary Education', Unpublished Masters thesis, Flinders University of South Australia.
2 This research project titled 'Forms of Racism' was funded by the Australian Research Council, whose support is gratefully acknowledged, as is the contribution of my co-researchers, Dr Alan Rice and Dr Margaret Woodward of Monash

University, Australia. Thanks also to John Knight for his comments on an earlier draft of this paper.
3 The names used of the schools teachers and children throughout this chapter are pseudonyms.
4 Usage of the terms 'Aboriginal people' and 'Aborigines' does not include Torres Strait Islanders, as all students at Ealing are Aborigines. However, even this usage masks the diversity among the students who, while identifying as 'Nunga' also identified with family, regional and language groupings such as 'Pitjantjatjara' and 'Kaurna'.

References

ANTHIAS, F. (1990) 'Ethnicity, Nationalism and Racism: Parameters of Collective Identity', Paper presented at an International Conference on Racism, Hamburg.
BARTH, F. (1969) *Ethnic Groups and Boundaries*, London, Allen and Unwin.
BERGHE, P. VAN DEN (1981) *The Ethnic Phenomenon*, New York, Elsevier.
BILLIG, M. (1988) 'Prejudice and Tolerance', in BILLIG, M. *et al.* (Eds) *Ideological Dilemmas*, London, Sage Publications, pp. 100–123.
BRANDT, G. (1986) *The Realization of Anti-Racist Teaching*, London, The Falmer Press.
BULLIVANT, B. (1981) *Race, Ethnicity and Curriculum*, Melbourne.
BULLIVANT, B. (1987) *The Ethnic Encounter in the Secondary School*, London, The Falmer Press.
COHEN, P. (1987) *Racism and Popular Culture: A Cultural Studies Approach*, Centre for Multicultural Education, London, University of London.
CONNELL, R., ASHENDEN, D., DOWSETT, G. and KESSLER, S. (1982) *Making the Difference*, Sydney, Allen and Unwin.
COOMBS, H., BRANDL, M. and SNOWDON, W. (1983) *A Certain Heritage*, Centre for Research and Environmental Studies, Canberra, ANU.
CROWLEY, V. (1990) 'Educational Inequality: A Cast-study of Aborigines in Secondary Education', Unpublished Masters thesis, Flinders University of South Australia.
GAERTNER, S. and DOVIDIO, J.F. (1986) 'The Aversive Form of Racism', in DOVIDIO, J.F. and GAERTNER, S. (Eds) *Prejudice, Discrimination and Racism*, New York, Academic Press, pp. 61–90.
GALBALLY REPORT (1978) *Report of the Review of Post-Arrival Program and Services*, Canberra, Australian Government Printing Service.
GILROY, P. (1987) *There Ain't No Black in the Union Jack*, London, Hutchinson.
GLAZER, N. and MOYNIHAN, D. (1970) *Beyond the Melting Pot*, Cambridge, MIT Press.
HALL, S. (1986) 'Gramsci's Relevance to the Analysis of Racism and Ethnicity', in *Journal of Communication Inquiry*, 10, 2, pp. 5–27.
HENRIQUES, J. (1984) 'Social Psychology and the Politics of Racism', in HENRIQUES, J. *et al.* (Eds) *Changing the Subject*, London, Methuen, pp. 60–90.
HUMAN RIGHTS AND EQUAL OPPORTUNITY COMMISSION (1991) *Report of the National Inquiry into Racist Violence*, Canberra, Australian Government Printing Service.
KALANTZIS, M., COPE, B. and SLADE, D. (1989) *Minority Languages and Dominant Culture*, London, The Falmer Press.
LAWRENCE, E. (1982) 'Just Plain Commonsense: the "roots" of racism', in CCCS, *The Empire Strikes Back*, London, Hutchinson, pp. 95–142.
LOGAN, L. *et al.* (1989) *Teachers in Australian Schools*, Melbourne, Australian College of Education. (The Logan Report)
MCCARTHY, C. (1990) *Race and Curriculum*, London, The Falmer Press.
MILES, R. (1989) *Racism*, London, Routledge.

NATIONAL ABORIGINAL EDUCATION COMMITTEE (1986) *Philosophy, Aims and Policy Guidelines for Aboriginal and Torres Strait Islanders Education*, Canberra, Australian Government Printing Service.

NEW SOUTH WALES DEPARTMENT OF EDUCATION (1983) *Multicultural Education Policy Statement*, Sydney, Department of Education.

NEW SOUTH WALES DEPARTMENT OF EDUCATION (1991) *Anti-Racism Education Policy Statement*, Sydney.

OFFICE OF MULTICULTURAL AFFAIRS (1989) *National Agenda for A Multicultural Australia*, Canberra, Australian Government Printing Service.

OMI, M. and WINANT, H. (1986) *Racial Formation in the United States*, New York, Routledge and Kegan Paul.

PETTMAN, J. (1992) *Living in the Margins*, Sydney, Allen and Unwin.

RIZVI, F. (1991) 'The Idea of Ethnicity and the Politics of Multicultural Education', in DAWKINS, D. (Ed) *Power and Politics in Education*, London, The Falmer Press, pp. 161–96.

SACHS, J. (1989) 'Match or Mismatch: Teachers Conceptions of Culture and Multicultural Education Policy', in *Australian Journal of Education*, 33, 1, pp. 19–33.

SMITH, A. (1981) *The Ethnic Revival*, Cambridge, Cambridge University Press.

SMOLICZ, J. (1984) 'Ethnic Identity in Australia: Cohesive or Divisive?', in PHILLIPS, D. and HOUSTON, J. (Eds) *Australian Multicultural Society: Identity, Communication and Decision-Making*, Melbourne, Drummond, pp. 129–139.

SPIVAK, G. (1990) *The Post-colonial Critic*, New York, Routledge.

SWANN LORD (1985) *Education for All: Report of the Committee of Inquiry into the Education of Children from Ethnic Minority Groups*, London, HMSO.

TROYNA, B. and WILLIAMS, J. (1986) *Racism, Education and the State*, London, Croom Helm.

TROYNA, B. (1988) 'Paradigm Regained: a Critique of "Cultural Deficit" Perspective in Educational Research', in *Comparative Education*, 23, 3, pp. 273–83.

WALLMAN, S. (1986) 'Ethnicity and the Boundary Process in Context', in REX, J. and MASON, D. (Eds) *Theories of Race and Ethnicity*, Cambridge, Cambridge University Press, pp. 226–245.

Chapter 14

Teaching about Equality, Inequality and Cultural Diversity in Australian and Pacific Contexts

David Dufty

Speaking to groups of student teachers in Australia today one is acutely conscious of their concerns about the current crises of contemporary society. Unemployment looms as number-one concern since they themselves, and many of their fellow students may not get jobs for some years. If they do they will be teaching youth facing imminent unemployment. Environmental issues concern and inspire many but the Earth Summit did little to assuage their worries. Wars in the Middle East and eastern Europe concern them for their numbers include Jews and Muslims, Serbs and Croats. Somehow the teacher and designer of curricula for teacher-education fields such as 'studies of society' and 'environment' must face up to these challenges and design courses which take into account current realities but within a conceptual and value-based framework that can help them to make sense of, and cope with, their personal, social and global futures. This, my colleagues and I have been trying to do in two contrasting settings: Sydney, Australia, and Honiara, Solomon Islands, and this curriculum concern is the subject of this chapter.

The Australian Context

Australia is a complex, multifaceted society with a broad resource base but currently its citizens are acutely aware of the recessed nature of the economy, of the considerable inequalities between people and of the lack of equitable access to those resources. What then are some of the contemporary indicators of social inequality and differences, and what are some of the repercussions and challenges? (Dufty, 1986).

Although average GNP per head may be relatively high, **inequality of income** is great, as in most 'western democracies' and the gap is becoming greater. Some 2 million people of Australia's 17 million people, at the time of writing, are said to live in poverty (Brotherhood of St. Lawrence, 1990; Edgar *et al.*, 1989; Gorton, 1978; Hollingworth, 1983; Saunders and Matheson, 1991). One in eight children consequently lives in poverty. Some 25,000 children are homeless. The top 1 per cent of population earns as much income as the bottom 21 per cent.

Social stratification or class, while multi factored concepts, are probably primarily determined by past and present income in a society where there is no formal aristocracy (Wild, 1978). The alleged land of 'mateship' is far from a classless society. The current recession has seen some notably rich people, such as the well-known Alan Bond, lose their wealth. A number of upper middle-class people have also suffered from corporate failures. Privatization and selling off of government assets, such as the Commonwealth Bank, may have assisted some small-scale neo-capitalists to own a small part of the farm. But the economic and social gap remains very great between those owning profitable industries or those in select positions in industry and government, and the average worker. People with very high incomes are able to live in elite suburbs, such as those surrounding Sydney harbour. High-income families are estimated to spend 40 per cent more on housing fuel and power, 45 per cent more on food, 46 per cent more on transport, 67 per cent more on clothing and 70 per cent more on recreation than low-income families. Many people are struggling to make payments on home mortgages or to keep up their rent payments and have little income left for other aspects of daily living.

Employment and unemployment remain the great dividers with a general unemployment rate running at more than 11 per cent of the workforce but very much higher rates exist amongst youth and also in particular towns and regions where industries have closed. At the time of writing the employment rate for 15 to 19 year-olds looking for full-time work was over 35 per cent. Because work is so important in the value system of young and older people, not having a job, or being retrenched early has a decimating effect on the psyche of many people. There is, in addition, much hidden unemployment including those who are discouraged and have given up looking for work, reluctant retired people, youth staying at school because of poor job prospects, married women who would like to work but have not tried.

Race remains significant. Aboriginal people fall very much into the lower-income groups and also suffer racial discrimination. World attention has been attracted by the notorious Aboriginal deaths in custody. 70 per cent of Aboriginal children come from poverty or near-poverty situations. One in eight Aboriginal 5 to 9-year-olds do not go to school. Few go on to the senior years of high school and fewer still to tertiary education. This is however an area of major national and world attention and current efforts for change are considerable. A multimillion-dollar project to follow on the Aboriginal deaths enquiry will attempt to eliminate institutional racism. Land-rights issues continue and the infamous doctrine of *terra nulius*, which denied any rights of the indigenous people to their land despite their thousands of years of occupation, has been challenged by recent court rulings. Fortunately, neo-fascist groups remain of little influence in Australia and 'white Australia' as a basis for immigration is primarily of historical interest.

Ethnic differences are a feature of this multicultural society and are celebrated in folkloric performances but have their darker side when ethnic conflicts flow on from the old countries. These are sometimes related to religious loyalties and conflict can break out within groups even more than between groups. Non-English-speaking individuals inevitably suffer disadvantage and programmes to cater for them are widespread. In contrast there is a demand for people with skills in Asian languages as a basis for an improved 'export culture'. Youth from migrant groups sometimes do outstandingly well at schools as they struggle for success in their adopted country but usually not until they have gained the power of adequate skill in English (Taylor and MacDonald, 1992). Refugees, family reunion and the nature and amount of additional immigration remain major areas of debate with skilled, English-literate migrants, preferably with capital, being looked on more favourably. Migrants still tend to cluster in selected suburban areas, new migrants taking over from old.

Educational differences are critical in modern society. A 'good education' remains an important source of social mobility for the successful students in state and private high schools but those from high-income families who attend high-reputation private schools may still possess advantages over their less favoured competitors. New systems of teacher promotion by local selection may disadvantage rural schools. Adult literacy is being tackled by the Technical and Further Education System (TAFE) and considerable progress has been made. More students are staying on at school but this is partly due to the lack of available jobs. There are now inadequate places for all those wishing, and qualified, to proceed to tertiary education.

Gender remains a major basis of difference, debate, discrimination and celebration (Baldock, 1988; Eastal, 1992; Kenway and Willis, 1990). Women have increased to 43 per cent of income earners but their incomes are still low compared with men's and few occupy high-level positions in business and government. Women groups of many kinds are active and men's action groups have appeared as part of a possible feminist backlash. Homosexual/lesbian issues continue to be raised. A major public debate has recently occurred in regard to the spread and treatment of AIDS, with remarks being made regarding money spent on AIDS in comparison with other medical demands such as Aboriginal health. Homosexuals have also recently been discriminated against in regard to the armed services. On the other hand, the 'Gay Mardi Gras' in Sydney has become a major event. Sex workers remain in ambiguous situations with attempts to legalize prostitution varying from state to state (Perkins, 1991). Popular magazines continue to titillate and the porn industry prospers. Churches ponder their attitudes to love, sex, homosexuality and women priests.

Age is an important element of difference. At one end, the ever increasing numbers and percentages of aged people create major differences in society. Pensioners have received regular increases but those depending on small investments as a substitute for regular payment of superannuation have found the returns from their investments falling rapidly due to the recession. Many have lost some or all of their savings. Organizations for pensioners and senior citizens and their votes constitute a strong force of 'grey power' and many leisure, tourist and adult-education programmes cater for the ageing. Numbers suffering from dementia tend to increase as life expectancy increases and full-time care is required for increasing numbers. Aged immigrants constitute special problems (Rowland, 1991). On the other hand, the aged can be perceived as a great source of wisdom and experience as in tribal societies. A few schools do make use of this wisdom. Young children are mentioned below but teen society continues to be a basis of differing interests and a major basis for media and retail activities both in responding to and moulding tastes. Pressures to succeed create great demands on youth and teenage suicide is a major issue.

Marital status and family relationships remain important factors in differences at a time when a family needs a double income in order to keep up payments on

David Dufty

the Australian dream of the family home. 56 per cent of two-parent families have both parents working. Large numbers of single parents struggle to maintain the health and happiness of themselves and their child or children. 61 per cent of sole parents receive government benefits. In 1986 54.50 per cent of single parents and their children lived below the poverty line. Single parents spent 37 per cent of their income on housing costs. 88 per cent of sole parents were women. Child-care facilities have improved but remain a high expense for many families (Picton and Boss, 1981; Jovanovich, Vimpani and Parry, 1989). Our conceptions of what a family is have changed and diversified.

Rural isolation has always been regarded as a basis of difference and some-times of disadvantage, however new forms of communications, including satellite dishes and the services of groups like the flying-doctor service, have greatly assisted the isolated. The current problem is rural poverty and the low world prices due to tariff agreements and subsidies in areas such as USA and the European Community. Many property owners have been forced off the land with consequent impact on country towns and further problems as rural dwellers try to relocate in urban areas. More generally, there are differences between interests and life-styles in the varied regions of Australia, for example as between say Hobart dwellers and north Queensland dwellers. This diversity, amongst other things, enhances our important tourist industry.

The disabled vary greatly in their needs and major efforts have been made by governments, NGOs and voluntary groups to cater for these varied needs (AGPS, 1990; AGPS, 1991). A current phrase used in the caring field is 'every-one's differently abled' and one is reminded of the remarkable and inspiring capabilities shown by participants in international sporting events designed for those who are different.

In addition to all of the above bases of difference there are many other differences in society based on varied **ideologies and interests**. These include political groups and conflicts — active but seldom violent. They also include the 250 religious groups identified through the census (Bouma, 1992) and the rich variety of interest groups identified through the yellow pages of the telephone book, the advertisements in the Saturday papers and the wealth of magazines at the newsagents, including a lively ethnic press, plus ethnic radio and television. All support a reasonably positive perception of Australia as a land of relative political freedom and of relative unity in its diversity. All highlight the current economic problems.

It is not only the 'facts' of difference, poverty and discrimination which create distinctive social climates for people but their perceptions of their situations. As a report by the Sydney City Mission points out, many are 'prisoners of poverty'. I have not attempted to define 'poverty' since poverty lines, as measured in income, will vary from time to time and place to place but those interviewed by the City Mission are well aware of its nature and repercussions:

I see poverty in terms of the inability of a family to cope with their present situation, be it financial, be it emotional or the inability to communicate with each other.

To me poverty represents the basic human right of a family to have food, clothing and shelter. When these things are missing in the family unit,

168

then all the rest of the social and economic deprivations follow: lack of co-operation in the family, family violence, children who flee from a difficult situation. (Sydney City Mission, 1989, p. 2)

As the Brotherhood of St. Lawrence stresses: 'poverty is not only a low level of income, it is a lack of choice, a lack of access and a lack of power.' (Brotherhood of St. Lawrence, 1990, p. 3).

One significant response to the above inequalities is to monitor cases of discrimination and to try to rectify these situations. For example, the Anti-discrimination Board of NSW (Annual Report, 1990–1) now acts upon discrimination in regard to:

- sex (including pregnancy);
- race (including 'racial villification');
- marital status;
- homosexual/lesbian;
- intellectual impairment;
- physical impairment; and
- compulsory retirement

but only in the following 'areas' or circumstances:

- employment;
- state but not private education;
- obtaining goods and service;
- accommodation; and
- registered clubs.

Another response to the above issues is to provide social services of various kinds. As compared with nineteenth-century society, a vast range of social services has been established in Australia to improve the lot of people who suffer through inequality and difference. There is no space to discuss these efforts, only to say that there is no room for complacency in a society where the poverty mentioned above still seems to be endemic in capitalist society and where the hope of an alternative ideal system of socialism or communism has been all but lost.

The deeply rooted problems related to unemployment and the recessed state of the economy are constantly debated in Australia today and clearly involve major social reforms, including such currently discussed options as special youth wages and a corps of young people employed in environmental and other projects.

All of the above data and issues merit a place in current curricula so that students in schools and teacher-education institutions can gain awareness of them, reflect on, and react to them. The problem is that as stated above they consist of 'one damn problem after another' and there is clearly a need for some structure if such studies are to be fully meaningful to students.

Responding to the Challenge: General Educational Responses

Education systems, schools and designers of curricula must respond to the challenges raised by the above data and issues. Children may come to school with empty stomachs unable to concentrate. Ethnic or racial conflicts may spill into the playground. On the other hand the school may be able to contribute to the reduction of racial conflict in a town where conflict has flared for many years. Cultural diversity is also of great value and adds to the richness of school life. As the editor of this book has said in his letter to contributors: 'teachers must acknowledge the intrinsic validity of all cultures/subcultures which merit recognition and respect as distinct and separate identities.' As part of the total curriculum, in schools and in teacher-education institutions, students need to become aware of the nature of inequality and the pluralistic society, as illustrated above, and knowledge of 'the facts' needs to be complemented by values education and by involvement in action, where appropriate. For example, students could be further involved in voluntary activities in regard to the aged or handicapped.

Governments also, in addition to their programmes of social services and antidiscrimination, need to help create an education system which itself contributes to the awareness of, and the reduction of, inequality. As a result of the work of interested groups and active political leaders there is concern and action about *equity* in education, or, as an influential NSW government document published in 1989 puts it, with both 'excellence and equity' (NSW Ministry of Education and Youth Affairs, 1989). This document reflects the current climate of economic rationalism but it also reflects a concern to 'ensure that appropriate education is available for all, especially education for employment. Its multiple and sometimes conflicting goals can be seen in reform strategies such as 'stronger discipline codes and more effective welfare policies in government schools' and 'greater diversity and choice of schools for parents and students both within the government schools system and between government and non-government schools'. Or more fully: 'the government is committed to the promotion of a general school culture which unashamedly promotes maximum effort and excellence of achievement and repudiates mediocrity and satisfaction with minimum levels of achievement. Equally it is committed to enhancing equality of opportunity for disadvantaged children, for example from non-English-speaking backgrounds and Aboriginal backgrounds, and for girls in those curriculum areas and subject levels where they are seriously underrepresented.' A more recent document from NSW entitled *Education 2000* (NSW Department of School Education, 1992) outlines major social changes in the society, including changes in income distribution, numbers experiencing disadvantage, long-term unemployment and disability, changes in the role of women, increased participation in the workforce by women, increased recognition of voluntary and unpaid work, increasing proportion of the population over 60 years, a higher growth rate of Aboriginal population relative to the general population, high levels of immigration, an increased priority to address inequalities amongst schools. It includes in its outcomes by 2000 that students demonstrate positive attitudes to cultural and linguistic diversity, support a cohesive and harmonious, multicultural society, reject discriminatory or violent behaviour and are skilled in the peaceable resolution of conflict.

The subject 'Australian studies' is currently being introduced in NSW (as a combination of history and geography) and also in other states as a compulsory element of the curriculum and this provides plenty of opportunity to stress the multicultural nature of Australian society. There is an emphasis on 'Australia's neighbours' but less emphasis on development and global education. Poverty needs to be studied in comparative, global as well as Australian contexts.

The Commonwealth government is increasingly important as a player in Australian education and is involved in the development of a National Curriculum framework in close cooperation wih the states. British ideas have been influential but we are assured that 'it is nothing like Maggie Thatcher's National Curriculum. No Standard Assessment Tasks. No testing at 7, 11, 14 or 16. No league tables of school results.' (Hannan and Wilson, 1992) A significant national report is the Finn Report (1990) which is concerned with post-compulsory schooling and with the concept of 'essential employment-related Key Areas of Competence'. It stresses the need to improve the participation of disadvantaged groups in post-compulsory training and identifies three national programmes which provide support for 'at-risk' students in the school system: the Disadvantaged Schools Programme (DSP), the Students at Risk Programme (SAR) and the Country Areas Programme (CAP). The Finn Report has been followed up by the Mayer Report (1992) *Employment-related Key Competencies: A Proposal for Consultation*. These competencies include language and communication, solving problems, using mathematics, scientific and technological understanding, cultural understanding, working with others and in teams, and career planning. There is no mention of skills in intercultural communication needed in a multicultural workplace, or in the major current industry of tourism, but there is a mention of understanding major global issues. What is also missing is adequate discussion of personal coping skills and an appreciation of the intrinsic worth of the individual so that people can carry on their lives during times of non-employment as well as employment. Yet another report is concerned with the implementation of an *Australian Vocational Certificate Training System* prepared by The Employment and Skills Formation Council (1992) which has long-range plans for a system of combining work and training for all those young people who are not currently participating in training programmes.

After years of paternalistic syllabus contributions by non-Aboriginals to Aboriginal Education at the State level, National Curriculum developments are now being placed firmly in Aboriginal hands. A nationally agreed philosophy and guidelines for Aboriginal and Torres Strait Islander studies K-12 is being undertaken by the states/territories coordinators for Aboriginal education under the federal government's reconciliation and schooling strategy. Gender has received major attention in the 1990 report *The National Agenda for Women: Maintaining the Momentum* and a project on gender equity in curriculum reform is being coordinated by the Commonwealth Department of Employment, Education and Training. Major Commonwealth initiatives have also been taken in education for literacy which is clearly highly relevant to issues of equality (Christie, 1990).

Responding to the Challenge: Designing Curricula in Studies of Society and Environment

Education about inequality could be a very confusing and depressing topic for students in schools and colleges unless it is seen as a part of a broader or more holistic understanding of how society is constructed and unless it is seen in terms of how people can change society and culture to make it more just and less alienating. In this section I would like to make use of case-study material which illustrates some possible approaches to the key area of studies of society and environment which try to assist students to see relationships and to make some sense of the world rather than perceiving current issues as chaotic and unsolvable.

Instead of suggesting that a National Curriculum in studies of society and environment should be based on the subjects of history and geography, the Australian Education Council (1992) has identified five conceptual strands, which is a step towards a national framework in this area. These strands are:

- culture and beliefs;
- systems: natural and social;
- resources: natural and human;
- place and space; and
- time: continuity and change.

They will be subject to further discussion before being accepted as the basis for any national framework. The linking of society and environment is most commendable. A notable omission in the strands, however, is 'the individual' or 'the person'. Without this concept it is extremely difficult to highlight the human-rights basic to any adequate study of pluralism, inequality and disadvantage and the positive role which each individual plays in influencing their own life and those of others. It also weakens the important person–people–planet link which is most relevant to the identity problems of modern youth. 'Civic education' or 'social-studies education' have been plagued by this failure to fully incorporate the individual human being and the planet in their rationales, hence my strong support for the 'holistic education' movement.[1] A basic argument of this chapter is that to cope with these divisive times it is necessary to have a world view that assists one to make sense and meaning of life on the planet.

For many years my colleagues and I have struggled with these problems of explaining both the complexity and the interrelatedness of human society, of balancing social-formation views of the individual with transformatory views of human possibilities. In doing this we have made use of diagrammatic models in order to express visually the all-at-onceness and interconnectedness of human process and in order to present a more democratic and interactive view of society rather than the linear and hierarchical models typified by diagrams showing the structure of government. Figure 14.1 provides an exemplar of this model, in this case one included in the document *Social Education in the Nineties* prepared for the Social Education Association of Australia (1990). A simpler version has now been used for ten years in the syllabus and in the teaching of the course 'society and culture', which is taught in NSW senior high grades.[2] It has its limitations but it has proved to be a very useful device for both students and teachers in trying to understand basic concepts like persons, society, culture and environment and their interactions. The 'society and culture' course includes a general section based on this model, 'depth studies', which includes optional studies of social inequality, prejudice and discrimination and of intercultural communication, and the widely acclaimed personal-interest project' which is a mini-research task done by the students but which is examined externally and requires a detailed and well-prepared report. (NSW Board of Studies, 1991). Students are expected to understand the nature and limitations of social research and the exercise has clearly been an empowering one to many students. Features of the teaching have also included visits between schools of clearly different class and ethnic backgrounds

Figure 14.1: Basic Components of the Social World and Their Interrelationships

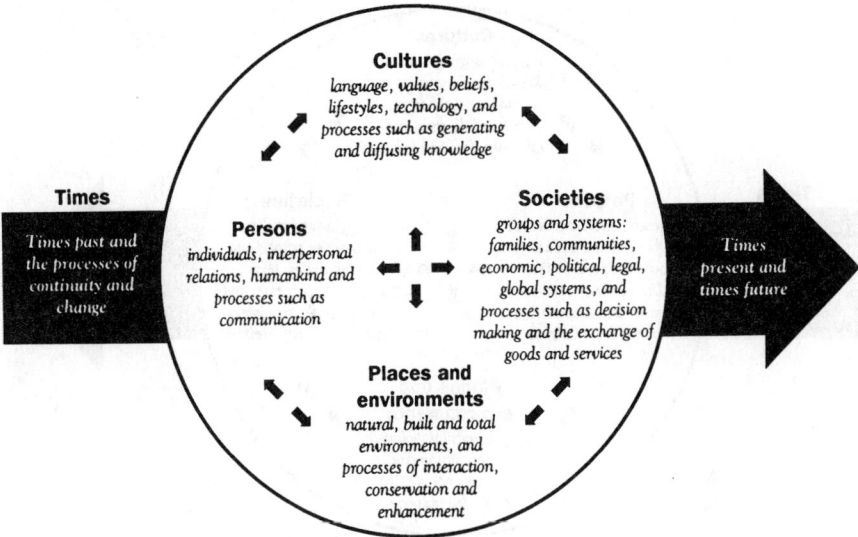

Cultures
language, values, beliefs, lifestyles, technology, and processes such as generating and diffusing knowledge

Times
Times past and the processes of continuity and change

Persons
individuals, interpersonal relations, humankind and processes such as communication

Societies
groups and systems: families, communities, economic, political, legal, global systems, and processes such as decision making and the exchange of goods and services

Times
Times present and times future

Places and environments
natural, built and total environments, and processes of interaction, conservation and enhancement

and consequent sharing of common interests and concerns. Outcomes and evaluations of this course, especially from the viewpoint of the pupils, have been very encouraging.

The model and the other parts of the course are aimed at bringing out various understandings relevant to equality, inequality and cultural diversity. For example:

- each person is unique and possesses a bundle of human rights;
- human beings are highly diverse in nature as are the cultures which they create;
- persons are not just formed by their environments but involved in a vital process of interaction between individuals and their social and cultural environments;
- human beings construct their social institutions and their cultures and are capable of modifying and changing them for the better;
- people and their social institutions and systems interact with natural environments and can work with nature to conserve and improve these environments;
- persons, societies and ecosystems are all interrelated in life on planet Earth and we must learn to think globally as well as locally and regionally; and
- everything changes and human beings have greatly influenced changes in the planet and can greatly influence planetary futures.

For the purposes of the course society is defined in terms of social relationships and institutions, and culture in terms of knowledge, the latter being sometimes

David Dufty

Figure 14.2: Values Related to Key Components

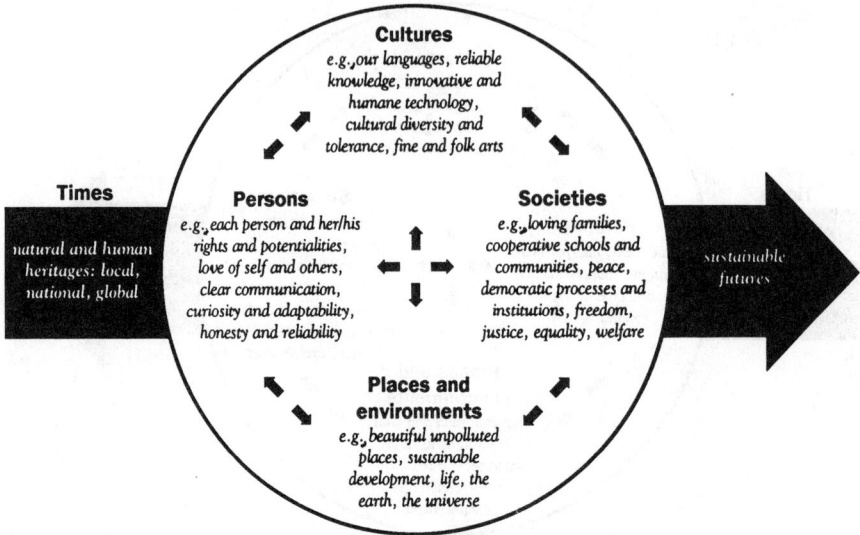

represented in the course diagrams by dots which permeate and surround other aspects of the model, as shown in Figure 14.2. Students are encouraged to build their own models. Discussion inevitably takes place as to whether such models are descriptive of social reality or highly idealized in nature. This leads on to a discussion of values. The model does not clearly emphasize values, although many of the above 'understandings' are value laden. In contrast to the relativistic days of 'values clarification' there is currently in Australia a much stronger move to identify substantive social values which presumably may be actually inculcated in schools rather than just personally clarified. (NSW Board of Studies, 1990). For example, the draft curriculum design brief mentioned above stresses *social justice*, *ecological sustainability* and *democratic process* as key areas of values underlying a future national framework in studies of society and environment.

Social Education in the Nineties (Social Education Association of Australia, 1990, p. 8) offered the model shown in Figure 14.2 as a basis for discussion. In this model the basic concepts shown in Figure 14.1 are used as a heuristic device to generate a range of value concepts. Other models generated were 'skills to cope with and influence the world' and 'actions related to the key components'. The models continue to be revised and we would welcome comments by others. For example, 'equality' is shown in Figure 14.2 as related to the structure of society rather than to the person as there are undoubtedly considerable differences between individuals. Equality is a value which must be intentionally built into the social structures of society so that we reduce institutional racism, sexism or class privilege and so that we reflect on whether, in certain circumstances, we should favourably assist people who suffer from such prejudice or disadvantage in order to give them greater access to material and non-material benefits of social systems, or in order to reduce rather than increase gaps in society.

174

Solomon Islands: Context, Challenge and Response

At the risk of moving too quickly in this argument, I would like to comment briefly on our attempts to validate the above models by applying them to the teacher-education programme at the Solomon Islands College of Higher Education, with the special interest in using them to bring out the richness and diversity of Solomon Islands society as well as its current issues and problems. The Solomon Islands are a small Pacific country which has one major urban centre, Honiara, but otherwise is mainly village centred. It has very limited bases for modernization apart from the declining copra industry and expanding tuna and timber industries. Foreign capital and foreign aid are vital to sustain the modern sector. The college students have little exposure to world events through press and television but at the outbreak of the the Gulf War some 400 people turned up to the college when a seminar was advertised on this topic, together with recent television coverage.

Curricula and teacher education in Solomon Islands still strongly reflect colonial influences. I found that my students were using Australian and British textbooks with their western concepts, values and case studies and had little formal knowledge of their own history, geography and culture. They of course carried with them a vast amount of knowledge in the three or four languages which they spoke and in the village culture which they carried into their church-run high schools and the urban institution of the College of Higher Education. Using the above models it was possible to generate a model for Solomon Islands studies and to put this into action by a curriculum which included such activities as making field trips to prehistoric sites, such as a cave quite close to Honiara which was quite unknown to the students and which introduced them to their thousands of years of cultural heritage. The base model was similar to the model in Figure 14.1 and this was then used to generate a number of questions about Solomon Islands society which were collated and included in the model shown as Figure 14.3 in order to generate further research, including personal-interest projects.[3]

We also expressed this in the form of a matrix, as shown in Table 14.1, which brought out more clearly the values and potential for praxis of the study.

Solomon Islands students were fully aware, and appreciative of, the cultural diversity of their island nation. They responded extremely well to the challenge of the personal-interest project which was carried out in their home villages during the mid-year break. This diversity was also utilized and celebrated in culminating our work in a multimedia production in the college auditorium. Groups from the various regions worked together to make a presentation about their culture. These were not just 'custom dancing' as was popular in the high schools but delved more deeply and widely into the culture and at times were critical about contemporary trends, thus appreciating that culture is both changing and changeable. The presentation included a coverage of the environmental beauty of the Solomons with plenty of critique of the destruction of the forests and the pollution of the lagoons by exploitative methods that could be changed to sustainable ones. The historical section began 3000 years ago with a return to the archaeological site (the Poha Cave) visited by the students and a presentation of poems they wrote in response to that moving experience. Allied to this presentation was a renewal of the shabby environment of the campus by painting the walls and then covering them with dramatic murals using traditional motifs.

David Dufty

Figure 14.3: Questions and Issues Raised by Solomon Islands

What languages are spoken in the Solomons? How do these languages help to shape our view of the world? What do Solomon Islanders believe? What do they value most? What are their unique customs and behaviours? Their expressive arts and literature? Their crafts and technologies? Are some technologies more appropriate to the Solomons than others?

Who am I? What does it mean to be a Solomon lalander, or a person from a particular group or island? Can I cope with the changes around me? How can I keep healthy? Who can I look to for help and leadership?

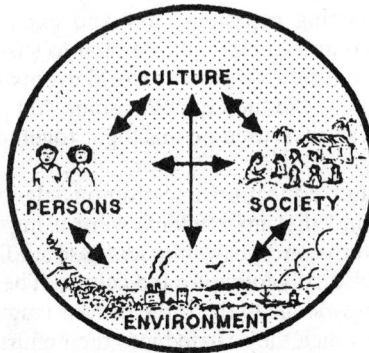

How important is the family in Solomon Islands society? Ethnic and Wantok groups? The Church? How can Intergroup relations be improved? How does our political system work? Our economic system? Our legal system? Our education system? How could they work better? How do we relate to other countries?

How does living in a country of many islands affect life here? The tropical climate? The cyclones? The volcanoes? How important are our forests, our rivers and seas, our soils and minerals? How are we using and conserving our resources. How are we affecting our ecosystems? Are our towns good places in which to live?

TIME ⟶

| How long have people lived here? | How important is kastom? | What past forces have influenced our story? For better or for worse? | What changes are occurring today? | What future development do we prefer? |

One of the most intriguing sessions relevant to this chapter was a presentation by a student on employment in the Solomons. Rural and urban work was discussed with appropriate statistics gleaned from the authorities and then the student concluded something was missing. Not a word on 'unemployment'. Back to the authorities but no figures were available for the concept was not a meaningful one despite the many 'Lius' who wandered around the town apparently temporarily fed and housed by 'Wantoks' in the suburbs. Unemployment was a western concept, a concept of the modernized world. It was recognized, however, that the number of such urban drifters was increasing and the problems of the modern world were being recreated here. But there were no 'homeless kids'. The concepts of 'development' and 'sustainable development' were explored. Further consideration needs to be given to the use of western concepts in non-western

Table 14.1: *A Matrix for Solomon Islands Studies*

	INFORMATION and INVESTIGATION	VALUING, FEELING, RELATING	CREATION and COMMUNICATION	PRAXIS (REFLECTIVE ACTION)
Interactions between PERSONS	E.g., Knowing about oneself as a Solomon Islander. Knowing about other Solomon Islanders: their hopes and problems	E.g., Loving one-self. Being at home with oneself. Loving, respecting, helping other people (and not only Wantoks).	E.g., Writing and expressing one's feelings. e.g. Through biographical writing, talking to and with others.	E.g., Learning skills in being, growing and doing.
CULTURE	Knowing about, and how to investigate, Solomon Islands culture and the cultures of subgroups.	Appreciation of Solomon Island traditions and arts. Valuing language.	Developing skills in one or more expressive arts. Maintaining and using language.	Critical appraisal of Solomon Islands Culture. Acting to conserve or modify Solomon Islands culture.
SOCIETY	Knowing about and investigating groups, institutions and systems, including global systems.	Valuing human rights, democracy, pluralism, honesty, commitment in Solomon Islands society.	Developing skills in one or more expressive arts. Maintaining and using language.	Using knowledge, values communication as empowerment in critiquing and helping to change Solomon Islands Society for the better.
ENVIRON-MENT	Knowing about the many parts of the Solomon Islands understanding Soloman Islands ecosystems and resources.	Loving this place: Its mountains, seas, birds, the future of this beautiful place.	Expressing this love and sense of place through varied media. Being 'vocal' in one's concern.	Acting thoughtfully and responsibly in the use and conservation of resources. Thinking globally and acting locally.
TIME	Knowledge and skill in studying the antiquity, diversity and richness of the Solomon Islands.	Appreciating heritage. Having empathy for past, present and future generations.	Gathering and contributing to the oral tradition. Keeping and writing records. Imagining preferable futures.	Actions to conserve what is best in our oral, written and material heritage. Actions to create preferable and sustainable futures.

situations and whether the models which were transferred from a modernized western culture to a very different situation were really appropriate or full of preconceptions which need to be completely rethought in discussion with, and mainly between, indigenous people. Then we must rethink our own work-related concepts.

The issues of teaching and curriculum, too briefly raised in this chapter, demand much more thought and dialogue. However, I consider that in any context they cannot be solved by creating formal history and geography courses centred on one's own nation, nor can they be solved by courses which treat the issues as a set of disconnected problems. Inequality and pluralism are universal features of human societies, despite current attempts to purify ethnic states by creating break-away nations. Basic economic, political and sociological understandings are needed, as well as concepts of time and place, in order to analyze and reflect on the data presented in the first part of this chapter (See also Andjamrozik, 1989; Castles, 1991; Castles *et al.*, 1990). As suggested in the title of David Purpel's book (Purpel, 1989) we also need 'a curriculum of justice and compassion' in which values and valuing are a basic part of the content and the processes. We need to share our experiences with those in other countries who are facing up to the curriculum issues raised by inequality, diversity and social change. Unfortunately there is as yet no international organization which shares a common interest in 'studies of society' and 'environment'. A major opportunity exists for a group to take up this challenge and to initiate networking in our electronic age.

Notes

1 For further details on holistic education refer particularly to the *Holistic Education Review* and the publications of the Holistic Education Press: 39 Pearl Street, Brandon, VT 5733–1007, USA and to the holistic network: Global Alliance for Transforming Education (GATE), 4202 Ashwoody Trail, Atlanta, Georgia 30319, USA.
2 Details of course available from the NSW Board of Studies, PO Box 460, North Sydney, Australia.
3 This study is more fully reported in *O'O Journal of Solomon Islands Studies*, 1990, 2, 2 (available from USP Centre, Box G23, Honiara, Solomon Islands).

References

ANDJAMROZIK, G. (1989) *How Australians Live: Social Policy in Theory and Practice*, South Melbourne, MacMillan.
AUSTRALIAN GOVERNMENT *Ethnic Youth: Their Assets and Aspirations (1987) Homeless Children (1989), Accommodation for People with Disabilities (1990), Social Justice Strategy: Towards a Fairer Australia (1990) Aboriginal Deaths in Custody, 1 and 2, (1992), Girls in Schools, 1, 2, 3, and 4. Report on the National Policy for the Educations of Girls in Australian Schools*, Canberra, Australian Government Printing Service.
BALDOCK, C.V. and CASS, B. (1988) *Women, Social Welfare and the State*, Sydney, Allen and Unwin.
BOUMA, G.D. (1992) *Religion: Meaning, transcendence and community in Australia*, Melbourne, Longman Cheshire.

BROTHERHOOD OF ST. LAWRENCE (1990) *Australians in Poverty: A Resource Book.*

CASTLES, F.G. (Ed) (1991) *Australia Compared: People, Policies and Politics*, Sydney, Allen and Unwin.

CASTLES, S. *et al.*, (1990) *Mistaken Identity: Multiculturalism and the Demise of Nationalism in Australia*, Sydney, Pluto Press.

CHRISTIE, F. (1990) *Literacy for a Changing World*, Hawthorn, Vic, ACER.

DUFTY, D. (1986) 'Remodelling Australian Society and Culture: A Study in Education for a Pluralistic Society' in MODGIL, S. *et al.* (Eds) *Multicultural Education: the Interminable Debate*, London, The Falmer Press.

EASTAL, P.W. (1992) *The Forgotten Few: Overseas Born Women in Australian Prisons*, Canberra, Australian Government Printing Service.

EDGAR, D. *et al.* (1989) *Child Poverty*, Sydney, Allen and Unwin.

EMPLOYMENT AND SKILLS FORMATION COUNCIL (1992) *Australian Vocational Certificate Training System*, Canberra, Australian Government Printing Service.

FINN REPORT (1990) *Review of Young People's Participation in Post-compulsory Education and Training*, Canberra, Australian Government Printing Service.

GORTON, S. (1978) *Out of Luck*, Sydney, Allen and Unwin.

HANNAN, B. and WILSON, B. (1992) 'The Development of a National Curriculum Framework', *Curriculum Perspectives*, 12, 2, pp. 2–3.

HOLLINGWORTH, P. (1983) *Australians in Poverty*, Melbourne, Nelson.

JOVANOVICH, B., VIMPANI, G. and PARRY, T. (1989) *Community Child Health and Australian Perspective*, Melbourne, Churchill Livingstone.

KENWAY, J. and WILLIS, S. (1990) *Hearts and Minds: Self-Esteem and the Schooling of Girls*, London, The Falmer Press.

MAYER REPORT (1992) *Employment-related Key Competencies: A Proposal for Consultation*, Melbourne, The Mayer Committee.

NSW BOARD OF STUDIES (1990) *The Values we Teach*, Sydney.

NSW BOARD OF STUDIES (1991) *Preparing and Presenting Your Personal Interest Project*, Sydney.

NSW MINISTRY OF EDUCATION AND YOUTH AFFAIRS (1989) Sydney.

NSW DEPARTMENT OF SCHOOL EDUCATION (1992) *Education 2000*, Sydney.

PERKINS, R. (1991) *Working Girls: Prostitutes their Life and Social Control*, Canberra, Australian Institute of Criminology.

PICTON, C. and BOSS, P. (1981) *Child Welfare in Australia: An Introduction*, Sydney, Harcourt.

PURPEL, D. (1989) *The Moral and Spiritual Crisis in Education: A Curriculum for Justice and Compassion in Education*, Grandby, MA, Bergin and Garvey.

ROWLAND, D.T. (1991) *Immigrants and Ageing in Australia*, Canberra, Australian Government Printing Service.

SAUNDERS, P. and MATHESON, G. (1991) *Ever-rising tide: Poverty in Australia in the 80's*, Social Policy Research Centre, University of NSW.

SOCIAL EDUCATION ASSOCIATION OF AUSTRALIA (1990) *Social Education in the Nineties*, Sydney, pp. 7–8.

SYDNEY CITY MISSION (1989) *Prisoners of Poverty: Report to the Nation*, Sydney.

TAYLOR, J. and MACDONALD, H. (1992) *Children of Immigrants: Issues of Poverty and Disadvantage*, Canberra, Australian Government Printing Service.

WILD, R.A. (1978) *Social Stratification in Australia*, Sydney, Allen and Unwin.

Chapter 15

Knowing Ourselves:
Practising a Pluralist Epistemology
in Teacher Education

Malcolm Reed and Michael Beveridge

The search for method becomes one of the most important problems of the entire enterprise of understanding the uniquely human forms of psychological activity. In this case, the method is simultaneously prerequisite and product, the tool and the result of the study. (L.S. Vygotsky, 1978)

We begin by situating Initial Teacher Training (ITT) for a pluralist society within the current structure of an ITT course, the Post-Graduate Certificate of Education (PGCE) of one year's duration. Understanding the architecture of teacher training is crucial to our task of constructing an appropriate curriculum.

Teacher education is under intense pressure to transform itself in order to meet new criteria and procedures for the accreditation of ITT courses nationally (Department For Education, 1992). We should assume that the model determined by the Council for the Accreditation of Teacher Education (CATE) of a minimum of twenty-four weeks spent 'on the premises of partner schools in full-time secondary PGCE courses' not later than 1 September 1994, requires some discussion of the role of a partnership curriculum which arises through collaboration between ITT institutions and their partner schools.

In the past, institutions of education have been exempt from curriculum planning in the sense which has governed the school curriculum since the Education Reform Act (1988) brought in the National Curriculum, which applies to the teaching of pupils aged 5–16. Post-16 education (further education) and graduate and postgraduate education (higher education) do not fall within the brief of the National Curriculum Council (NCC) and the School Examinations and Assessment Council (SEAC). However, the reconstitution of CATE in 1990 and the demise, as of 1 September 1992, of the local CATE committees which formerly 'approved' ITT courses, leave us in no doubt that ITT is becoming rigorously controlled by a central accreditatory body whose criteria are laid down and approved directly by the Secretary of State for Education and his chosen advisers. However, whilst an institution of teacher education must respond to the National Curriculum, it is not yet bound by a similar 'National ITT Curriculum' written by CATE. There are a number of structural and political reasons why this has not yet happened. Therefore, our central theme in this chapter is that, while we fully support attempts to improve educational standards, it is impossible to impose homogeneity on the teaching process without reducing it to ineffective mono-logue. And, most crucially, nowhere in education is this clearer than in multiethnic contexts.

Currently, assessment of ITT courses occurs through approval of accreditatory mechanisms and contacts, not through approval of epistemological contents and persuasions. Although validation of a course's content is necessary, it is 'not a sufficient condition for the Secretary of State's approval'. A major condition of approval requires the assessment of a broad range of 'competences of teaching', not dissimilar to those previously laid down by CATE. 'The progressive develop-ment of these competences should be monitored regularly during teacher train-ing'. Therefore, we detect an *assessment* structure which suggests a 'hidden' imperative that teacher educators *teach* the development of competence. We wonder on what pedagogic basis ITT will develop competences in intending teachers such as:

> an awareness of individual differences, including social, psychological, developmental and cultural dimensions

> a self-critical approach to diagnosing and evaluating pupils' learning, including a recognition of the effects on that learning of teachers' expec-tations (DFE, 1992)

This is a significantly different undertaking to that of assessing competence.

The axiomatic relationship that exists between the assessment of competence and its teaching, with the actual processes of development remaining undescribed in curriculum legislation, requires both teachers and teacher educators to contextualize their pedagogic understandings of how competence is achieved within the imposed assessment structure. We might note that, as of September 1992, all that will have been implemented by curriculum legislation that might inform actual teaching of pupils and the training of teachers refers to accreditation rather than pedagogy. The history of independent pedagogic practice which has played such a significant role in the development of plural responses to plural needs for most of this century is being increasingly overwritten, but it has not yet been discounted.

Such relative independence has allowed training institutions to formulate their own curricula in response primarily to criteria for initial teacher training determined by CATE since its genesis in 1984. Note the plural form of 'curriculum'. Each training institution may interpret the criteria in accordance with the needs of their intake, their pedagogic determination (towards active learning, or reflec-tive learning, for instance) and the requirements of their partner schools. We should stress that we do not claim that this is in fact what happens in all cases, merely that the possibility exists.

A rich diversity of curricular organization exists centred around the intention to make a coherent response to the needs of intending teachers spread across a broad range of subject disciplines; within an even broader range of schools and the many communities which are represented by the pupil intake from any train-ing institution's catchment area. The catchment area may define a set of priorities to be addressed by a notional training curriculum, determined largely by the demands made by the school population on trainees during teaching practice. Attempts have been made to organize curricula addressing the needs of these populations. For instance, throughout the 1970s and for part of the 1980s (therefore pre-CATE) the University of London's Institute of Education ran an 'alternative' course which prioritized the training of teachers for the 'inner-city' London population. However, initial teacher training has never been organized nationally to respond directly to specific socio-economic, ethnic and linguistic descriptions of the school community. It is likely, then, that any curriculum developed for ITT will address the broadest base of educational priority in its attempt to prepare intending teachers to meet any eventuality in whichever school in which the trainee intends to teach. One might begin to question, as Her Majesty's Inspectorate (HMI) have done, whether this is a satisfactory state of affairs, and whether, indeed, such preparation is anything more than cursory (Department of Education and Science, 1991).

Given that we have identified such a broad base to be catered for by the initial training curriculum and questioned whether the notion of a single curriculum actually fits the historical development of teacher training nationally, we should recognize that the task in hand is to propose a future curriculum with an identifiably pluralistic intention: a curriculum pedagogically geared toward pluralism. Whereas there exists a plethora of expressions of pluralist pedagogy, the structure of initial teacher training remains relatively uniform at PGCE level of entry, generally comprising a subject specialism with an option to study a second method or subsidiary subject. These subject specialisms are contextualized within a broader framework of educational studies (also termed 'professional' or 'contextual' studies).

This approach builds difficulties into ITT. Whilst subject specialisms have invested some consideration of issues of social diversity through gender, ethnicity, class and disability with respect to their particular subject field, it is not at all clear that these considerations share a common objective. We might draw a distinction between changing the database of representations in textbooks and analyzing the language which serves to represent the field of any given classroom enquiry. It is now generally recognized that pupils cannot be expected to accept any portrayal of themselves in a subordinate socio-economic role in school texts, but it is the very language of learning which is the more direct field of communication and cognition, and it is this which pupils and teachers contest daily. Understanding the diverse representations of language in initial teacher education will help to clarify practical objectives in the classroom. Questions which articulate how a group of learners situate themselves differently in relation to the micropolitics of learning are only beginning to be explored by teachers actively engaged in researching their own classrooms. These are all dynamics of actual practice which require reflection and articulation *in vivo*, in the lived experience of teaching and being taught. We need to ask whether such experience can only arise from school practice and also what collaborative dialogue needs to occur between the school and their higher education partners.

Although the new CATE criteria suggest that ITT is only just becoming school-based and implies a clear division between ITT theory and school-based practice, ITT courses have worked closely with schools for many years (Gilroy D., 1992). Subject-method lecturers are almost always experienced classroom teachers who have been formally trained to teach and thereby practise theory and theorize practice. Practising classroom teachers are theorists and teacher-educators are practitioners, not least when they share the domain of the classroom whether in college or at school. This actuality is the essence of the collaborative dialogue which already exists in teacher education far beyond initial training. Practising teachers bring lived experience of teaching into Higher Education. Such 'praxis' is rather more than 'theory': it may well be the remaking of theoretical discourses to which higher education generally gives so much credence.

Issues of social diversity continue to be explored within ITT *in vitro* from psychological, philosophical, historical and sociological perspectives within the framework of educational studies. The extent to which intending teachers import and export concepts fashioned in both educational studies and subject methods can only be guessed at, as can the sense that is made of understandings drawn from distinctly different epistemological and experiential bases.

Most students have recognized the schism between the two strands of their training and consider the subject-specific training to refer to applied methods of educational practice, whilst the brief of educational studies remains one of context. The distinction that arises is one of cognitive function: does the understanding gained from learning within the context of educational studies function adequately when applied to subject-method understandings? How do we know what to do in practice, and how do we avoid practising through miscognition?

We begin to recognize an epistemological divide; distinguishing between knowledge of the system and knowing how to apply knowledge. Epistemology is 'concerned with the discourses of knowledge', (*Chambers Twentieth Century Dictionary*, 1977) and discourse is defined as:

> the socially and historically conditioned practices of groups of human beings using language to articulate views on their worlds; discourses are always situated, that is, permeated by intentions, conceptual frameworks, and the pressures of history. No discourse can be neutral. (Burton, 1989)

We wish to discover the plural nature of these discourses as they arise in education and particularly in the context of educating intending teachers about education.

It is obviously intellectually unhealthy to perpetuate the schism between the two discourses which seems to divide subject methods from educational studies. The content of teacher training in the somewhat simplistic form we have given it so far may only exacerbate this divide. It is more than likely that macropolitical issues of social, psychological and historical identity and representation, distinguished by class, gender, ethnicity and disability, are *described* within the epistemological discourse of educational studies, yet supposedly *applied* micropolitically within that of subject methods and school practice.

A further result is the division of each enquiry concerning identity and representation into coded parts, with each part examined through a tension between its sociological description and its political function. Thus, educational studies may deal taxonomically with ethnicity and racism, gender and sexism, and less distinctly with class and disability, through a series of discrete lectures and/or seminars. If subject methods are aligned to, or contextualized alongside, educational studies, then there might possibly be some focus of agreement between the two epistemological discourses. But such agreement is unlikely; nor is it entirely satisfactory for two reasons.

First, the dichotomy between subject methods and educational studies represents much more than that between two linked, yet estranged, branches of a single curriculum. The 'curricula' of teacher education are not, in fact, varieties or plural versions of a single, integrated human science called education. They do not exist due to a common epistemological centre or within a common functional context. Neither are they plural simply because distinct institutions of education have existed within a freedom of organization from any overriding National Curriculum for teacher education. The curricula are, in Bakhtin's sense of the term, 'heteroglossic': they arise in formal relation to, and struggle against, the many discourses which entwine, align and oppose throughout the history of the meaning of education itself — as a science, as a language, as a practice (Bakhtin, 1981; Rice and Waugh, 1989; Burton, 1989). Put simply, the many discourses which constitute, say, English as a subject on the school curriculum, are not necessarily the same, or mean the same, as those which constitute the sociology of education within educational studies. Again, even within a narrowed-down focus on the 'sociology of education', what is recognized as the constituent representations of sociology at one institution will differ at any other. Likewise for what is taken to be English, or Maths, or whatever we choose to regard as a subject or a method anywhere in the world. There will be similarities and differences, of course, but no simple agreement of discourse.

The second reason why simple agreement between subject methods' and educational methods' curricula cannot be assumed is due to a misrepresentation of the meaning of 'constituency'. Not only do the discourses arising from sociology of education lie in opposition and overlap within the field taken to describe sociology and across other fields, such as the study of English literature or the teaching of a modern language, but they never constitute a single discourse in themselves.

The detached sociological view tends to focus on, and relate to, particular discourses, such as race and gender, as coded descriptors of culture and society, in order to fashion a scientifically objective language of representation. Yet, each discourse, each 'lens' (Hall, 1978, cited in Hardy and Vieler-Porter, 1990) has its own history of representation which is never truly objective, given that it is a mediated fabrication, frequently made and agreed upon by observers who are neither politically neutral, nor psychologically detached. The problem for anyone encountering their own representation is the story of what the observer thought was being observed, narrated within codes chosen to express that observation in language. By employing a code, for instance, the 'cultural' code, 'which is the presence in the text [and in oral discourse] of the accepted knowledge of our culture' (Barthes, 1975, cited in Rosen, 1985), one *constructs* an 'acceptable representation for 'our' culture. Since culture itself arises out of a multifaceted history of significance, whosoever employs the code does so for a variety of intentions which may or may not include an understanding from actual experience of what 'being' and 'belonging to' the discourses of others entails. To complicate matters further, no one exists merely within a single discourse, no one is simply 'white' or 'black': we are women and men, of a certain age, with a complex sexuality, living within, and moving between, diverse communities, employed or not, more or less physically and mentally able, and most of all constantly seeking deliverance from exploitation through misrepresentation and miscognition. Therefore, we can all be said to occupy contingent and centrifugal positions in the representational code-system: the codes construct each other, they 'play' within each other (Donald and Rattansi, 1992).

Of course, it is possible to detach oneself from this complicated reflection on language and be reassured that 'it's just a problem of words', which gives us the popular discourse of the 'problem'. Yet the oft-cited 'race', 'gender', or 'class problem', the 'something out there, but not my problem', only disguises that which is integral to our society: our unease with, and suppression of, 'difference'. In this way language is withdrawn from the social world. Yet, to reflect on language is to reflect the diversity of meaning in the social world of language users, which is, ultimately, to reflect social difference in all its complexity:

> The social world is the locus of struggles over words which owe their seriousness — and sometimes their violence — to the fact that words to a great extent make things, and that changing words, and, more generally representations . . . is already a way of changing things. Politics is, essentially, a matter of words. That's why the struggle to know reality scientifically almost always has to begin with the struggle against words. What very often happens is that in order to transmit knowledge, you have to use the very words that it was necessary to destroy in order to conquer and construct this knowledge: you can see that inverted commas are pretty insignificant when it comes to mark such a major change in epistemological status. (Bourdieu, 1990)

Ignoring or misunderstanding the complexity of the representation of 'difference' endorses the very monocentric stereotyping we need to explore and redress as educators. Therefore, it is a matter of critical urgency that we begin to think beyond the simplistic dichotomy of discourses concerning inequalities found in current teacher education. We must indicate to intending teachers that they can understand the complex of discourses which constitutes, for example, the function of racism in education. However, when that complex is referred to only partially in a discrete lecture or seminar on the educational studies' programme, here today and gone tomorrow, this can only perpetuate miscognition. In the attempt to make a sum of these parts, one ends up reconstructing a patchwork of sociological and ideological concepts: a cloak of intellectual darkness.

To train intending teachers to think contingently, in order to recognize the centrality of inequality, prejudice and 'rough justice', which permeates and constructs this society, requires the application of critical methods of deconstruction upon the social and historical frameworks of education as it is practised, *with* intending teachers and *by* them. We need to teach that there are no easy answers, no comfortable ideologies which will change the society we inhabit and perpetuate. As Paul Gilroy points out, in his examination of contemporary antiracism:

> The first question I want to ask . . . is whether it does not collude in accepting that the problems of 'race' and racism are somehow peripheral to the substance of political life. My view, which locates racism in the core of politics, contrasts sharply with what can be called the coat-of-paint theory of racism. (Gilroy, 1987)

> This is not, in fact, a single theory but an approach which sees racism on the outside of social life ... racism is always located on the surface of other things. It is an unfortunate excrescence on a democratic policy which is essentially sound and it follows from this that, with the right ideological tools and political elbow grease, racism can be dealt with once and for all, leaving the basic structures and relations of British economy and society essentially unchanged. (Gilroy, 1992)

If intending teachers begin to fit onto their pupils a set of preconceived notions of racial or sexual identity, or for that matter any aspect of social identity, this represents the failure of the training institution and its lack of a clear, coherent epistemology. That the National Curriculum wilfully ignores the political complexity of the nation (Hardy and Vieler-Porter, 1990), or seeks to impose a limited ethnocentric ideology on the nation, must be taken as an opportunity to put to use critical methods as the tools of reflective thought embedded in the intending teacher during training. The integrative epistemology on offer needs to support the practice of teaching and contest 'easy' notions of class, ethnicity, gender, sexuality and physical and cognitive ability.

Stuart Hall's 'new ethnicities' arise from detailed examination of the 'relations of representation' and enable us to counter simplistic and, therefore, discriminatory representations of identity:

> What is involved is the splitting of the notion of ethnicity between, on the one hand the dominant notion which connects it to nation and 'race' and, on the other hand what I think is the beginning of a positive conception of the ethnicity of the margins, of the periphery. That is to say, a recognition that we all speak from a particular place, out of a particular history, out of a particular experience, a particular culture without being contained by that position ... We are all in that sense, ethnically located and our ethnic identities are crucial to our subjective sense of who we are. But this is also a recognition that this is not an ethnicity which is doomed to survive, as Englishness was, only by marginalizing, dispossessing, displacing and forgetting other ethnicities. This precisely is the politics of ethnicity predicated on difference and diversity. (Hall, 1992)

The key to our thinking is the right of those people who have been subjected to a history of representation beyond their epistemological control to determine their own identity. The erstwhile 'object', excluded from, or assimilated indifferently into, the picture, now narrates representation from the perspective of 'subject'. Thus, the language of representation and identification has to articulate a pluralist objectivity, whilst reorienting itself to place its excluded subjects as controllers of their discursive destinies.

This absence of discursive control happens all of the time in schools; the identity of the pupil or colleague is immediately recognized as an 'other' and categorized according to a repertoire of 'false images', a photokit of labelled descriptions with an emergency pack of pedagogic solutions, often received during teacher education and enhanced through contact with powerful philosophies of remediation experienced during school-based training. This inflexible instinct, often full of the best of intentions to 'save the other' from obscurity and 'place' them within the known world and the world of knowledge, acts before it has asked the most basic of questions to open a dialogue and assesses before it has begun to get to know.

The message to teachers should be: pupils don't want or need to know what you think about them; they want to know how you can help them to think for themselves. The discourses in the mind of the teacher depend upon the 'logic of representation' invested in, and accepted by, that teacher in their learning about 'self' in relation to 'others'. Yet these psychological narratives, these sociological stories, all bound up in thought and language and identification, worry away at each other and are born out of each other. Instead of clarifying the identity of the pupil, they constrain and immobilize children's right and desire to know for themselves about themselves. However, such psychological and social complexity of 'being' and 'becoming' can denote a site of great potential for both the pupil and the teacher, a complex of discourses of self and history with multiple narratives awaiting exploration if each allows the process of education to bring the communication of such a complexity to fruition.

A dialogic exchange between a pupil and teacher recognizes that learning is a two-way process of sharing understanding and experience. Underachievement generally arises when a learner only receives a monologic version, which is no exchange at all. Monologism perpetuates the standard history and the 'acceptable' content, accounted for in the 'standard' language. The National Curriculum appears to be emphasizing monologism in its insistence of the facts to be learnt rather than the questions to be asked. We must not make the mistake of believing that because knowing an answer *can* indicate understanding, it always *does*. Where is there a place, a locational psychology of pluralist discourse, for the pupil *and* the teacher, without a history of dialogue and of questioning representation? In a monologic world of received wisdom, what is the point of making a record of one's understanding? What psychological dynamic of individuality within plurality remains to drive learning through discursive literacy?

Amidst all the *brouhaha* surrounding the supposed decline of 'standards of literacy', it is worth recalling how teachers have met the needs of multiethnic and multilingual pupils through the practice of dialogue, often with outstanding results for pupils whose learning histories are battlegrounds of institutional misrepresentation and miscognition. John Hardcastle in 'What was necessary to explain' discusses for us the learning exchange which took place when a 14-year-old boy called Tony, who, whilst born in England, had been raised and educated mainly in a rural Jamaican community, chooses to write his autobiography under the assumed name of 'Paul'. Following Carolyn Steedman's argument in *The Tidy House* (1982) that we may read children's writing 'for evidence of individual psychologies in certain social circumstances', Hardcastle writes:

> Tony, I think, was engaged in a similar way, working with the symbols
> of his social realities and putting together a version of personal history
> that made sense for him. As he wrote he drew upon the conventions of
> autobiography as he knew them, and he had met these in different settings
> and at different moments in his development, both in and out of
> school ... Autobiographical traditions have different distributions within
> the wider culture. The value placed upon them varies according to context.

And — over and above this — they have been elaborated variously within different social histories, which have been shaped in this specific instance by colonial and post-colonial relationships of domination and subordination. It is a matter of social history that some people's stories have been articulated and valued while others have been relegated to the margins. For Tony it was never a matter of choosing between alternatives, school and community, London and Jamaica, as ways of representing the self. (Hardastle, 1992)

Hardcastle's work with Tony is essentially dialogic. Tony openly writes into the 'space' and 'play' of a learning environment which encourages the discourse of difference, both cultural and textual. However, there is no *laissez faire* liberalism in the pedagogy, no hint of such dialogue being beyond the pale of 'learning correct English usage', as the criticism so frequently levelled at teachers of English goes. The achievement of full literacy is not being subtly disempowered by placing writing within the bounds of another monologism, the 'every word which isn't correct is the betrayal of Standard English' syndrome. Unless learning to write is understood within a theory of grapholexis, the function of error or miscue in written language is frequently misunderstood as a deliberate act of sabotage by 'other' dialects with teachers portrayed as willing accomplices. The grapholect of Standard English is not the exclusive sytem that arbiters of cultural purity wish to 'correct' us into believing:

A modern grapholect such as 'English', to use the simple term which is commonly used to refer to this grapholect, has been worked over for centuries ... It has been recorded massively in writing and print and now on computers so that those competent in the grapholect today can establish easy contact not only with millions of other persons but also with the thought of centuries past, for the other dialects of English as well as thousands of foreign languages are interpreted in the grapholect. In this sense, the grapholect includes all the other dialects: it explains them as they cannot explain themselves. The grapholect bears the marks of the millions of minds which have used it to share their consciousnesses with one another. Into it has been hammered a massive vocabulary of an order of magnitude impossible for an oral tongue. (Ong, 1982)

Tony writes towards grapholexis, as do all pupils who are learning to write in English or any other written language. It may be that certain 'non-standard' syntactic forms and vocabulary arise and are documented, but this is what learning to write is all about: a continuous *approchement* within the grapholect. Confusing learning to write the grapholect by insinuating that learners are automatically wrong in their exploration of its many discursions and conventions misunderstands the pluralist dialogue we all practise by confirming what is and rethinking what is not acceptable in our writing to other readers and users of the grapholect. Learning to place one's orality within the grapholect is not a deliberate attempt to taint the 'national language' with non-standard stock, and what a perverse linguistic eugenics it is that pretends otherwise. To *write* in a non-standard variety of English is to begin to construct a non-standard grapholect, unless one already exists, in which case it will almost certainly be evolving through a process of assimilating variance. The grapholect of Standard English has no monoglossic heritage which underwrites its syntactic and semantic making across the breadth of its written usage, unless for ideological reasons one pretends to rewrite linguistic history after the event (Cameron and Bourne, 1988).

It may seem by now that we are a long way off the mark of a pluralist curriculum for ITT. In fact, we are at the heart of pluralism. Understanding how language is pluralistic by nature and intention and how language *is* learning need to be made the bedrock of all teachers' training: the epistemological base on which any subsequent understanding of social difference must rest.

It is through such awareness that teachers have asked the questions which bring their own practice to account. Mary Bousted, in researching her own classroom practice, writes:

> I am forced to confess that for a long time I remained unconvinced by the weight of evidence documenting patterns of participation, along gender lines, to whole class question and answer sessions. Although I readily accepted that girls might remain quiet and passive, in *other* teachers' classrooms, I was convinced that girls in *my* classroom did participate actively in whole class discussions ... My complacency was jolted only by the gathering of 'hard' evidence ... I felt there were two main lessons to be learnt from my own evidence. The first was that in spite of my efforts to be what Barnes calls an 'interactive' teacher — one who is aware that students will learn if the teacher values their knowledge and opinions and uses these as a basis for their teaching, I was denying opportunity for my students to make their knowledge available to themselves, and to me. My domination of the discussion gave the students the primary role of listeners ...
>
> The second lesson that I had to learn was that my classroom was a place in which *some* boys dominated classroom talk. Only half the boys in the class (five out of ten) achieved speaking turns [yet] had an almost complete monopoly on student talk and contributions. I discovered that what I thought of as 'Whole Class Discussion' was in fact small group discussion with teacher participation. The rest of the class became the audience for the speakers in the discussion. (Bousted, 1989)

The teacher then goes on to change these dynamics of different appropriation of oracy space by exploring strategies for shared classroom discourse which require both the teacher and the pupils to redescribe, reassess and reconstruct deeply embedded social manifestations of micropolitical power. Hegemonic indifference, as displayed by many boys and men in relation to women, for example, can be strategically disarmed of its practised suppression of 'others' by establishing the proactive power of different discursive perspectives. These may recount immediate histories of subjection to indifference within the context of learning to share the learning space. Finding strategies which work to change the social reality of classrooms, requires intervention to activate and positivize the powerfully different discourses actually being subordinated and monologized within every classroom (Moss, 1992).

What these teachers share with many other teachers in all subjects is an emancipatory pedagogic consciousness of the predicament of pupils and teachers trapped by theoretical persuasions which have objectified language and learners as static and systematized. For those of us who have learnt that the classroom is never subordinate to the curriculum or the forces that shape the curriculum, teaching is a paradigm of liberation, of making and remaking theory through practice, of breaking free in as many ways as possible to secure the full learning potential of all our students. This is the 'object' of teaching in a pluralist society and the goal of training. The reality of the classroom should always be the final site for such a reconstitution of the multiple discourses of educational studies as integral to, and contextualized within, subject methods. Since, as we have seen, the route is by no means straightforward, we need to return to a methodological path which might guide us to such fruitful practice.

The practising of theory whilst theorizing through practice denotes an orientation towards praxis:

> Praxis is, of course, a word with a history ... I use the term to mean the dialectical tension, the interactive, reciprocal shaping of theory and practice which I see at the center of an emancipatory social science. (Lather, 1986)

However, whilst praxis-orientation at research level might shift the epistemology of the ITT institution towards a sense of integrated curriculum, teacher education happens on a double front, both within the classroom of the institution and within the school classroom. Our praxis is multilocative: it occurs in a number of places. Therefore, it is essential that the ITT curriculum is praxially orientated in relation to the practices of schools in their implementation of the National Curriculum. This does not mean a subordination of the ITT curriculum to the discourses of the National Curriculum, which constitutes assimilation; we require dialogue and collaboration, since in most instances we need to work at a metacurricular level: one which knows how to teach how the National Curriculum might be taught. The double front holds a double bind, since we also need to know how to teach what the National Curriculum avoids, which is, paradoxically, pluralist praxis.

Initially, the National Curriculum prescribed content according to levels of attainment; now it prescribes modes of assessment to measure attainment. What the National Curriculum does not describe is the process by which a pupil learns to attain the level. It does not show the teacher how to teach or the learner how to learn — only that which is to be taught and learnt and how it is to be assessed. So, pluralist praxis is still free to determine an ITT curriculum which reflects the transformative processes by which any pupil comes to learn.

> It becomes necessary, then, to emphasize practical activity in concrete reality (activity that never lacks a technical intellectual dimension, however simple it may be) as a generator of knowledge. The act of studying social as well as individual character functions independently of its subjects' awareness of it. Basically, the act of studying, a curious act of the subject facing the world, is an expression of a form of existing. Since human beings are social, historical beings, they are doers, they are transformers, they not only know, but they know that they know. (Freire and Macedo, 1987)

We want to point out that this principle governs all learners, whether the teacher educator, the intending teacher or the school pupil, all of whom, in the praxial dialogue, are studying each other. It is within these dialogues that learning exists, and the articulation and recording of these dialogues accounts for the learning that is taking place. Assessment is, therefore, an ongoing and multitypic discourse: the praxis of tutelage, conference, coursework and final examination.

It is useful, in passing, to recognize the danger to such a praxis being legislated in the name of assessment in the National Curriculum, since this demonstrates how far away we are being taken from process-based learning. The accumulation of pupils' achievements in response to the process of learning within the Programmes of Study is a generative and documentary function of the curriculum. Coursework reflects the variance of learning over a Key Stage: diachronically over time; dialectally according to user; and diatypically according to the type of language used (Halliday and Hasan, 1989; Carter, 1990).

There is a legitimate place for national standardized testing at the end of a Key Stage: we need documentation of pupils' performance under closed conditions of examination and we need final comparisons of performance. However, we need most of all an assessment culture which recognizes that longitudinal documentation of pupils' progress is superior to final performance testing since it is the only research data which demonstrates how and why children learn variously *within* the context of the curriculum.

The widespread replacement of assessment through coursework by a final, standardized test cuts to the core of learning through language across the school curriculum. It replaces the generative function of learning with a sterile regurgitation of memorabilia, measured according to a standardized marksheet; it dismisses thinking and recording within the process of learning for a sad response of curtailed memorization after the learning event has happened.

Assessing learning after the event is a fitting note on which to end. It implies that understanding is success, misunderstanding is failure and that each side of the learning dialectic is readily quantifiable. Yet pupils, teachers and teacher educators learn through the quality of dialogue kept open within the dialectic. Understanding failure does not reveal a failure of understanding. Knowing that we need to know better what knowing all of our selves means, what learning to know is, and what differences arise in the pursuit of practising our understanding, is no less than respect for the many minds that will determine the cultural future of this nation. Pluralism has always been with us and no amount of pretence at homogeneity will deliver education in a way that will stand the test of time.

Note

We wish to thank Lynn Raphael Reed for her editorial suggestions and critical reading of this chapter.

References

BAKHTIN, M.M. (1981) *The Dialogic Imagination*, Austin and London, University of Texas Press.

Malcolm Reed and Michael Beveridge

BARTHES, R. (1975) *S/Z*, London, Jonathan Cape.
BOURDIEU, P. (1990) *In Other Words: Essays Towards a Reflexive Sociology*, Cambridge, Polity Press, p. 54.
BOUSTED, M. (1989) 'Who talks?', in *English in Education*, 23, 3, Sheffield, National Association for the Teaching of English, pp. 41–2.
BURTON, M. (Ed) (1989) *Enjoying Texts: Using literary theory in the classroom*, Cheltenham, Stanley Thornes, p. 109.
CAMERON, D. and BOURNE, J. (1988) 'No common ground: Kingman, grammar and the nation', in *Language and Education*, 2, 3, Clevedon, Multilingual Matters.
CARTER, R. (Ed) (1990) *Knowledge about Language and the Curriculum: The LINC Reader*, London, Hodder and Staughton.
DES (1991) 'Training Teachers for Inner City Schools: A Report by HMI', London Department of Education and Science.
DFE (1992) 'Initial Teacher Training (Secondary Phase)', London, Department For Education, pp. 2–3 and Annex A, 2.1, 2.6.4, 2.6.7.
DONALD, J. and RATTANSI, A. (Eds) (1992) *'Race', Culture and Difference*, London, SAGE Publications for the Open University.
FREIRE, P. and MACEDO, D. (1987) *Literacy: Reading the Word and the World*, London, Routledge and Kegan Paul, p. 78.
GILROY, D.P. (1992) 'The Political Rape of Initial Teacher Education in England and Wales', in *Journal of Education for Teaching*, 18, 1, Sheffield, JET.
GILROY, P. (1987) *There Ain't No Black in the Union Jack*, London, Hutchinson GILROY, P. (1992) 'The end of antiracism', in DONALD, J. and RATTANSI, A. (Eds) *'Race', Culture and Difference*, London, SAGE, p. 52.
HALL, S. (1978) 'Racism and reaction', in *5 Views on Multi-Racial Britain*, London, Commission for Racial Equality.
HALL, S. (1992) 'New Ethnicities', in DONALD, J. and RATTANSI, A. (Eds) *'Race', Culture and Difference*, London, SAGE, p. 258.
HALLIDAY, M.A.K. and HASAN, R. (1989) *Language, context, and text: aspects of language in a social-semiotic perspective*, 2nd ed., Oxford, Oxford University Press.
HARDCASTLE, J. (1992) 'What was necessary to explain', in KIMBERLEY, K. *et al.* (Eds) *New Readings: Contributions to an understanding of literacy*, London, A. and C. Black Ltd, pp. 133–4.
HARDY, J. and VIELER-PORTER, C. (1990) 'Race, Schooling and the 1988 Education Reform Act', in FLUDE, M. and HAMMER, M. (Eds) *The Education Reform Act 1988: Its Origins and Implications*, London, The Falmer Press.
KIMBERLEY, K., MEEK, M. and MILLER, J. (Eds) (1992) *New Readings: Contributions to an understanding of literacy*, London, A. and C. Black Ltd.
LATHER, P. (1986) 'Research as Praxis', in *Harvard Educational Review*, 56, 3, Harvard, p. 258.
MOSS, G. (1992) 'Rewriting Reading', in KIMBERLEY, K. *et al.* (Eds) *New Readings: Contributions to an understanding of literacy*, London, A. and C. Black Ltd.
ONG, W.J. (1982) *Orality and Literacy: The Technologising of the Word*, London, Methuen, p. 107.
REED, M. (1986) 'Sound and System', in TCHUDI, S.N. (Ed) *English Teachers at Work: Ideas and Strategies from Five Countries*, New Jersey, Boynton/Cook.
ROSEN, H. (1985) *Stories and Meanings*, Sheffield, National Association for the Teaching of English, p. 34.
ROSEN, H. (1992) 'The Politics of Writing', in KIMBERLEY, K. *et al.* (Eds) *New Readings: Contributions to an understanding of literacy*, London, A. and C. Black Ltd.
RICE, P. and WAUGH, P. (Eds) (1989) *Modern Literary Theory*, London, Edward Arnold.
STEEDMAN, C. (1982) *The Tidy House*, London, Virago.
VYGOTSKY, L.S. (1978) *Mind in Society*, London, Harvard University Press, p. 65.

Chapter 16

Teacher Training and Social Justice: Early Attempts to Develop the Teacher-Democrat

Alex Robertson

From classical times, literature on the education of the young has identified teachers as the moral and intellectual mentors whose purpose was to prepare them for an appropriate place in society, with corresponding attitudes and skills. By the time systematic teacher training evolved in the nineteenth century induction to classroom practice derived from the priorities implicit in that clear ideology. However much the emphasis on teaching technique increased in colleges it was always secondary to the personal qualities of the trainee teacher. Slowly at first, major changes in perception have occurred until it has now become uncommon to write philosophically, let alone idealistically, about teachers and the contribution they should make to the character of society. The reader wishing to be reminded of the serious attempts to address changes to teacher training in the recent past cannot do better than consult the impressive volume edited by William Taylor *Towards a Policy for the Education of Teachers.* (Taylor, 1969). To read again Bantock, Boyle, Britton, Collier, Maclure, Morris, Taylor and Vaizey, among many others seeking a new synthesis, is to realize it was a time when old assumptions were challenged and practice moved, sometimes too quickly for comfort, into uncharted waters. The effect of this, when added to the revolution of the last decade, has created a new context of teacher education and training which few have yet addressed. An exception is Professor Stewart Ranson in his important paper *Towards a Charter for Public Education.* (Ranson, 1989).

However, in general, teachers are struggling to clarify and formalize the implications of the new order. Government has interpreted the long period of adjustment to political, educational and societal change as symptomatic of loss of direction, and judged that training has moved too far from the grassroots of the profession. The proposed school-related realignment may or may not be wise, but it is a very partial response to the dilemma of the trainer and the teacher in the classroom 'What does society expect of the teacher in the 1990s?'

It is strange, perhaps, in a period of profound change, how persistent among politicians and others, has been the old belief that teachers are powerful change agents. Policy makers and reformers have enlarged the social responsibilities placed on schools in proportion to the increase of pressures in society. This has occurred despite the persuasive argument of Musgrove twenty years ago that schools are under-powered for such responsibilities (Musgrove, 1971). A complicating factor has been an equally persistent view that the young cannot be expected to understand the privileges and responsibilities of democratic society without having their consciousness raised as part of their experience in school. The American philosopher, John Dewey, has been the most influential exponent of this view. As educational philosophy is currently little valued in professional training (in contrast to earlier in the century) it is worth giving a short quotation:

> It is quite clear that there cannot be two sets of ethical principles, or two forms of ethical theory, one for life in the school, and the other for life outside the school. As conduct is one, the principles are one also. (Findlay, n.d., p. 21)

This fits well with the assumption implicit in this book that teachers and those who train them should play some part in awakening students to those principles which supply the ethical base on which society rests and which contribute significantly to its sense of justice and political cohesion. The consensus of opinion earlier this century was that such awareness in students was unlikely to result from traditional training programmes and that a new and enriched concept of teacher professionalism should be developed. To be technically proficient in a subject and an efficient communicator are important skills. However, they have little to do with an understanding of such issues of social justice as problems associated with class, gender, ethnicity, internationalism, drug taking, violence or environmentalism, with which contemporary society is profoundly concerned.

It has been characteristic of the last forty years that university one-year training programmes have concentrated on a minimum level of technical expertise and confidence-building. Despite the evidence of Clegg, Douglas, Floud, Halsey, Hargreaves, Jackson, McGeeney, and a stream of others in the 1960s and 1970s emphasizing the social nature of schooling, the dimension of what the teacher was being trained to *be* as well as to *do*, has never gained an appropriate place in the debate. Despite the successes of the best B.Ed. courses — and perhaps because of them — uncertainty over the role of the lecturer was sharpened and the old dichotomy between theory and practice continued to cause disquiet, to the extent that government could argue for drastic action to restore a balance.

This chapter examines the work in the first half of this century of the Education Department at the University of Manchester. A historical perspective of how an earlier generation addressed the challenge of responding to social and political pressures in the training of teachers may raise some interesting questions, not without significance to the strategies presented in this volume. The preoccupation was not then with inequality (though it might surprise many how near to a modern outlook some thinking was becoming) but the problem was the same logistically: how could a response be made to the implicit belief that teachers were agents of social improvement?

At Manchester, receptiveness to social problems was mainly a response by the first generation of lecturers around the turn of the century, men and women of extrovert personality and radical views about education and the contribution the teaching profession could make to society. Their work was often inspired by Herbart and Froebel. Certainly at Manchester, and probably in other industrialized urban areas, university colleges developed a sense of responsibility to the community. Professor Samuel Alexander, the eminent philosopher, played a major part in the selection of four professors of education, Withers, Findlay, Sadler and Smith, all of whose writings are permeated by an awareness of the social aspects of schooling and a sense of mission for their department and the teachers they trained.

Alexander actively supported the womens' movement in Manchester and was instrumental in developing a hall of residence to encourage female enrolment at the university. The master of method, H.T. Mark, a national authority on moral education, became the president of the Manchester branch of the Men's Association for Women's Suffrage. On its national committee were leading Liberal Mancunians, the industrialist William Mather and the editor of the *Guardian*, C.P. Scott, both of whom, supported by their able wives, had taken a leading part in developing the training work in the university. Catherine Dodd, the mistress of method, radical in her feminism, politics and support for progressive teaching methods, lost no opportunity for confronting the women students with new ideas and experiences, and as the first woman on the academic staff, played no small part in accustoming the university to innovation and the need to adapt to social change.

Education staff played a significant part in the movement to extend higher-education opportunities through extra-mural teaching and contributed to the university settlement in the very deprived area of Ancoats, a work in which their students played a supportive role. It is less well understood than it should be, that the educational initiatives which were derived from Froebel and to a lesser extent, Montessori, developed in Britain associated with social change. This was related in particular to improvement in the conditions to which many urban children were condemned and which diminished their opportunities to benefit from education. Froebelism as a dynamic force, social and political as well as educative, as symbolized by the McMillan sisters in London, permeated the Education Department at Manchester until the 1920s.

The students worked in an environment with a powerful institutional ethic which was consciously promoted by the staff. Student teachers knew that their lecturers were themselves involved in important and controversial issues of the day. An early example which caught the imagination of staff and students was the Free Kindergarten Movement, largely inspired from the United States and dedicated to improvement in the lives of poor working women and their children. One respected member of staff gave up her work to found a kindergarten in a Manchester slum which became for many years a notable experiment in child and parent care. Most important, it was regularly visited by students in training.

Similar in character in that it began with a desire to aid those for whom access to education was frustrated by circumstance, was Irene Goldsack's work from 1919 to train teachers of the deaf. To bring this vital but marginalized work into the Education Department was itself proof of commitment to education in a broader context. Radical though the initiative was, the choice of lecturer was more so, for Goldsack was the most innovative worker then in the field of educating the deaf, and the university had to resist much traditionalist professional opposition. As the work developed in conjunction with her future husband, Alexander Ewing, and gained an international reputation, it never lost its devotion to the ideal of relieving suffering as well as creating educational opportunities for the handicapped (Ewing Mss).

It is no longer possible to judge how far the students in the department from 1890 to the 1920s were influenced by the environment in which they studied, but two things are clear. The organization and atmosphere in the Education Department was collegiate. The staff had no inhibitions about creating a dynamic ethos within which the technicalities of training took place in an environment in which the students could mature with a sensitivity to professional responsibilities and challenges.

Short extracts from addresses by the professors who ran the department from 1903 to 1933 demonstrate the range of thinking on these matters.

> Every school is a community, a corporate society; and the individual comes out from the school bearing the stamp, deep down in his whole spiritual life, of the influences of those who govern and guide that society. This element, then, in the teachers' training cannot be left to chance. (Findlay, 1903, pp. 16–17)

> What the pupils want is a course vivid with practical experience and full of sound history and competent economics. The important thing is to kindle their interest in scientific methods of social investigation; and to make them see that the problem of social reform is very urgent and very complicated; that ill-formed or partisan talk darkens counsel. (Sadler, 1908, p. 34)

> A mastery of his material is only one branch of the master's interest. He must have also a social interest in education. He is the organ of the community for handing on its life . . . in our own day that is no easy task. It demands a wide outlook and broad sympathies. (Smith, 1913, pp. 37–8)

It was noteworthy how the department tried to adapt to allow these ambitious aims to be developed. For much of the first thirty years of the century the department was merged with a demonstration school of local children. The students were immersed in that atmosphere, with the theoretical education course growing out of the issues confronted in the school. It was hoped that in such a positive atmosphere professional attitudes could be inculcated early in the student's career. There were many problems, among them the conservative nature of the university and some lecturers and teachers. But the greatest problems were ethical:

> I will not lead children to answer questions on conduct before the questions arise . . . abstract thinking upon any field grows out of concrete experience. (Findlay, 1908, p. 26)

This comment by Findlay revealed the dilemma. A liberal political system and, most persuasive of all, new understanding of how children learn, raised doubts about the propriety of persuading teachers to raise controversial issues with the immature. The clumsy attempts by some school authorities in the recent past to implement positive anti-discrimination policies are modern examples of what Findlay had in mind.

The middle years of the century at Manchester were dominated by Professor

Richard A.C. Oliver who was appointed to the chair in 1938. His significance as an educator is only now becoming clear. It is interesting to observe from the perspective of history a continuation of that social dimension of education which had been foreshadowed in the Manchester department so long before. (Pearson *et al.*, 1989). Oliver was preoccupied by the interrelationships of the educational process, the work and preparation of the teacher and the kind of society appropriate to a democracy. His views as expressed in 1942 were very similar to those of Findlay who died in that year.

> A democracy recognises the equal right of everyone to share what opportunities for a good life the efforts of the society can provide. The only inequality between one and another which it recognises is the inequality laid down by nature in people's varying natural capacities and endowments. (Oliver, 1942, p. 47)

The language of 'equal rights' and 'inequality' are those of the second half of the century. The theme is that set out by Findlay in his major work *The Foundations of Education* (1927) that the education system and the teaching profession must find a way to promote the values of society. Findlay's latter years had been deeply scarred by events in Germany from where he had learnt so much in his youth. One can sense a fear that in a very ideological age the integrity of the young was to be sacrificed. He noted wryly that some still believed that one could ' "make" children free' (Findlay, 1927, pp. 41–2) and wrote angrily to the journal *Child Life* in 1934 after a German contributor had praised the Hitler Jugend and linked it to the ideals of Froebel.

Oliver's paper *Planning Education* (1942) is a radical statement which advocated recasting the educational system, to include a 'single common school', a greatly enriched concept of the youth service, smaller classes, nursery education and improved welfare. It also contained a critique of the special place examination or 'IQ' test, which, with the other points, were to become such a focus of the debate on inequality:

> It determines whether we shall earn a wage or a salary, whether we shall have a week's holiday at Blackpool, or a fortnight or more in the Lakes or on the Continent.

He hoped it would be abolished (Pearson *et al.*, 1989, p. 50).

Committed to a democratic society Oliver never doubted that the schools should play a part in the extension of social justice. Logically the training experience must prepare the student for this; only when it had been internalized could he 'tackle intelligently . . . what and how to teach' (Oliver, 1943, p. 7). It is not unimportant to record that another stimulus to Oliver's views on equality came, as for many others, from Christian belief and he quoted the 'Ten-point Programme' of the main church leaders in 1940:

> Every child, regardless of race or class, should have equal opportunities of education, suitable for the development of his peculiar capacities. (Pearson *et al.*, 1989, p. 51)

Oliver lost no time in addressing the challenge. The impetus for his important book *The Training of Teachers in Universities* (1943) lay in the work of the Association for Education in Citizenship, a national pressure group headed by the Manchester business man, Sir Ernest Simon (Oliver, 1943, Preface). Oliver accepted the view that had emerged from various government reports that:

> teaching is essentially the arrangement of the child's environment in such ways that he will have experiences which the teacher believes will change him in the desired ways.

The answer was not only to teach civics but to imbue the life of college and school with the vitality of democratic principles. It followed that teacher professionalism of the future needed a full commitment to democratic ideals and the sensitivity and ability to transmit them with implications far beyond the classroom. Such an outlook could not be introduced to student teachers in the same way as classroom techniques. This must have contributed to Oliver's view that teacher training in universities should extend over at least four years and that academic and professional studies should be integrated. It also gives particular significance to the emphasis Oliver placed on general education in both secondary schools and universities, for he was doubtful of the value of intensive subject specialism for most teachers.

It is no coincidence that he contributed an article to the first volume of the *Universities Quarterly*. He asked:

> Can the universities train specialists and yet imbue them with some of the wisdom garnered from the past to guide them in the problems of the present? (Oliver, 1947, p. 144)

It was the challenge of this task and the uncertainty whether it was being attempted, which provoked W.H.G. Armytage in the same journal a decade later to ask 'Can Education Departments Educate?' A century earlier, Matthew Arnold had urged lecturers to open students' minds; Armytage made the same point in a characteristically trenchant way:

> a good teacher needs more than mere technique, he needs a high outlook, he must not be what Ortega calls a sub-man. (Armytage, 1954, pp. 388–395)

Oliver devised a programme to achieve this and believed the extended training course would give many opportunities to increase maturity and develop awareness in student teachers. Interestingly, the process depended to a marked degree on the traditional principles of a liberal education extended to include professional training. It is noticeable in the work of both Findlay and Oliver that specific contemporary issues are not given much prominence. This was from recognition that emphasis in society would alter and what was needed was a form of training capable of adaptation to changing circumstances. This also explains why Oliver set such store on carefully balanced educational experiences in the new training course and wished to extend teachers' experience of the world through a period in commerce or industry before taking up an appointment (Oliver, 1941, p. 9).

While neither Findlay nor Oliver believed that teachers could be made aware and sensitive by prescription, they did believe that young men and women would accept as part of professional training values and practices which would predispose them to see their influential job in a particular way. In a memorandum to the Vice-Chancellor in 1941 Oliver wrote:

If it was not clear before, the war has shown that teachers have much wider functions in the community than merely teaching children in class . . . they have been revealed as social workers with functions far beyond the schools. It is clear that to fulfil their responsibilities they need more than a narrowly specialised training. (ibid., p. 8)

There would be a number of specifically educational options across the years of the degree course. With our later familiarity with the Bachelor of Education degree, Oliver's proposals have lost their power to surprise, but this was not the case in 1943. It is not possible here to explore the rich mix of child study, health, psychology and social studies which Oliver planned. Despite Findlay's efforts, the evaluation of practical teaching was still disappointingly traditional. Oliver wanted to find more sophisticated methods of assessment, appropriate to the much more complex role of the school teacher and a notable amount of departmental research time was devoted to this. Awareness of children's needs, introduced in psychology lectures, should be evaluated by studies derived from observation in classrooms, and the student's 'laboratory notebook' should be a perceptive record, from which short papers on specific issues or problems could be written or used for discussion in the seminars which were a feature of the Manchester training programme. As well as encouraging the student to synthesize the various aspects of the work, this:

would do something to train him in that objective attitude to problems of education which is one element in the make-up of a good teacher. (Oliver, 1943, pp. 21–2)

The probationary year was of little value, he believed, and should be merged into the college-based training and carried on with the support of LEAs and the staff of colleges after certification. It is interesting to record that with the recent abolition of the probationary year, the Education Department introduced in 1992 a Teaching Studies Programme very similar to that suggested by Oliver.

That Findlay's experiments were ahead of their time and Oliver's were made impossible by decisions of the Ministry of Education, is irrelevant to the theme of this chapter. Both men had responded to pressure to reconsider the purpose of teacher training, particularly in regard to a more egalitarian society. They believed profoundly that a liberal education accompanied by a liberal approach to vocational training, was capable of producing men and women of sensitivity, perception and good will, who would meet the social challenges of the twentieth century with tolerance and self-confidence. At the end of the century many in the United Kingdom are both less optimistic and less confident of the ability of schools and teachers to influence society.

Alex Robertson

References

ARMYTAGE, W.H.G. (1954) 'Can Education Departments Educate?' *Universities Quarterly*, 9.

EWING MSS, Papers of Sir ALEXANDER EWING, JOHN RYLANDS University Library, Manchester (JRUL).

FINDLAY, J.J. (1903) *The Training of Teachers*, Manchester, Sherratt and Hughes.

FINDLAY, J.J. (1908) 'The Growth of Moral Ideas in Children, in SADLER, M.E. (Ed) (1908) *Moral training and Instruction in Schools*, London, Longmans Green and Co.

FINDLAY, J.J. (1927) *The Foundations of Education*, 2, University of London Press.

FINDLAY, J.J. (n.d.) *Educational Essays of John Dewey*, London, Blackie and Son.

MUSGROVE, F. (1971) *Power and Authority in English Education*, Methuen, London.

OLIVER, R.A.C. (1941) *Memorandum on Possible Future Developments*, Paper to the Vice-Chancellor, JRUL Archives.

OLIVER, R.A.C. (1942) '*Planning Education*', in PEARSON, R. *et al.* (Eds) (1988) *The Psychologist as Educator*, University of Manchester, School of Education.

OLIVER, R.A.C. (1943) *The Training of Teachers in Universities*, University of London Press.

OLIVER, R.A.C. (1947) 'General Education in the Universities', *Universities Quarterly*, 1, p. 144.

PEARSON, R. *et al.* (1989) *The Psychologist as Educator*, University of Manchester, School of Education.

RANSON, S. (1989) 'Towards a Charter for Public Education', BEMAS Conference, Leicester, September.

SADLER, M.E. (1908) *Moral Instruction and Training in School*, 1, London, Longmans Green and Co.

SMITH, H.B. (1913) *Education as the Training of Personality*, Manchester University Press.

TAYLOR, W. (1969) *Towards a Policy for the Education of Teachers*, London, Butterworth.

Notes on Contributors

Gajendra K. Verma is professor of education, and Dean of the Research and Graduate School in the Faculty of Education, University of Manchester. He has previously taught at the Universities of East Anglia and Bradford. He has written and researched extensively in the fields of ethnicity and education, curriculum evaluation, self-esteem and identity. A member of the Swann Committee, he has also served on a number of national committees concerned with education.

John Eggleston has been responsible for teacher education at the Universities of Leicester, Keele and Warwick. Currently professor of education at the University of Warwick, he is chairman of the Central Television Education Committee and deputy chairman of the Design and Technology Association. Previously he has been a member of the DES Assessment of Performance Unit and of the Executive Committee of the Universities Council for Teacher Education. He has written extensively in the fields of teacher education and equal opportunities.

Roger Iredale is the chief education adviser at the Overseas Development Administration where his work includes close involvement with education projects supported by the British aid programme and coordination with other donors. His career in education has involved teaching and teacher training for most age groups from primary through secondary, further and adult education. He has lectured at the Universities of Algiers and Leeds, and spent two years in South India.

David Freer, although educated initially in Birmingham, has taught in schools, colleges and universities in Southern Africa since 1956. He has held a variety of posts directly concerned with the education of teachers. He was senior lecturer at Bulawayo Teachers' College, the University of Zimbabwe, and Rhodes University. Appointed professor of education at the University of the Witwatersrand in 1981, he has been dean of the Faculty of Education there since 1987. His research interests include curriculum development, curriculum evaluation and multicultural issues.

Carl A. Grant is professor in the Department of Curriculum and Instruction and Afro-American Studies at the University of Wisconsin-Madison. He was selected in 1990 as one of the top leaders in teacher education by the Association of

Teacher Educators. His major professional interests include multicultural education; race, social class and gender and school life; and pre-service and in-service education, areas on which he has researched and written extensively.

Ann Hickling-Hudson is a Jamaican/British citizen with experience as an educator in the Caribbean, Britain and Australia. She lectures at the Queensland University of Technology, Australia, in 'sociology of education' and in 'education for a multicultural society'. Her research has primarily been in comparative and international education.

Marilyn McMeniman is a senior lecturer in education at Griffith University, Australia. Her primary research interest is in language education in a cultural context.

Lionel Orlikow is director of the education programme at The Winnipeg Education Centre and associate professor at The University of Manitoba. The centre is an innovative teacher-education initiative mandated to recruit and train teachers from Aboriginal, recent immigrant and urban poor communities. He is currently a school trustee for the Winnipeg School Division and a former Deputy Minister of Education for the province of Manitoba.

Jon Young is an associate professor in the Department of Educational Administration and foundations in the Faculty of Education at the University of Manitoba. He teaches and writes in the areas of antiracist education and critical perspectives in educational administration.

Iram Siraj-Blatchford is currently lecturer in education at the University of Warwick. She has taught in primary schools and in higher education. She has published widely on the issue of inequality and teacher education. Her current research is focused on developing feminist, antiracist epistemologies in research.

Clem Adelman is professor in the Faculty of Education and Community Studies, Reading University. His published research ranges from early childhood to higher education and includes the methodologies of participant research, action research, case study and evaluation. He has taught pre-service and in-service teachers and, with the support of the CRE and DES established in 1983, AIMER, the national database on multicultural and antiracist teaching materials in the faculty.

Ivan Reid is Schofield professor and head of the Department of Education at Loughborough University. His educational career commenced with secondary-teaching, but has mainly been involved in teacher education and particularly in-service education. He taught sociology at Edge Hill College of Education, the sociology of education at the Universities of Bradford and Leeds. He has authored several books, a large number of articles and is an executive editor of *The British Journal of Sociology of Education* and the executive editor of *Research in Education*.

Hans de Frankrijker is lecturer at the Centre for the Study of Education and Instruction, Faculty of Social Sciences, University of Leiden, The Netherlands.

He teaches courses in sociology of education and educational policies. He has published in the areas of teacher education and multicultural education.

H. Wilfred Campbell is senior lecturer in the Department of Psychology at the University of Nijmegen. Since 1987, he has also been director of the Research Institute of the Foundation Studia Interethnica, Utrecht. He has taught at the Universities of Utrecht, Groningen, and Nijmegen, The Netherlands. He was research fellow at the Bell Telephone Company, New Jersey, USA, 1975–6. He has published in the area of ethnicity and education.

Fazal Rizvi is an associate professor in education at the University of Queensland in Australia. He is a philosopher of education with research interests in issues of cultural policy and education, and has written number of monographs and papers on racism, multiculturalism, democratic reforms in education and ethics and educational administration.

Vicki Crowley is a lecturer in Aboriginal studies at the University of South Australia. She is currently a doctoral student at the University of Queensland working on issues of racism and its articulations.

David Dufty, formerly professor in the School of Teaching and Curriculum Studies, University of Sydney, is now a writer and consultant in the area of studies of society and environment working from his home in Killcare, NSW, Australia. During 1990 and part of 1991 he was a lecturer and curriculum consultant at the Solomon Islands College of Higher Education in Honiara. His recent writings include guide books for teachers and student teachers on integrated studies, on teaching about the greenhouse effect, the oceans, and politics in Asia.

Malcolm Reed trained at the London Institute of Education on the 'alternative' course in 1980 and completed an MA (Ed) there in 1985. He taught English full-time in Hackney, East London, from 1981 to 1990, when he was appointed lecturer in education (English method) at the University of Bristol, School of Education. He is responsible for coordinating the PGCE English programme.

Michael Beveridge is professor and head of the School of Education at the University of Bristol. He has published extensively in the area of language and communication especially in relation to children with special needs.

Alex Robertson is a senior lecturer in Education at the University of Manchester. He is a historian who has had much experience of the training of teachers in a College of Education and a University Department. His research interests include the response of University Education Departments to social factors in education and he has published papers on this topic. Recently he has been involved with a linkage with the University of Madras.

Index

Singh, J.S. 23
Singh, M.G. 64
Siraj-Blatchford, Iram 89–98
Sleeter, C.E. 45, 47, 51, 61, 66
Smith, A. 149
Smith, B.O. 42
Smith, D.J. 12
Smith, H.B. 196
Smith, P.C. 46
Smith, S. 84
Smolicz, J. 150
Snowdon, W. 156
socialization 8–10, 13, 48, 63, 75, 80, 101
sociology 109–14, 115, 184
Solomon Islands, teacher education in
    175–8
Solomon, P. 86
South Africa, apartheid and teacher
    education in 28–40
specialism, subject 35–6, 38, 62, 71,
    76–7, 90–1, 95, 109, 111, 182–4,
    190, 198–9
Spivak, G. 158
Staples, R. 52–3
Steedman, Carolyn 187
stereotyping 4, 11, 13, 21, 47, 67, 73,
    103, 145, 154, 157, 185
systems of education 1–2, 5, 17–18, 20,
    28–31, 35–8, 41, 126

Tajfel, H. 134
Taylor, J. 167
Taylor, W. 110, 113–14
Taylor, William 193
teaching practice 23, 43–5, 65, 73, 75,
    79, 90, 97, 111, 128–9, 139, 142,
    182–3, 195–7, 199
Teunissen, J. 125
Thomas, B. 79
Thorman, J. 49
Tolbert, S.M. 16
tolerance 3, 17, 40, 50, 65, 106, 145,
    148, 155, 157–9, 199
Tomlinson, S. 12, 116

Troyna, B. 73, 81, 116, 154, 159
Tucker, A. 66
Turner, J.C. 134

university 11, 32, 34–8, 40–1, 43–4, 49,
    53, 60, 62–3, 66–7, 70–1, 75–6,
    78–84, 90, 92, 95, 97, 101, 109,
    112–13, 125, 194–9
USA
    multiculturalism and teacher
        education in 41-55, 61, 104

values 6, 8, 13, 16–17, 59, 63, 72–3, 79,
    105, 108, 133, 135–6, 148–50, 162,
    166, 170, 174–8, 197, 199
Verma, Gajendra K. 1–5, 122
Verspoor, A.M. 23–4
Vieler-Porter, C. 184, 186
Vimpari, G. 168
Vlug, V. 136
Vygotsky, L.S. 180

Walker, S. 91
Wallman, S. 149
Watson, K. 130
Waugh, P. 184
Webster, J. 81
Weil, S. 94
Wells, G. 84
Wiggan, L. 86
Wild, R.A. 166
Williams, J. 95, 159
Williams, L. 78
Willis, S. 167
Wilson, B. 171
Winant, H. 161
Woods, C.A. 36
Wormald, E. 113
Wright, C. 105
Wyatt, J. 78

Young, Jon 70–85

Zeichner, K. 80–1